RCEA

I want to dedicate this book to
my fans all over the world . . .
because a song feels best
when it is shared.

DOLLY PARTON

MY LIFE IN LYRICS

S·O·N·G·T·E·L·L·E·R

DOLLY PARTON with ROBERT K. OERMANN

CHRONICLE BOOKS
SAN FRANCISCO

PREFACE

BY ROBERT K. OERMANN

MY GRANDMOTHER SOLD ALL KINDS OF records in her music store in the mountains of Western Pennsylvania, so I grew up knowing about the classic country stars of the 1950s.

In Pittsburgh in the 1960s, country's syndicated TV programs came on after the cowboy movies on Saturdays. On *The Porter Wagoner Show*, Dolly Parton gamely pitched ads for a health tonic or a laundry detergent and sang tenderly.

I pushed country music aside when I was a teenager; I was obsessed with the sounds of R&B. Grandma sold those kinds of records, too.

By 1971, I was living in St. Louis amid country fans. That was the year that Dolly released "Coat of Many Colors." I wept the first time I heard it. I realized that this was soul music of another kind.

I was clerking in a St. Louis record store when Dolly released "My Tennessee Mountain Home," "Jolene," and "I Will Always Love You." Then came "The Seeker." Soul music, indeed.

It was a wonderful era to be reintroduced to country music. Dolly was part of a new generation of songwriters who were transforming the art form. Kris Kristofferson and Tom T. Hall were among them.

I thought to myself, "If this is what country music is now, I need to go to Nashville." Once Dolly and her peers opened the door, I found a world of songwriting artists waiting for me on the other side.

I arrived in Music City to work at the Country Music Hall of Fame just as Dolly was embarking on her quest to conquer the pop universe. The first time that I interviewed her, I couldn't face her. She was so beautiful that I was afraid I would forget my name if I looked into her eyes.

That didn't last long. Over the years as a music journalist, I kept remembering why I'd been fascinated by her in the first place. It was her songwriting.

I raised my glass the first time I heard her empowering lyrics for "9 to 5" in 1980. This was a lyricist at the peak of her power.

In 1986, Emmylou Harris called from an LA recording studio to tell me that something extraordinary was being created. It became a stunning album called *Trio*, and there was Dolly in its center alongside Emmylou and Linda Ronstadt.

As the world transitioned into a new millennium, Dolly wrote songs that renewed her connection to her mountain roots. The insights about that music that she shared during our interviews made me admire her more than ever.

You can't exist in the Nashville music community and not develop a profound respect for songwriters. Only the very rare and gifted among them continue to craft consistently creative works over six decades, as Dolly Parton has done. Just one example from each of those decades can illustrate: "Down from Dover" (1969), "To Daddy" (1975), "Appalachian Memories" (1983), "Eagle When She Flies" (1991), "Raven Dove" (2002), and "Why" (2018). In a town full of co-writers and collaborators, she impressively wrote all of those songs, and more, alone.

Over the years, I have interviewed Dolly for dozens of television documentaries, press kits, and magazine features. Those experiences always leave me filled with warmth, optimism, and, most of all, respect. And I still get a lump in my throat every time I hear her sing "Coat of Many Colors."

Songteller celebrates what I like best about Dolly Parton. It's the chronicle of one of our greatest American songwriters, told as only she can tell it.

INTRODUCTION BY DOLLY PARTON

MY NAME IS DOLLY PARTON, AND I AM A SONGWRITER.

That is how I express myself. In a song, I can go anywhere and do anything.

As a songwriter, I am influenced by everything around me—by the people around me, by the feelings of people I know, and by my own joys and sorrows. In my songs, I've touched on a whole lot of subjects. I've put so many songs out there, and they are there for anybody who wants to listen.

I write a lot from my own heart. But I also just have a big imagination. When I was young, we didn't go to the movies, so I just created my own stories. It's kind of embedded in me to make up songs and stories. I'd read something in a book or hear something and think, "What would happen next? What kind of story would that turn out to be?" And ever since I was a small child, I have had the gift to rhyme things.

I used to love to go to graveyards a lot. I'd read somebody's name on their stone or see the grave of a little kid and wonder what their story was. I'd create lives for all of those people in the graveyard, just invent stories in my head for them. A creative mind just likes to do that, I guess.

These days, inspiration can strike at any time. I might hear a great title, think a great thought, see a great story on TV, or hear something on the news and think, "Somebody needs to write a song about that." And that somebody is usually me. That's why I always try to keep a little notepad or a tape recorder beside my bed or in my purse. Because I never know when something's going to hit me.

People ask me, "Do you have to be in a particular place to write a song?" I don't. I can write anywhere, anytime, any place. I don't have to be in any particular environment. Noise or anything else around me can't stop me. On my tour bus, on an airplane, in the bathtub, or just about anywhere, the writing comes all the time. Because it does, I always try to be open to it and always try to be ready. I stay close to my guitar or a tape recorder, so that I can always remember a melody if it comes to me.

My preference is to take time off to do nothing but write. But that's a luxury I don't have much anymore. I used to have more time to do that, to go off by myself. I love to sit around for hours, alone

with a good cup of coffee, and just do my thing. Because when I do, boy, I can really do some serious writing then.

I just go into my "God space." Most songwriters have a zone that they go into. I call it my spiritual zone. I feel like I'm closest to God when I write. I have to leave myself open for the songs to come in or go out. But God doesn't hand you everything. You have to do the work. Still, every once in a while, something special happens. A great line will just come to me, and I'll go, "Hey, thank You, Lord. I know I didn't think of that."

I know I'm skilled at writing, and I have been writing for, Lord, hundreds of years! But I just love it when that spark happens. I get so excited that I wish I could call somebody and say that new line to them. But I learned years ago that people aren't interested in the process. You have to wait until the song is done.

I am a singer, an entertainer, and a businesswoman. But if I had to choose just one thing to be, I would choose to be a songwriter. I could happily just sit in my house forever, enjoy life, and write songs. The songs lead to everything else. Everything that I am starts with that song. No matter who you are as an artist, if you don't have a great song, you're not going anywhere.

I decided to call my book *Songteller* because that pretty much sums me up. I love songs, I love to tell stories, and most of all, I just love to write. It's just who I am. I am a "song teller."

I have often said that my songs are my children and that I expect them to support me when I'm old. Well, I am old, and they are!

But I do take my songwriting seriously. I am so proud that I am able to write. I know there are many songwriters in this world who are much greater than I am. But I know for a fact that no writer in this world enjoys it more than me.

At the end of the day, I hope that I will be remembered as a good songwriter. The songs are my legacy.

CHAPTER

1

MY TENNESSEE MOUNTAIN HOME

DOLLY PARTON WAS BORN JANUARY 19, 1946, IN THE GREAT SMOKY Mountains of East Tennessee. This is a landscape of misty valleys, deep forests, bright meadows, lofty vistas, dark hollows, and abundant Appalachian flora and fauna. But in these scenic hills and vales are pockets of the worst rural poverty in America.

Dolly Parton was raised in small, unheated shacks and cabins without indoor plumbing, electricity, or running water. The family lived with no telephone, automobile, television, or other modern convenience, except for a battery-powered radio. Rural electrification and paved roads did not come to the area until the 1950s.

She is one of twelve children born to an unskilled, illiterate laborer and subsistence farmer and his wife in Sevier County. The Partons' clothes, food, and toys were homemade. So was their entertainment.

Dolly began writing songs as a toddler. She started entertaining local audiences around age eight. At age ten, she began appearing on radio and TV in Knoxville. She launched her recording career at thirteen, which is also when she made her pilgrimage to Nashville to appear on the Grand Ole Opry.

These are the Dolly Parton compositions that reflect her hardscrabble upbringing. Also here are the songs that track the child prodigy's journey out of deprivation and into the spotlight.

I fantasized about being a famous country singer ever since I was a child. I'd put a tin can on a stick as my "microphone" and pretend the front porch was my stage. Then I'd sing to whatever was in the front yard—human, animal, or dirt.

Little Tiny Tasseltop 1952

DOLLY COMPOSED HER FIRST SONG when she was around age six. It was an ode to her corncob doll with corn-silk hair. Her mother, Avie Lee Owens Parton (1923–2003), wrote its lyrics down for her. Avie Lee saved dozens of songs Dolly wrote as a child. One of them, "Life Doesn't Mean That Much to Me," has a strikingly adult lyric mourning a fallen soldier. Dolly's highly musical mother not only encouraged Dolly to pursue songwriting, but also influenced her daughter's singing style.

Little tiny Tasseltop
I love you an awful lot.
Corn-silk hair and big brown eyes,
How you make me smile.

Little tiny Tasseltop,
You're the only friend I've got.
Hope you never go away.
I want you to always stay.

People in the mountains still know how to make corncob dolls. These ones in my museum at Dollywood look just like Tasseltop, the subject of my first song.

Ever since I was a small child, I've always had the gift to rhyme. So I was making up songs before I could even write. I would rhyme everything, whether it was whatever was on the table, what was on the floor, what the kids were doing.

I grew up in a very musical family, especially on my mother's side. So it was just natural for my mom to always be singing. My mother had that old-timey voice, and she used to sing all these songs that were brought over from the Old World. They were English, Irish, Welsh folk songs where people tell stories.

Mama had this haunting voice, and Lord you would feel it. There's a famous old folk song called "Two Little Orphans" about two little kids who come up to the door and are frozen to death because nobody's answering. Mama would emphasize those moments in the lyrics when the two little orphans are "talking." It was really like being there if Mama was singing it.

That's how I try to sing, too. I want you to feel it when I'm telling you the story. Mama singing all those old-timey mountain songs was just embedded in my soul, in my psyche. I call it my "Smoky Mountain DNA."

Early on, I would listen to all of those songs and all of those stories. I started to write songs, I guess, because I picked up so many things.

My first song was called "Little Tiny Tasseltop." It was about a corncob doll that my mama had made me and put a little dress on and put corn-silk tassels on for hair. Daddy made eyes with the fire poker from the fireplace. But I loved that little doll.

I expressed myself and my feelings through writing—I'm sure what I was thinking was, "Well, Tasseltop has to have a song about her." So I wrote, "Little tiny Tasseltop, you're the only friend I got. Big brown eyes and corn-silk hair, how you make me smile." You know, whatever feelings I was experiencing about that doll.

Mama wrote that down, because Mama would encourage me. She said, "That's really good." I must have been five or six when I wrote "Little Tiny Tasseltop." We found it years later in a shoebox. Mama kept a lot of stuff I wrote that I don't even remember.

Later on, when I started playing guitar and writing more serious songs at age seven, whenever somebody would come around Mama would say, "I want you to hear this song this little thing has made up. It's really good." And that just made me want to get more attention. Because there were so many of us, any special attention was good. So I learned early on to get attention through my songwriting. Because Mama was very encouraging.

I love seeing the expressions on kids' faces when they meet me. I guess because I'm blonde and sparkly, they think I'm a character from a fairy tale come to life. So when I made my first children's album, I decided I should look like a fairy princess on its cover by wearing this dress, complete with wings.

I Believe in You 2017

THIS IS THE TITLE TUNE of Dolly's children's album. When she was eight, her uncle Bill Owens replaced her homemade instruments by giving little Dolly her first real guitar. This aided her early songwriting efforts.

Just like that little story that we've all
read about
That says I can, I think I can, and I am
here to shout
That there's a little engine inside all of us
That says we can do anything if we just
don't give up.

CHORUS
Woo-woo, woo-woo, woo-woo-woo.
I can do it, so can you.
Woo-woo, woo-woo, woo-woo-woo.
I believe in you.

Now this big ol' world is full of dreams
and possibilities,
And the train of life is filled with hopes
and opportunities.
So stay on track and don't look back.
Just learn the rules and know the facts.
Clickety, clickety, clickety, clack
I believe in you.

REPEAT CHORUS THREE TIMES

I always had something inside me that believed I had something important to do. I didn't know exactly what that was.

One of the first little books I remember is *The Little Engine That Could*, which talked about "I think I can, I think I can." Well, since that time I've always thought that I am the little engine that did.

By the way, that's the first book that we give out through my Imagination Library program. It's all come about because of the faith instilled in me by Mama saying, "Through God all things are possible." And because of the message of that little book. So when I got ready to write songs for my children's album I thought of "I believe in you. I can do it, so can you."

I think it's so important to instill in children to have faith and to know there are great things out there. Greatness is out there, greatness you can tap into. But it has to start from in your heart.

My uncle Bill was one of Mama's younger brothers. He loved music, and he loved playing. He used to come to our house all the time . . . when it was time to eat on Sunday or when he needed a place to flop.

He was fascinated that I loved music just as much as he did. I would sing my songs to him, because I knew he wrote songs, too. So he was like a kindred spirit. He saw that I had potential.

We always had just old instruments around with the strings busted. But I would make anything work. Uncle Bill thought, "If she's that serious about this, she's gotta have a real guitar and learn to play it really good."

I remember I got these deep old blisters and calluses from practicing. Oh, it was so painful trying to learn. I kept saying, "It hurts." And he kept saying, "No, you're going to have to learn. You gotta wait until those ol' calluses harden until you won't feel it anymore, and that's when you're going to be serious. You can't cry and complain about that. You're going to get blisters."

But I loved that little baby Martin Guitar. I remember loving that thing like it was a piece of my body, a piece of my soul. I just made friends with it.

Uncle Bill had this big ol' red Gretsch electric guitar, and he was good. He kind of fancied himself that he was going to be a star. He was a very handsome boy, with black hair and a spit curl. So he had this billing as "Little Billy Earl with the Spit Curl."

So Little Billy Earl with the Spit Curl used to take me around to places like the county fair or to where a local radio station was going to have some sort of little musical thing on a truck bed outside of a store, different places.

That's when I thought, "Well, I have to believe in me." And I believe that all of us can do whatever it is that we set out to do.

Coat of Many Colors 1971

RELEASED IN THE FALL OF 1971, this song hit No. 4 on the country charts and served as the title tune of a Top 10 hit country LP the following year. Shania Twain and Alison Krauss later sang it, as did Emmylou Harris, the Oak Ridge Boys, and others. It inspired a highly rated NBC TV movie in 2015.

Back through the years I go wanderin'
once again,
Back to the seasons of my youth.
I recall a box of rags that someone gave us,
And how my mama put the rags to use.

There were rags of many colors, but every
piece was small,
And I didn't have a coat, and it was way down
in the fall.
Mama sewed the rags together, sewin' ev'ry
piece with love,
She made my coat of many colors that I was
so proud of.

As she sewed, she told a story from the Bible
she had read,
About a coat of many colors Joseph wore,
and then she said,
"Perhaps this coat will bring you good luck
and happiness."
And I couldn't wait to wear it, and mama
blessed it with a kiss.

My coat of many colors that my mama made
for me,
Made only from rags, but I wore it so
proudly.
Although we had no money, I was rich as
I could be
In my coat of many colors my mama made
for me.

So with patches on my britches and holes
in both my shoes,
In my coat of many colors, I hurried off
to school,
Just to find the others laughing and making
fun of me
In my coat of many colors my mama made
for me.

And, oh, I couldn't understand it, for I felt
I was rich.
And I told them of the love my mama sewed
in every stitch.
And I told them all the story mama told me
while she sewed,
And how my coat of many colors was worth
more than all their clothes.

But they didn't understand it, and I tried
to make them see
That one is only poor, only if they choose
to be.
Now I know we had no money, but I was rich
as I could be
In my coat of many colors my mama made
for me

My coat of many colors that my mama made
for me,
Made only from rags, but I wore it so
proudly.
Now I know we had no money, but I was rich
as I could be
In my coat of many colors my mama made
for me.
. . . Made just for me.

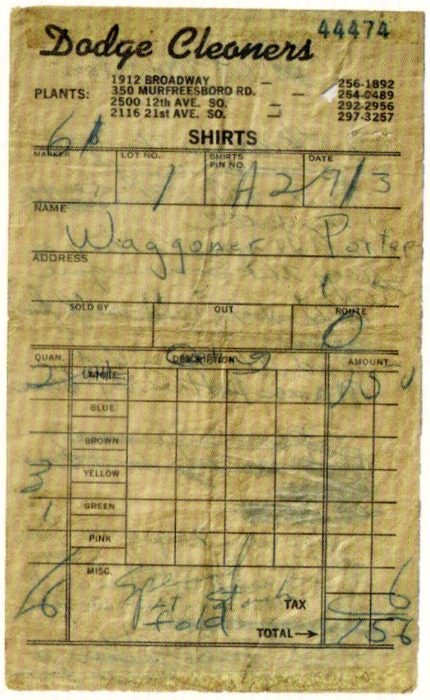

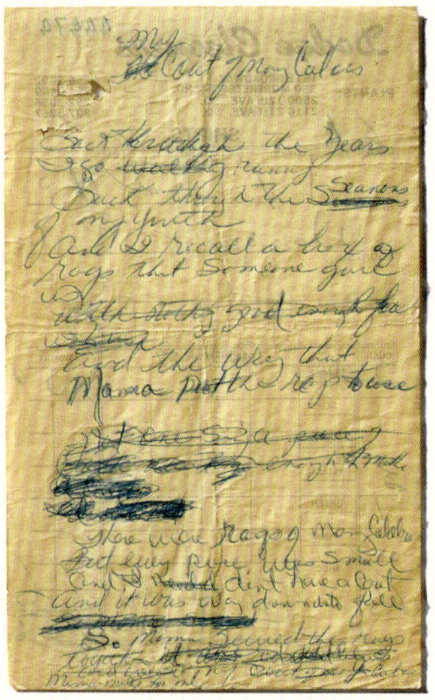

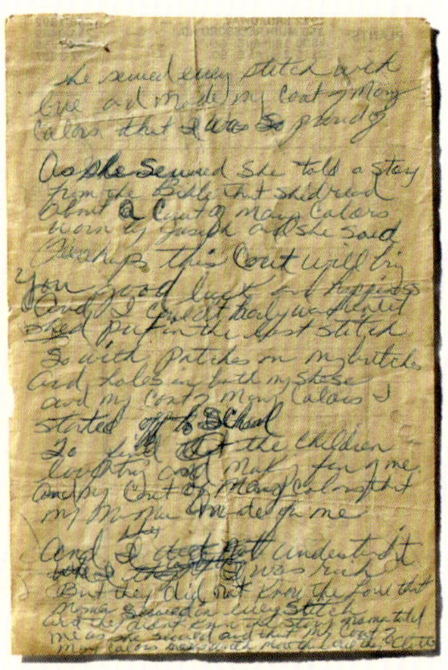

I'll grab whatever is handy when a song strikes me. In this case, it was Porter Wagoner's dry-cleaning receipt, which was on the tour bus. I scribbled down my original lyrics for "Coat of Many Colors" right then and there.

When I was a young child, there were a lot of poor people who grew up in our area. But then we started going to a bigger school, where there were other children who had more things than we did.

My mom made me this little coat. In order to make me proud of that little coat, I know now, she told me the story about Joseph from the Bible and his coat of many colors. So I thought, "Well, if it's from the Bible, and Joseph was an important person, it has to be very special and important."

Then when I went to school, the kids did not see that. They just made fun of my little coat. I had seen so much more in that coat than what Mama had sewn, things sewn into my body, my soul, my everything. Mama had made it and told the story and made it all seem so real. It was so mind-warping and heart-shattering to me when they made fun of it. In my mind, I thought I looked just like Joseph. But the kids didn't, and it crushed me.

I was trying to tell them in my own way, "It ain't about golden riches. You can be rich in love. In all sorts of wonderful things, you can be rich." But the kids didn't get that.

It's amazing how kids can be cruel without knowing that they are. As they say, "Everybody loves to hate." Everybody loves to pick on something. And once you get a little kid down, everybody thinks, "Well, let's pile in on that."

When I was feeling bad enough as it was, they locked me in the coat closet and wouldn't let me out. And I was so afraid of the dark as a kid.

That was a traumatic thing for a child of that age—to be shattered and to try to put those pieces back together, trying to teach a bunch of kids who didn't want to know.

I was even kind of hurt and angry at my mama, because I felt that she had sort of told me a fib. I even expressed that to her. So that's when Mama said, "Look, don't you ever say we are poor. We are not poor people. Now, we don't have as much material stuff as other people do, but wealth is not measured by a dollar." She explained the whole thing to me and again made me feel proud of my little coat.

So that little song is like a world of things. It teaches about bullying, about love, about acceptance, about good parents. That little story has even been written into a schoolbook to teach children about being different, that it's all right to be different. And that you don't make fun of other people. You have to accept everything and everybody.

At the time, I thought, "Why is this happening?" Now I know it was so I could write that song. It really is true that "God works in strange and mysterious ways His wonders to perform." You never know when you're going through things what is actually going to turn out to be a blessing. So it's worth the suffering.

"So that little song is like a world of things. It teaches about bullying, about love, about acceptance, about good parents. That little story has even been written into a schoolbook to teach children about being different. You have to accept everything and everybody."

My Tennessee Mountain Home 1973

A NO. 15 COUNTRY HIT, this is the title tune of Dolly's concept album about her Smoky Mountain girlhood. It was later revived by folk and pop star Maria Muldaur and by country rock's Earl Scruggs Revue, as well as by Dolly's early childhood favorite, Rose Maddox.

Sittin' on a front porch on a summer afternoon
In a straight-back chair on two legs, leaned against the wall.
Watch the kids a-playin' with June-bugs on a string,
And chase the glowin' fireflies when evenin' shadows fall.

CHORUS
In my Tennessee mountain home,
Life is as peaceful as a baby's sigh.
In my Tennessee mountain home,
Crickets sing in the fields nearby.

Honeysuckle vine clings to the fence along the lane,
Their fragrance makes the summer wind so sweet.
And on a distant hilltop, an eagle spreads its wings
And a songbird on a fencepost sings a melody.

REPEAT CHORUS

Walkin' home from church on a Sunday with the one you love,
Just laughin', talkin', makin' future plans.
And when the folks ain't lookin', you might steal a kiss or two,
Sittin' in the porch swing, holdin' hands.

REPEAT CHORUS

The Chasing Rainbows Museum at Dollywood has recreations of the rooms of "My Tennessee Mountain Home," some using our original furniture. My uncle Louis took the photo of the real house for the cover of my 1973 album.

I love being a mountain girl, a country girl. And I've written so many songs about it. "My Tennessee Mountain Home" really talks about sitting on a front porch, leaning back like we used to, singing, and having peaceful times. There were hard times, too. But when you grow up in the mountains, you're not working every second. If it's right after supper and you're with your mom and dad, everything seems to be calm. There are those moments when you talk about peaceful things—lightning bugs out in the fields, kids running around doing whatever, and thinking back.

We would all set out on the porch and play music. We were always together, singing songs. Whether it would be aunts and uncles, cousins, brothers and sisters, we would kind of branch out into little groups. Whether it was a little trio that was asked to go sing at a funeral, or if it was a bunch of us that were asked to go play at a barn dance, we could do it. And we certainly all used to sing in church.

Most of us in the household learned to play early on. Every time anybody would show up, any uncle or aunt who knew how to play an instrument, I'd have them show me how to play a little bit on the banjo, the guitar, an autoharp, or whatever instrument was around. I wanted to find different sounds, so I would just have anybody help me. Because I wanted to write songs.

One of my favorite lines in this song is "Life is as peaceful as a baby's sigh." We always had plenty of babies, and there's nothing like holding a little baby after he's bawled his head off and finally gone to sleep.

My Tennessee Mountain Home

1 Sittin on the front porch on a summer
afternoon
In a straight back chair on two legs
leaned against the wall
I watch the kids a playing with June
bugs on a string
And chase the glowing fireflies when evening
shadows fall

Cho
In My Tennessee Mountain Home
Life is as peaceful as a baby's sigh
In my Tennessee Mountain Home
Crickets sing in the fields nearby

2 Honeysuckle vine cling to the fence along
the lane
And their fragrance makes the summer
wind so sweet
And On a distant hilltop an eagle spreads
it's wings
And a song bird on a fence post
sings a melody

Repeat Chorus

These really are my daddy's work boots. He is so precious to me, and I'm so glad I got to hold on to this little bit of him. The shoes inspired a song, and my daddy inspired me.

"You don't really realize how many people can't read and write. Me telling the story about my daddy instilled some pride in people who felt like they had to keep it hidden like a secret."

Daddy's Working Boots 1972

THIS IS AN ELEGY for Dolly's hard-working father, Robert Lee Parton (1921–2000). It appeared on her LP *My Tennessee Mountain Home*.

My dear, hard-workin' Daddy works his life away for us.
That's the way that Daddy shows to us his love
And Daddy's two hard-workin' hands,
They're callous and they're sore.
And Daddy's working boots
Have walked a million miles or more.

As long as I remember, I remember Daddy workin',
Workin' on the job, or either on the farm,
Trying to provide for the family that he loves.
And Daddy's working boots
Have taken many steps for us.

CHORUS
Daddy's workin' boots have served as his foundation,
Though, just like him, they're tired and worn.
For years they've helped him stand.
Daddy's workin' boots have filled their obligation.
They've walked that rocky road
With a mighty, mighty man.

Dear Lord above, I know up there my Daddy's got a mansion.
And a great reward that's long been overdue.
And when it comes my Daddy's time to be with You in Heaven,
Won't You let him walk Your golden streets
In a pair of brand-new golden boots?

REPEAT CHORUS

My daddy was so precious. He really did make his living by the bend of his back and the sweat of his brow. Daddy always wore these big old hard-working boots, which I have in the museum at Dollywood. I wrote the song "Daddy's Working Boots," and even one called "The Dinner Bucket" about his lunch pail and what we remember about him.

Daddy raised that whole family on his brains and hard work. He was such a smart person. I always thought that if Daddy had an education, there's no telling what he could have been. Because he knew how to barter, he knew how to bargain. He knew how to make everything work, and he knew how to count money. He knew exactly what everything was worth, how much he was going to make from that tobacco crop, what he could trade, and how he could make it all work.

My dad couldn't read and write, and he was always kind of ashamed of that. But it's not a thing to be ashamed of, because in my daddy's case, he grew up in a family of fifteen kids, back in the mountains. You had a one-room schoolhouse, and it was sometimes a mile away. Kids had to go to work in the fields to help feed the family. Because of the weather and because of conditions, a lot of kids couldn't go to school.

So he influenced me to start the Imagination Library. I got him involved helping me with it, and he felt so great about that. I told him, "Daddy, there are probably millions of people in this world who don't know how to read and write, who didn't get the opportunity. Don't be ashamed of that. Let's do something special."

You don't really realize how many people can't read and write. Me telling the story about my daddy instilled some pride in people who felt like they had to keep it hidden like a secret. I get so many letters from people saying, "I would never have admitted it" or "I was always ashamed."

Whenever I make appearances for the Imagination Library, I love to read stories or sing to the kids. They call me "The Book Lady," and Daddy loved that nickname.

Daddy got to live long enough to see it doing really well, and he just loved it when kids would call me "The Book Lady." He took pride that he was a part of that. And I wanted him to, because he was my inspiration for doing it. I think deep down inside, my daddy was prouder of that than he even was of my career.

When I started it with my dad, I thought, "Well, maybe we can do it for a county or two." Then we went all over Tennessee, and then we got into Canada. We're in places all over the world now. We've given away 130 million books so far, and it's still growing.

I'm certainly no educated person. I've just got a high-school education. I hated school, because I wanted to get out and make my music.

My songwriting and the Imagination Library are the two things I'm proudest of in my life. They're what I hope to be remembered for.

And I take great pride in Daddy. I get a lot of my spirituality and my music from my mom. But I've got my daddy's nerve and determination and work ethic. The biggest reason that I work is for my family. I want to be there for them, just like Daddy. I'll work 'til I fall dead, just like my daddy. And I work for my family, just like my daddy. Daddy was very, very special.

ABOVE: Robert Lee Parton is surrounded by his family in this photo. Mama is holding baby Rachel on her lap. Can you tell that's me standing second from the left?

BELOW: The state of Tennessee offers a license plate, with proceeds going to the Imagination Library that I started with Daddy.

Dr. Robert F. Thomas 1972

THIS SONG ON DOLLY'S *Tennessee Mountain Home* album praises the country doctor who brought her into the world. He was paid with a sack of cornmeal for delivering her at home. He was a mountain physician who worked for little money throughout his life to care for the poor in East Tennessee. Today, Dolly supports a Sevier County charity fund named in honor of Dr. Robert F. Thomas (1891–1980).

CHORUS

Dr. Robert F. Thomas,
May his name forever stand.
Dr. Robert F. Thomas
Was a mighty, mighty man.
And he enriched the lives
Of everyone that ever knew him.
And in my song, I hope to sing
Some of the praise that's due him.

Dr. Thomas was a man the Lord must have appointed
To live among us mountain folks in Eastern Tennessee.
And he delivered more than half the babies in those mountains.
Among those babies, he delivered me.

There was no way to drive along the roads back in those mountains.
But Dr. Thomas got there just the same.
He often rode on horseback, to get where he was needed.
But if he had to walk, he always came.

REPEAT CHORUS

Dr. Thomas was a friend, a neighbor, and a doctor,
Though he seldom got a dime for all he'd done.
And I remember lots of times we sent for Dr. Thomas,
But I don't recall a time he didn't come.

They say a man is judged by the deeds he does while livin',
A judgment when he stands before the Lord.
And I know Heaven holds a place for men like Dr. Thomas,
And I know he'll receive his just reward.

REPEAT CHORUS

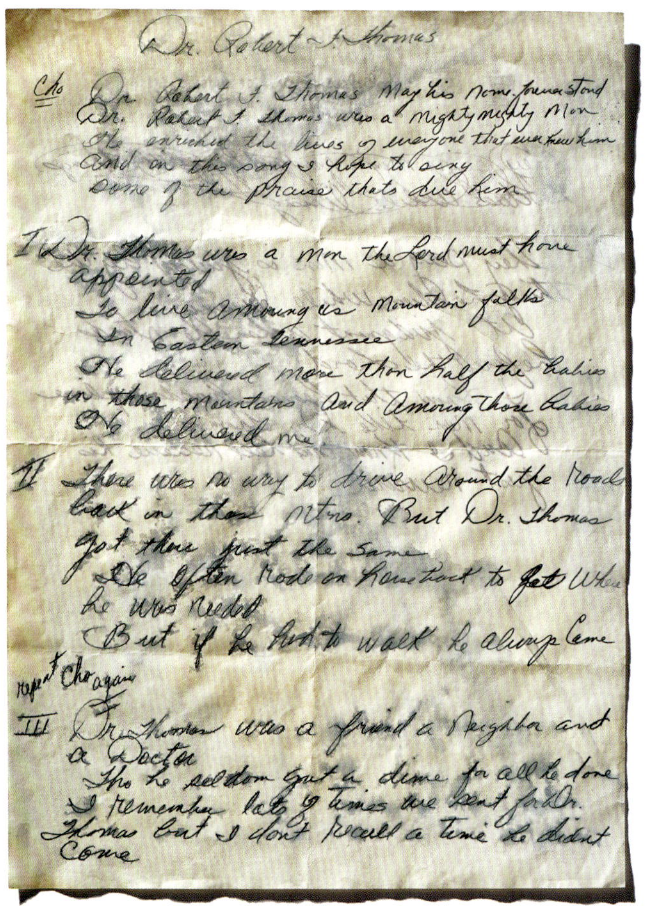
Dr. Robert F. Thomas

Cho Dr. Robert F. Thomas May his name forever stand
Dr. Robert F. Thomas was a mighty mighty man
He enriched the lives of everyone that ever knew him
And on this song I hope to sing
Some of the praise thats due him

I Dr. Thomas was a man the Lord must have appointed
To live among us mountain folks
In Eastern Tennessee
He delivered more than half the babies
in those mountains And among those babies
He delivered me

II There was no way to drive around the roads
back in those Mtns. But Dr. Thomas
got there just the same
He often rode on horseback to get where
he was needed
But if he had to walk he always came

repeat Cho again

III Dr. Thomas was a friend a neighbor and
a Doctor
Tho he seldom got a dime for all he done
I remember lots of times we sent for Dr.
Thomas but I don't recall a time he didnt
Come

Dr. Robert F. Thomas carried this black doctor's bag with him when he went up into the mountains to care for the poor folks. He brought me into the world, and I've tried to keep his memory alive.

Dr. Thomas was a missionary and a very educated city man. I think he was born and raised in New York. He had been sent overseas with his family. His son got some disease that was so severe that they came back to the United States. He was a Methodist, and the church decided to send him somewhere else. They sent him to the Smoky Mountains because of the poor people there.

He pastored a church and had a little clinic beside the church. It was in a community called Pittman Center. There were so many poor people who lived up in those mountains that he always kept a horse, because that's the only way he could get to those folks.

He was such a wonderful man. But he would go up into those mountains with those country people, and a lot of them would hold a gun on him: "If my wife dies or my daughter dies, you're going to die, too." There's lots of stories about him.

But anytime you cut a leg half off—you couldn't go all the way to Knoxville to the nearest hospital—you'd go get Dr. Thomas. He was the one who snipped your tonsils or did whatever. I still remember that antiseptic smell in his little clinic by the church. He was there to save those poor people of the mountains, and he was kind of a savior to us.

There were twelve of us kids. Six of us were born at home, and six of us were born in hospitals. I'm one of the older ones. I have a sister and two brothers older than me. A lot of the kids, my grandma or my aunts would help deliver. But if you had problems, you had to send for Dr. Thomas.

I was born on January 19, and it was snowing. When I was trying to be born, Mom was having trouble so Daddy had to ride his horse out to Pittman to get Dr. Thomas to ride with him back to our place. He certainly couldn't drive there. Dr. Thomas came and helped deliver me. Daddy didn't have any money, but we always raised corn and had cornmeal. So I always make a joke that "Dr. Thomas was paid for with a sack of cornmeal, and I've been raking in the dough ever since."

I Remember 1972

THIS SONG ABOUT DOLLY'S PARENTS is included on the 1972 album *My Tennessee Mountain Home*. The Partons' twelve children are Willadeene (b. 1940), David (b. 1942), Denver (b. 1943), Dolly (b. 1946), Bobby (b. 1948), Stella (b. 1949), Cassie (b. 1951), Randy (b. 1953), Larry (1955–1955), Freida (b. 1957), Floyd (1957–2018), and Rachel (b. 1959).

I remember, I remember
I remember Mama and Daddy most of all.

I remember meadows and fields of golden wheat
I remember songbirds and sugarcane so sweet.
I remember lots of things that often I recall.
But I remember Mama and Daddy most of all.

I remember gingerbread my mama used to bake.
I remember homemade toys that Daddy used to make.
Yes, I remember many things that often I recall.
But I remember Mama and Daddy most of all.

I remember Mama and Daddy most of all,
In our little country home they filled with love.

I remember Mama and Daddy most of all,
And all the things they did to make life happier for us.
Yes, I remember lots of things that often I recall,
But I remember Mama and Daddy most of all.

I remember candy that Daddy used to bring.
I remember songs my mama used to sing.
Oh, I remember many things that often I recall,
But I remember Mama and Daddy most of all.

I remember Mama and Daddy most of all,
And how they taught us children right from wrong.

I remember Mama and Daddy most of all,
How they used to hope and pray they'd live to see us grown
Oh, I remember many things that often I recall,
I remember Mama and Daddy most of all.

I remember, I remember.
I remember Mama and Daddy most of all
. . . Most of all.

In the back row, left to right, are Randy, David, Willadeene, Rachel, me, Mama, and Daddy. Seated in front are Cassie, Stella, Denver, Freida, Floyd, and Bobby. The twelfth child was Larry. He was to be "my baby" to care for, but he died at birth.

Through all the hard times and everything we went through, we had Mom and Daddy. They were bigger than us. They were wiser than us. And we felt like no matter what was going on, it was going to be all right, because we had Mom and Daddy.

Mom and Daddy got married when Mama was fifteen and Daddy was seventeen. By the time they were thirty-five and thirty-seven years old, they already had twelve kids, one set of twins. That's working really, really fast.

I always joke that I had to memorize my brothers' and sisters' names. We were born eighteen months or two years apart. Mama loved Daddy. Even if she had had birth control, she probably wouldn't have used it. And, obviously, she didn't.

I remember one time the doctor gave my mom a diaphragm. I was always such a curious kid, always so nosy. I remember finding that diaphragm under their mattress and thought, "What is that?" Somebody told me years later, and we laughed about it. I said, "Well, I don't know what she used it for. She must have drunk tea out of it, because she certainly didn't use it for birth control!"

They loved us, every one of us. They were overjoyed with every new baby. And every one of us older kids got to say, "Okay, you take care of this one, and you get to take care of that one."

"I Remember" pretty much tells its own story. It's just about the love that our parents had.

I've written so many songs about my parents. There's one song I wrote called "It Ain't Easy Being Dad" about my daddy. And it ain't easy being "Mom" either, especially when you grow up like we did.

It's never easy, no matter where you grow up. But to really maneuver that brood of kids, in that part of the world, with no real money coming in, just trying to survive without dying in the winter of pneumonia or worse, it's a lot to think about, a lot to write about, a lot to be grateful for. I think about my mom and dad all the time.

In the Good Old Days (When Times Were Bad) 1968

RELEASED AS A COUNTRY SINGLE in late 1968, this song rose to No. 25 on the charts. It became the title tune of Dolly's third solo album and was also included on 1972's *My Tennessee Mountain Home*. Country stars Merle Haggard, Jeannie Seely, and Skeeter Davis have also recorded this lyric.

We'd get up before sun-up to get the work
done up.
We'd work in the fields 'til the sun had gone
down.
We've stood, and we've cried as we helplessly
watched
A hailstorm a-beatin' our crops to the
ground.
We've gone to be hungry many nights in
the past
In the good old days, when times were bad.

CHORUS
No amount of money could buy from me
The memories that I have of then.
No amount of money could pay me
To go back and live through it again.

I've seen Daddy's hands break open and
bleed.
And I've seen him work 'til he's stiff as a
board.
I've seen Mama layin' in sufferin' and
sickness
In need of a doctor we couldn't afford.
Anything at all was more than we had
In the good old days, when times were bad.

We've got up before and found ice on the
floor
Where the wind would blow snow through
the cracks in the wall.
And I couldn't enjoy then, havin' a boyfriend
I had nothing decent to wear at all.
So I long for a love that I never had
In the good old days, when times were bad.

REPEAT CHORUS

In the good old days, when times were bad.
In the good old days, when times were bad.

Here I am at age three, "outstanding in my field." I still love to be out in nature, because I find inspiration there.

One of my favorite songs that I think is so descriptive is "In the Good Old Days (When Times Were Bad)." Even that title I love.

I remember Mom and Daddy working so hard, and I remember Mom used to get depressed. We didn't understand that until we were older. Every fall, she was thinking about winter coming on, not knowing if we were going to get sick and die. And Mama would always be in sickness.

We lived in these old, cold-ass houses, where we slept with our clothes on. You had to sleep dressed. Daddy wouldn't let us get up until he'd built a fire and had it going. I remember us saying, "Daddy, is the fire hot?" We had to wait. When we were little, we'd pee the bed and then go to school with those clothes on.

The snow would come in through those cracks in the wall. Mama and Daddy would have to thaw the water from the water bucket in the kitchen. That's how cold it was in those old houses.

Just like the song says, "No amount of money could buy from me, the memories that I have of then. No amount of money could pay me to go back and live through it again."

All of that environment and lifestyle that I was born into I've been able to use in my songwriting. Because my heart and mind are always open to every feeling.

As a songwriter and as a person, I have to leave myself wide open. I suffer a lot, because I am open to so much. I hurt a lot, and when I hurt, I hurt all over. Because I can't harden my heart to protect myself. I always say that I strengthen the muscles around my heart, but I can't harden it.

I just draw from everything I ever was—exactly where I'm from, how it all happened, and exactly who I am—because that's why I'm here today.

Early Morning Breeze 1971

DOLLY HAS RECORDED THIS PASTORAL song twice, once on 1971's *Coat of Many Colors* album and once on her 1974 *Jolene* collection.

I open up my door to greet the early morning sun.
Closing it behind me and away I do run
To the meadow where the meadowlark is singing in the tree.
In the meadow I go walking in the early morning breeze.

I cup my hands to catch a multi-colored butterfly
Perched upon the petals of a flower growing wild.
Freeing it, I watch it as it flies away from me
To visit with the flowers in the early morning breeze.

Rainbow colored flowers kiss the early morning sun,
The astor and the dahlia and the wild geranium.
Drops of morning dew still linger on the iris leaves
In the meadow where I'm walking in the early morning breeze.

Misty-eyed, I look about the meadow where I stray
For it's there I find the courage to greet the coming day.
For there among the flowers, I kneel gently to my knees
To have a word with God in the early morning breeze.

A rainbow colored meadow kissed with early morning sun,
The astor and the dahlia and the wild geranium.
Drops of morning dew still linger on the iris leaves
In the meadow where I'm walking in the early morning breeze.

Wildflowers 1987

DOLLY'S PROFESSIONAL JOURNEY BEGAN when Uncle Bill Owens (b. 1935) took her to Knoxville to audition for entrepreneur Cas Walker (1902–1998). The colorful grocery mogul and controversial politician hired her at age ten to become a regular on his radio and TV show, the *Cas Walker Farm and Home Hour*. When she performed there during the summer months, Avie Lee's sister Estelle Owens Watson (1921–1993) looked after little Dolly. Married duo entertainers Carl & Pearl Butler (1927–1992 and 1927–1988) also took Dolly under their wings. (The Butlers are noted for the country classics "Don't Let Me Cross Over," "Crying My Heart Out over You," and "If Teardrops Were Pennies.") This song first appeared on the 1987 LP *Trio*, which Dolly recorded with Linda Ronstadt and Emmylou Harris.

The hills were alive with wildflowers, and I
Was as wild, even wilder than they.
For at least I could run.
They just died in the sun,
And I refused to just wither in place.

Just a wild mountain rose
Needing freedom to grow,
So I ran, fearing not where I'd go.
When a flower grows wild, it can always
survive.
Wildflowers don't care where they grow.

And the flowers I knew
In the fields where I grew
Were content to be lost in the crowd.
They were common and close. I had no room
for growth.
I wanted so much to branch out.

So I uprooted myself from my home ground
and left,
Took my dreams,
And I took to the road.
When a flower grows wild, it can always
survive.
Wildflowers don't care where they grow.

I grew up fast and wild,
And I never felt right
In a garden so different from me.
I just never belonged. I just longed to be
gone.
So the garden one day set me free.

I hitched a ride with the wind,
And since he was my friend,
I just let him decide where we'd go.
When a flower grows wild, it can always
survive.
Wildflowers don't care where they grow.

Just a wild, rambling rose
Seeking mysteries untold,
No regrets for the path that I chose.
When a flower grows wild, it can always
survive.
Wildflowers don't care where they grow.

That's me and Uncle Bill on stage together during my teen years. Notice his spit curl.

Well, let me start by talking about Cas Walker. Cas Walker was an old raccoon hunter who started selling groceries door-to-door with a wheelbarrow. He was a real character. Eventually, he started his own chain of supermarkets. He was smart. He thought, "How am I going to sell my groceries? Well, I'm going to buy some time on the radio."

So he rented this theater in Knoxville, Tennessee, and put together this radio show [on WIVK]. He hired local bands and singers to come be on it. And eventually, he went on TV.

My uncle Bill said, "Well, we gotta take you down to the Cas Walker show," and that's where I got my first shot. Bill and I went down there, me with my little guitar and him with his big ol' Gretsch guitar. It was 1956, and I was ten years old. My two big numbers at the time were "I Love a Tall Man" by Rose Maddox and the George Jones song "You Gotta Be My Baby," which was a hit that year.

I went out and sang "You Gotta Be My Baby" and, I mean, the crowd loved me! They just applauded and applauded. I looked back at my uncle Bill, because I didn't know what to do. He said, "Just sing it again!" So I sang it two or three times.

After that, we were walking in the parking lot and I said to Uncle Bill, "I think they like me. I think I might could be a star." He said, "Well, I think you might could be, too." And I was so proud.

So I went to Cas Walker and said, "I want to work for you." He said, "Well, then you've got a job, because you're the only person that ever said they would 'work.'" He used to pay me $5 a show out of his pocket.

My mother's sister, my aunt Estelle, was married to a construction worker named Dot Watson, and they lived in Knoxville. After my big debut with Cas Walker, she would let me stay with her and would take me back and forth to the shows. And when

This is me and Uncle Lester posing on the hood of his car. He was a truck driver and gave me money to buy clothes for shows in the early days.

she couldn't, I could catch the city bus up the hill from where she lived. I was a little bit scared, but I enjoyed the fact that I was kind of independent and doing things we never did in the mountains.

Two other people who were very important to me at the time were Carl and Pearl Butler. They worked there at the Cas Walker show. They just loved me, and I loved them. They used to take me to their house to eat. I still have some film footage of me being there at their house in Knoxville. They also hired Uncle Bill to play guitar for them.

Dorothy Gable was a well-to-do woman in Knoxville who took an interest in me, too. She gave me and my uncle Bill money to pay for some self-made records and stuff.

A lot of times, I don't get to talk about the people who were behind the scenes. They don't always get the just dues that they deserve. But there's always great people who help you along the way.

I remember thinking at the time, "This is what I'm gonna do." So my mind took to wondering about where I was going to go next, where my dreams were going to take me.

When I wrote the song "Wildflowers," it reminded me of that time. Because I can draw from my childhood, roaming those fields. I knew the difference between beautiful garden flowers and the ones that grew wild. So I thought that made a really good base for singing about my dreams.

I've always been a wildflower, and I've always loved that song. It's going to live forever, I hope.

Puppy Love

(Bill Earl Owens / Dolly Parton) 1959

WHEN DOLLY WAS THIRTEEN YEARS OLD, two landmark events occurred. First, her debut commercial recording was released. Her uncle Henry Owens (1931–2003) arranged a recording session in Louisiana. This resulted in Dolly's first single, released on April 20, 1959. Very much in the hepped-up Brenda Lee rockabilly style, it's a teen-romance tune. On the single's flip side was "Girl Left Alone," which Dolly co-wrote with Uncle Bill and Aunt Dorothy Jo. The second big occasion occurred when Bill snagged her a guest appearance on the Grand Ole Opry in Nashville.

CHORUS
Puppy love, puppy love,
They all call it puppy love.
I'm old enough now to kiss and hug
And I like it, it's puppy love.

Pullin' my pigtails makes me mad.
When you kiss me, makes me glad.
You turn to leave and make me sad.
Still, you're the sweetest sweetheart I've
ever had.

REPEAT CHORUS TWICE

Sometimes you won't even carry my books.
The next time you see me, you'll rag on my
looks.
You're meaner to me than a mean ol' crook.
And I must confess, I'm really hooked.

REPEAT CHORUS

My first record was called "Puppy Love," and it was on Goldband Records in Lake Charles, Louisiana. I had an uncle named Robert Henry, and he was stationed in the Air Force down there. My musician uncles had found this recording studio. They said, "You need to come down here and make a record."

Well, how am I going to get to Louisiana? Mama's got a houseful of kids. Daddy ain't gonna want me to go, so we kind of had to sneak around. There was nobody to take me. This was my big chance, and I would beg anybody and everybody to take me, because Uncle Henry was sending me the money to go.

My grandma was beginning to get senile at that time. She dipped snuff and carried a can with a lid on it to spit in. She had never been anywhere. But she was the only person who could take me. I was just twelve, but I begged and begged, "Mommy, you've got to let me go, because this is my big chance."

So me and Grandma get the tickets and get on the bus in Sevierville to go to Louisiana. We don't know anything or anybody. We got off the bus and got lost. The bus leaves us there in Birmingham. My grandma was just a nervous wreck. She didn't know what to do or how to talk to anybody.

We'd eaten the little food we'd brought. People offered us potato chips or whatever. I was just shaking. I'm just a little country kid, and I don't know how to talk to people either. So I go up to the man at the depot and tell him where we're trying to go. He told us we would have to wait. I remember us sleeping in the bus station with Grandma crying.

Well, we finally got to Lake Charles. And then I got to make "Puppy Love." I fell in love with the little boy that was [Goldband executive] Ed Shuler's son, Johnny. He was the prettiest thing I had ever seen. We were about the same age, and that was my first big crush. My first big love and my first record.

When "Puppy Love" came out, it only got played locally. I remember the first time I heard myself on the radio. I about killed myself. I was sitting up on the counter, and the radio was on. I jumped off the counter and slid and fell trying to get to the radio to turn it up.

Uncle Henry became "John Henry III." He also sang and wrote. After he got out of the military, he worked at Dollywood for years. But I'll always thank him for that first record. My uncles were very prominent in my life.

My uncle Bill thought, “Well, we’ve made a record now. The next move is we’ve gotta go to Nashville and the Grand Ole Opry.”

So we’d go on trips back and forth to Nashville in whatever beat-up old car that Uncle Bill would have, anything that could take us there. I remember this one car [a 1953 brown Ford with a bashed-in passenger side and a blue, replacement front fender]—I think the very car that took me to the Opry—my side was wired together. You couldn’t get out of that side. I’d have to slide over and get out of the driver’s side.

Uncle Bill was really good at talking to people and convincing people. And who’s going to say “no” to a little kid? So we finagled around until [Opry star] Jimmy C. Newman gave us one of his spots on the Grand Ole Opry.

I was thirteen years old. Johnny Cash introduced me, and I thought he was the sexiest thing that ever was. That’s when I first felt hormones raging. It was his charisma and me being a growing girl. It was the first time a man had ever made me feel like a woman.

It was a special time. Being on the Grand Ole Opry was a dream. That was *something*. My daddy loved the Grand Ole Opry, and I just wanted to be on it so they could hear me back home.

My original handwritten lyrics for “Puppy Love” have survived all these years. For some reason, when the record came out, the songwriting credit read “Owens.” But my uncle Bill did help me with that one.

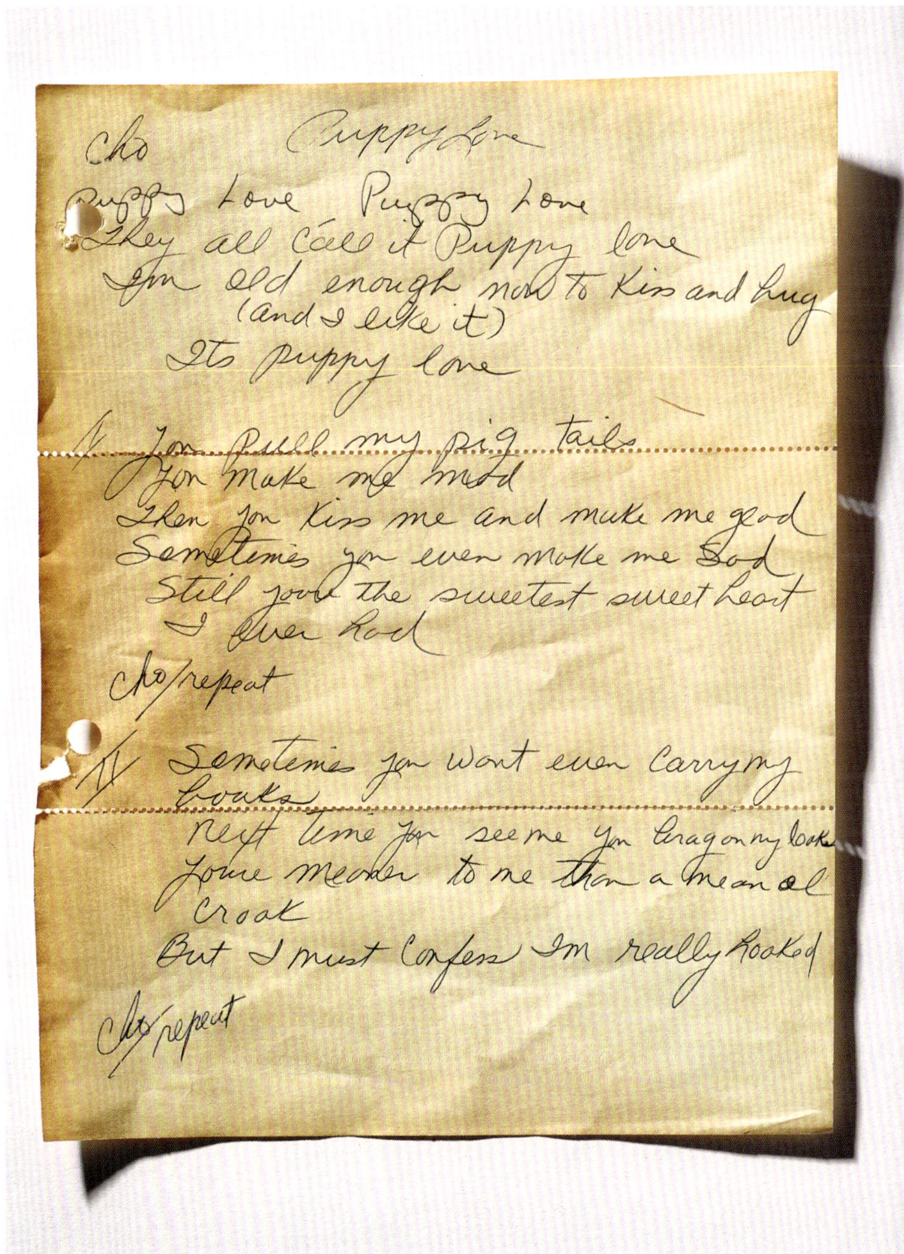

Cho Puppy Love
Puppy Love Puppy Love
They all call it Puppy love
I'm old enough now to kiss and hug
(and I like it)
Its puppy love

I You pull my pig tails
You make me mad
Then you kiss me and make me glad
Sometimes you even make me sad
Still you're the sweetest sweet heart
I ever had
cho/repeat

II Sometimes you won't even carry my books
Next time you see me you drag on my looks
You're meaner to me than a mean ol crook
But I must confess I'm really hooked
cho/repeat

Paradise Road 1998

AFTER "PUPPY LOVE" CAME OUT, young Dolly was on her way. She continued to appear on Knoxville television, record tunes at local radio stations, entertain at East Tennessee community events, and set her sights on Music City. "Paradise Road" was featured on her 1998 CD *Hungry Again*.

I grew up dirty, and I grew up poor.
The wolf didn't even hang around our door.
Not a crumb to spare,
And the cupboard bare.
But I had the gift of imagination.
I could change my situation.
Anytime I chose,
I could always go
Down Paradise Road.

I found a kingdom deep within,
A place to dream and to pretend.
And to prepare
For the world out there.
A dream can dress you when you're ragged,
Fill you up when hunger's naggin'.
I warmed my soul
When life was cold
On Paradise Road.

Paradise is a state of mind.
The sun shines warm and all the time.
And the rain don't flow,
And the wind don't blow
On Paradise Road.

A place no one can take from me,
A place of everlasting peace,
Where dreamers go,
It's never closed,
Paradise Road.

Paradise is a state of mind
Down the road of life and time.
And the friends we meet
Make the travelin' sweet
On Paradise Road.

Sometimes now when the world is mad,
I find that place I've always had
Inside my soul.
It's paved in gold,
Paradise Road.

I grew up dirty, and I grew up poor.
The wolf didn't even hang 'round our door.
Not a crumb to spare,
And the cupboard bare.
But I had the gift of imagination.
I could change my situation.
Anytime I chose,
I could always go
Down Paradise Road.

"Paradise Road" is one of my favorite songs because it kind of talks about my thoughts, my dreams, my plans. It really sums up what I was thinking, about getting out into the world and doing whatever I had to do.

It came about because of something I said as a kid to a man who lived up the mountain from us. I was jumping around on the road because I felt I had made a connection with God in this abandoned old church down below us. It was the first time in my life when I felt like that outside of a church service. I remember I was just dancing around, and my uncle Vonnie Owens, who owned the sawmill above us, said, "Where are you going on this fine day?" I said, "I'm on the road to Paradise!"

My idea in the song was that it has always been my imagination that I knew was going to get me out. Whatever I can't deal with, I've always had the power to imagine that it's different. Until I can make it so. That's kind of how I live my life to this day. I can always go to dreamland in my mind. I've always got my fantasy life, and I've always got my dreams. I can plan and dream until I can make it come true.

That's my 1964 prom dress. I couldn't wait to graduate from high school so I could get busy on my musical career. My freshman, sophomore, junior, and senior school photos show my various 1960s hair experiments.

CHAPTER 2

DOWN ON MUSIC ROW

BRIMMING WITH OPTIMISM FOLLOWING HER DEBUT SINGLE AND Opry guest appearance in 1959, Dolly returned to East Tennessee to continue her teenage musical endeavors. She made tapes of her tunes at WIVK in Knoxville and WSEV in Sevierville, and she and Uncle Bill traveled back and forth to Music City with those tapes, hoping to get someone interested in their songs and in her voice.

She continued appearing on the *Cas Walker Farm and Home Hour*, making $20 a week by this time. Doggedly pursuing her country music aspirations, she ignored the teasing of her high school classmates, who were doing the Twist and swooning over teen idols like Elvis, Fabian, and Ricky Nelson.

During one Nashville visit, she briefly recorded songs for Mercury Records at age fifteen. Around the same time, she recorded some Kitty Wells songs for the budget label Somerset Records. Dolly was eighteen when she moved to Nashville for good.

In Music City, Uncle Bill continued to shepherd her. Carl and Pearl Butler (of the *Cas Walker* show) had also relocated to Nashville by this time and had scored a No. 1 country hit in 1963 with "Don't Let Me Cross Over." Motherly Pearl remained in Dolly's corner, feeding her, championing her talent, and loaning her stage clothes. Dolly took part-time jobs as a receptionist at a neon sign company, a waitress in a family restaurant, and a singer on a local early-morning TV program.

The tide began to turn in 1965 with a recording pact at Monument Records and a songwriting contract with the Combine Music publishing company. Combine secured recordings of her songs by several established country stars.

Here are the songs that introduced her to the Nashville music industry. They include her first award-winning composition, her first self-penned single to make the country hit parade, and the first of her much-admired story songs.

This photo was taken at a recording session for Monument Records around 1965. In case you're wondering, yes, that's my real hair.

(It May Not Kill Me but) It's Sure Gonna Hurt

(Dolly Parton / Bill Owens) 1962

DOLLY'S FORAYS INTO THE NASHVILLE MUSIC SCENE throughout her teen years resulted in a few events that turned out to be false starts. Buddy Killen (1932–2006) signed her as a staff songwriter to his publishing company when she was fifteen and then secured a contract for her with Mercury Records. Because of her unusual, piercing, girlish soprano tremolo, he perceived her to be a pop novelty vocalist and had her sing this self-composed teenybopper single. It was released when she was sixteen. Dolly can also be heard on a cheaply made "supermarket" LP of her singing the songs of country superstar Kitty Wells.

It may not kill me, but it's sure gonna hurt.

Since my baby left me, I don't know what to do.
Just couldn't believe my eyes when I saw him with you.
He left me for you, oh, he's treating me like dirt.
It may not kill me, but it's sure gonna hurt.

CHORUS
It's sure gonna hurt to lose you, my poor heart's in pain.
Don't see how you could abuse me. It's driving me insane.
Oh, you're both out paintin' the town red.
Well, I'm paintin' it, too,
But I'm not paintin' the town red,
I'm paintin' it blue.

It hurts to lose everything to such a little flirt.
It may not kill me, but it's sure gonna hurt.

REPEAT CHORUS

It hurts to lose everything to such a little flirt.
It may not kill me, but it's sure gonna hurt.
It's sure gonna hurt.
It's sure gonna hurt.

Believe it or not, I actually got a royalty check from my days writing songs for Tree Publishing. It was only for a dollar and two cents. I'm surprised I even made that much, since nothing I wrote in those days was a hit.

My uncle Bill and I had been going back and forth to Nashville all my young years. We'd take along whatever food we had and go, trying to get people to record us, to listen to us. We would sleep in the car. My bedroom was in the back, and his was in the front seat.

Buddy Killen, who owned Tree Publishing Company at that time, is one of the people who gave me my very first shot at the big time, so to speak. He took an interest in my songs, and he took an interest in me.

When I was fifteen, he got [Jerry Kennedy to produce] a record of me called "(It May Not Kill Me but) It's Sure Gonna Hurt." They put the single out on Mercury Records, but nothing happened and it didn't do much. Buddy said, "Go on back home. You gotta finish school."

During that time, it came to my attention that they were doing these [tribute] records of [unknown] artists doing other people's songs. Because I was a nasally kind of singer, somebody said, "Well, maybe this little girl can sing Kitty Wells songs." So I did.

I needed the money. I was doing anything I could to pick up a little bit here and there. They paid me just $200 or $300. I don't remember the exact amount. But it was enough for me and my aunt to get to Key West, Florida, to see my uncle, who was in the service there. That's where I got my first suntan—sunburn, actually. But anyway, a good time was had because of that money.

I think I recorded all those songs in an hour and a half. I was just a kid and, you know, you do what you do.

But those records have lived forever. They are not that good at all. They are terrible, actually. They're awful. I hate the way I sound on them. But I do love Kitty Wells, and I love those songs. And those things are stepping-stones to a bigger career.

Down on Music Row 1972

ON JUNE 21, 1964, Dolly Parton became the first member of her family to graduate from high school. The day after the ceremony, she boarded a bus for Nashville, carrying only her clothes and a folder of her songs. The lyrics in this song describe her early experiences trying to make it on Music Row. "Chet" and "Bob" refer to Chet Atkins and Bob Ferguson, the music executives who eventually signed her to RCA Records. But the references to the Country Music Hall of Fame are poetic license, since it didn't exist when Dolly was new in Nashville. The song appeared on her LP *My Tennessee Mountain Home*.

CHORUS
Down on Music Row,
Down on Music Row,
If you want to be a star
That's where you've got to go.

I could feel a change a-comin'.
So I left my hometown a-runnin'
With my ol' guitar a-strummin'
All the songs I wrote.

I was on my way to Nashville,
I just couldn't hardly wait 'til
I could sing my songs
To the folks on Music Row.

I got into Nashville early,
Sleepy, hungry, tired, and dirty.
And on the steps of RCA
I ate a stale sweet roll.

In the fountain at the Hall of Fame
I washed my face and I read the names
In the Walkway of the Stars,
Down on Music Row.

REPEAT CHORUS

I waited there 'til eight o'clock
When office doors became unlocked.
And then I started walkin' down
The streets of Music Row.

Just a-walkin' up and down the street
Tryin' to find out who to meet
To help me get on record
And to hear the songs I wrote.

But I found the goin' rough.
Everyone was all tied up,
Either in a conference
Or in the studio.

They said that I could leave a tape,
But they'd suggest I didn't wait,
'Cause everyone was awful busy
Down on Music Row.

But I could feel that change a-comin',
So I just kept right on a-hummin'
With my ol' guitar still strummin'
All the songs I wrote.

And then Chet and Bob down at RCA
Well, they listened to my songs that day,
And they both told me that I was on my way
Down on Music Row.

REPEAT CHORUS

In "Down on Music Row," I sang about Chet and Bob. Here they are in 1967, watching me sign a contract to record for RCA. That's Chet Atkins standing and Bob Ferguson seated next to me. Porter Wagoner is leaning above Bob.

It was always my dream that when I graduated from high school that I was going to move to Nashville. My daddy wouldn't have let me go before then anyway. He'd have sent a posse after me if I had left home. So I stayed in school, even though I didn't like it. I couldn't wait to go. I was eighteen. I was a grown woman then. So I got on that bus.

I had never been away from home on my own. And I didn't know what was awaiting me. I didn't know what I was going to do. But I knew I didn't have to worry about being poor, because I couldn't have been any poorer than we were there at home.

I thought, "I can make a living. I can do something. I can be a waitress. I can do whatever."

By that time, Uncle Bill was working out of Nashville. He was working on the road [as a guitarist] with Carl & Pearl Butler and different people.

I knew that I could always come back home. I'd always be welcomed. But I told my folks that I wasn't going to come home until I had something to show for it. So I headed out to follow my dream.

Put It Off until Tomorrow

Recorded by Bill Phillips (Dolly Parton / Bill Owens) 1966

DOLLY PARTON AND BILL OWENS came to the attention of Combine Music, which signed them as staff writers making $50 a week apiece. In 1966, country star Bill Phillips (1936–2010) made "Put It Off until Tomorrow" their first songwriting hit by taking it to No. 6 on the charts. The father-daughter duo the Kendalls returned it to the Top 10 in 1980, and it has gone on to become a minor country classic. The song earned a BMI Song of the Year award, Dolly's first show-business accolade. There was one life event that Dolly did not "put off until tomorrow." A month after her first songwriting success hit the charts, she married Carl Dean on May 30, 1966.

Put it off until tomorrow, whoa-whoa,
you've hurt me enough today.

You say our love is over,
That you have found another
You say you're going away.
But leave me tomorrow, whoa-whoa,
You've hurt me enough today.

You've hurt me enough today
I can't believe the words you say
But I must accept the fact
You won't be coming back.

So stay just one more day.
Loneliness isn't far away.
Put it off until tomorrow, whoa-whoa,
You've hurt me enough today.

Put it off until tomorrow, whoa-whoa,
you've hurt me enough today.

OPPOSITE PAGE: This is the photo that Mama took of me and Carl on our wedding day in 1966.

BELOW: The one and only music-business event that Carl ever attended with me happened just a few months later, when Bill [Owens] and I got BMI Awards for "Put It Off until Tomorrow."

Uncle Bill used to write a lot of good songs. We wrote a lot together going back and forth to Nashville. I would write stuff down or bang it out on the dashboard while he was driving. We wrote "Put It Off until Tomorrow" during one of our trips to Nashville.

It was our first big record. Bill Phillips was on Decca Records at the time, and he recorded it. We'd sent Bill Phillips the demo [demonstration recording] of Uncle Bill singing the lead vocal and me singing harmony. And he said, "Whoever that girl is singing the harmony, I want her on this record."

We were just excited, as songwriters, that he'd heard it. That they wanted me to sing on it was another little springboard.

It's become a great little classic song. People seem to love, "Put it off until tomorrow; you've hurt me enough today."

I love being tied to that song with Uncle Bill, because we went through so much together. We wrote a lot of songs together, but that one will always be special to me.

Back in 1966, I was writing for Fred Foster at Combine Music, and I was on his Monument Records label. I was starting to have a career with him.

At the time, I had been dating Carl Dean, who I had met the first day I got to Nashville. I'd left two boyfriends back home, and I thought the last thing I wanted was a boyfriend. So the first thing I do, the first day in Nashville, I meet Carl. And I fell for him, and he fell for me.

Fred Foster was going to invest in me as a young artist. So I told him that I was thinking of getting married. He said, "No, you're not getting married. You can't get married, because I'm going to invest all this money and this is your big shot." So Carl and I went to Ringgold, Georgia, and got married. And didn't tell Fred.

A year or so later, after I started doing well, Fred said, "Now aren't you glad you didn't get married?" I said, "I've been married for two years. I got married the same weekend you told me not to!"

That BMI Awards banquet was the first and only time that Carl ever went with me to any music event. We went to BMI to get the award for "Put It Off until Tomorrow." He dressed up, wore a tuxedo, and went with me. After it was over, he started ripping off stuff before we even got to the car. He said, "I'm happy for you. I want you to do what you want to do. But don't ever ask me to go to another one of them damn things, because I ain't going." And he never has.

The Company You Keep

Recorded by Bill Phillips (Dolly Parton / Bill Owens) 1966

BILL PHILLIPS FOLLOWED DOLLY'S "Put It Off until Tomorrow" with another rendition of one of her songs, again co-written with Uncle Bill. She and Uncle Bill rewrote it specifically as a follow-up hit for Phillips, who took it to No. 8 on the country hit parade.

Yes, you're known by the company you keep.

You say you're doing nothing wrong.
I don't believe you are.
I'm only trying to help you, sis
Before you go too far.
'Cause I think you're an angel,
But folks think that you're cheap,
'Cause you're known by the company you keep.

Please listen to your big sister.
I feel I know what's best for you.
I feel that I must warn you, sis.
That's the least that I could do.
I'm not accusing you of anything.
I know it's fun, you see,
But you're known by the company you keep.

The company you keep, keeps you out too long.
Mom and Dad don't go to sleep until you get home.
Sis, you're gettin' in too deep.
You'd better look before you leap.
'Cause you're known by the company you keep.

Sis, you're gettin' in too deep.
The road of life is steep.
And you're known by the company you keep.

I'm in No Condition

Recorded by Hank Williams Jr. 1967

FUTURE COUNTRY SUPERSTAR HANK WILLIAMS JR. was eighteen years old and in the early years of his recording career when he hit No. 60 with this single of a Dolly song. Others who recorded early Dolly songs include the Stonemans ("You're Gonna Be Sorry"), Jean Shepard & Ray Pillow ("Who in the World"), Crystal Gayle ("You"), and Dick Curless ("Golden Girl").

Don't look at me with love in your eyes.
Go look at somebody that can make it worthwhile.
I'm hurt from a love affair I didn't want to end.
I'm in no condition to try to love again.

Don't smile at me, because it's no use,
'Cause I don't have a smile that I can give to you.
Someday you might look me up, but let me be 'til then.
For I'm in no condition to try to love again.

I'm in no condition to try to love again.
The man I love just broke my heart,
And it must have time to mend.
He gave me the breeze. Now he's gone with the wind.
I'm in no condition to try to love again.

No, I'm in no condition to try to love again.

This is what Hank Williams Jr. looked like when he recorded my song "I'm in No Condition"; of course he looks a lot different now.

More Love than Sense

Recorded by Kitty Wells (Dolly Parton / Bill Owens) 1966

BILL PHILLIPS WAS A MEMBER of the Kitty Wells and Johnny Wright road show. That is perhaps how Dolly's idol, Kitty, became aware of her songwriting. Known as "the Queen of Country Music," Kitty Wells (1919–2012) was the role model for all female country singers of Dolly's generation. Kitty recorded this song on December 20, 1966, but it was unreleased at the time and remains so. This is the first time its lyrics have been in print.

If I had any sense at all, I would have been gone by now.
But I love you so much I just couldn't leave, somehow.
You do me every way, every time you get the chance.
But I guess I have more love for you than I've got sense.

You always treated me just every way but right.
You go out on the town, leave me home at night.
Neighbors are talking over their backyard fence
Saying, "She must have more love for him than she's got sense."

CHORUS
I've got more love than I've got sense, that's plain to see.
Everybody knows you're cheating, including me.
I didn't want to believe it, but now I'm convinced
That I must have more love for you than I've got sense.

REPEAT CHORUS

I think I am one of the lucky few who ever had her picture made with both the King and Queen of Country Music, Roy Acuff and Kitty Wells. Along with Patsy Cline, Kitty was the most important star to pave the way for female country artists like me. I was beyond thrilled when she recorded one of my early songs.

Kitty Wells was always a favorite of mine. I used to sing her songs all the time when I was growing up. Along with Roy Acuff and all those folks, she was one of those people that we used to listen to on the Grand Ole Opry. So you can imagine how excited I was when she liked my song.

Kitty was probably the first female in country music to sing about defending the women. There was a song called "The Wild Side of Life" that talked about God making honky tonk angels. She did an answer to it, "It Wasn't God Who Made Honky Tonk Angels," saying that it was men who brought women down. She got recognized for standing up for women.

I just loved her sound. She recorded a lot of great country songs that had a lot of heart and a lot of soul. Just hearing a woman sing on the radio at that time was great. She was singing songs that spoke to us as girls and as women. She was a legend.

Fuel to the Flame

Recorded by Skeeter Davis (Dolly Parton / Bill Owens) 1967

POP AND COUNTRY STAR SKEETER DAVIS (1931–2004) scored a No. 11 hit with this Dolly tune in the early months of 1967. She later became the first artist to record an entire LP devoted to Dolly's songs. Many of the songwriter's hits sung by others—"Fuel to the Flame," "Put It Off until Tomorrow," "I'm in No Condition," and "The Company You Keep"—were all also recorded by Dolly Parton for inclusion on her debut album, 1967's *Hello, I'm Dolly*.

You kindle the fire of love inside me
Each time our lips meet.
I'm not strong when we're alone,
Your kisses make me weak.

You must know how I must feel
But do you feel the same?
Every time you kiss me
You add fuel to the flame.

My eyes light up when I see you.
I burn with desire.
Each time you're near
You say you care.
But still, I'm not sure.

But please don't ask me to love you
If you're not gonna change my name.
Every time you touch me
You add fuel to the flame.

This fire you started inside of me
Has reached my very soul.
You're adding fuel to a flame
That's already burning out of control.

When you give me your name,
I give you everything.
Every time you kiss me
You add fuel to the flame.

Yes, every time you touch me
You add fuel to the flame.

Skeeter Davis had a record that was a classic all over called "The End of the World" [1963]. So when she took an interest in my songs, it was so big for me. She was a very sweet lady, too. She really liked my songwriting, so we sent her "Fuel to the Flame." She recorded it, and it did pretty good.

I will always treasure that, because she kind of recognized me as a songwriter before everybody else. She was so big at the time, so that said a lot for me as a writer. I felt like when she did a complete album of my songs, a few years later, she really helped establish me in town. People began to take me seriously as a writer when she did that.

Don't Let It Trouble Your Mind 1969

THIS SONG APPEARED ON DOLLY'S ALBUM *In the Good Old Days (When Times Were Bad)*. In 2015, the acclaimed, four-time Grammy-nominated, African American folk star Rhiannon Giddens recorded her version of the free-spirited lyric.

Our love affair is bittersweet,
Insecure and incomplete.
And I've often wondered why your leaving's been so long delayed.

It's all become so complicated.
Maybe you feel obligated.
And out of sympathy for me, you stay.

CHORUS
But I had rather live alone
Than live with someone who doesn't love me.
And I'd rather have you go than stay
And put me down, thinking you're above me.
Our love affair is so wound up
It's best that we unwind.
And if you don't love me, leave me.
And don't let it trouble your mind.

You've waited much too long to leave,
Afraid of how I'd take it.
And I'm deeply touched by your concern,
But I think I can make it.

It won't be easy for a while,
But I'll forget in time.
And if you don't love me, leave me.
And don't let it trouble your mind.

REPEAT CHORUS

Something Fishy 1967

DESPITE THE FACT THAT SHE'D BEEN TURNED DOWN as a vocalist by every major record company on Music Row, Dolly was signed to Monument Records, an independent label owned by Fred Foster (1931–2019). Like Buddy Killen before him, Foster initially viewed Dolly as a pop act. He released a string of singles of her singing songs written by others in that vein. With "Something Fishy," she scored a country success with one of her own compositions for the first time. A No. 17 hit included on her *Hello, I'm Dolly* LP, the song is a lighthearted ditty about suspecting a philandering husband. It has much the same tone as "Dumb Blonde," her rendition of a Curly Putman tune that had marked her country chart debut a few months earlier.

There must be something fishy goin' on.

You said you were goin' on a fishin' trip with some old friend.
You said that you'd be home tonight, somewhere around ten.
Well, here it is, it's two o'clock, and you're still not at home.
I think there's something fishy goin' on.

I think that I'm a sucker, that's swallowing your line.
I try to make myself believe that it's all in my mind.
But you never ask me if I'd like to go along.
So there must be something fishy goin' on.

CHORUS
There's something fishy goin' on,
On these fishing trips you're goin' on.
I'm gettin' tired of stayin' home alone.
Some night when you come home
And discover that I'm gone,
You can bet there's something fishy goin' on.

I guess some large-mouth bass left that lipstick on your shirt.
I don't think you're a fisherman, honey, I think you're a flirt.
Well, if you're goin' fishin', then why don't you bring 'em home?
I think there's something fishy goin' on.

REPEAT CHORUS

I used to walk up and down the streets of Music Row, trying to get signed by a label. I had done that little record with Buddy Killen on Mercury, but after I moved to Nashville, I was not getting any real bites until I walked into Fred Foster's office. I was pretty raw at the time, but he saw something in me, some potential.

Since I was young, he thought that maybe I could do rockabilly or teenager-y stuff. So at first, he recorded a series of records on me that I was not that comfortable with. I would eventually grow into being able to do that, but at the time, I was just so country. I never thought about doing anything outside of that. Well, after "Put It Off until Tomorrow" became such a big country hit [for Bill Phillips], I said, "I told you I should be doing country music."

Fred asked Curly Putman to write a country song just for me. So Curly's "Dumb Blonde" became my first chart record. I loved Curly dearly and will always be appreciative of that song. It was the one that kind of put me on the map.

When I wrote "Something Fishy," I guess I was probably trying to think of something commercial that would at least be in keeping with the success I'd had with "Dumb Blonde." I was trying to do something a little more up-tempo, something that had a little bit of spunk.

"Dumb Blonde" was "This dumb blonde ain't nobody's fool." "Something Fishy" was "You think you're going to fool me? I'm too smart for that. You say you're going fishing. I think there's something fishy going on. You think you can fool me because I'm a girl, like I don't have enough sense to know what you're doing?"

Fred Foster saw potential, spent time, spent money, groomed me, and recorded my first album, *Hello, I'm Dolly*. He wrote a wonderful liner note on the back of it, which I'll always treasure. He liked me and took an interest in my career, and I'll always be grateful for that.

ABOVE RIGHT: Producer Fred Foster took the cover photo for my first album. In his liner notes on the back of the album, he predicted stardom for me. That meant so much to me that I still have those notes, framed, to this day.

OPPOSITE PAGE AND ABOVE LEFT: Within a very few years, I had stage outfits like this one being custom designed by Nashville dressmakers Lucy Adams and Ruth Kemp. This was one of my favorites, just sweet and simple. You can see I'm starting to like those rhinestones!

Your Ole Handy Man 1967

ONE OF THE EARLIEST OF DOLLY'S LYRICS featuring an assertive woman, this song on *Hello, I'm Dolly* calls out a husband who makes his wife do all the work at home.

I have to mow the lawn, and I have to wash the car.
And I'd just like to know, just who you think you are.
I'm gettin' tired of waggin' that old heavy garbage can.
Your woman's gettin' tired of being your ole handy man.

I have to run your water, and I have to wash your back.
And I have to scrub the tub, after you have had your bath.
You're as helpless as a baby, but I love you, understand.
I'm just gettin' tired of being your ole handy man.

CHORUS
Your woman's gettin' tired of being your ole handy man.
Now, I know you've got ten fingers, but where's your helping hand?
I've just made a decision. I've stood all I'm gonna stand.
Your woman's gettin' tired of being your ole handy man.

I do everything for you. You never help yourself.
And I think I'd die from shock if you raised a hand to help.
Well, I'm not gonna keep it up, if that's what you got planned.
Your woman's gettin' tired of being your ole handy man.

REPEAT CHORUS

Comedian Speck Rhodes is behind me during this 1969 Grand Ole Opry appearance. That's the year that I became a member of the Opry cast.

Daddy Won't Be Home Anymore 1967

DOLLY WROTE THIS DURING THE HEIGHT OF THE WAR IN VIETNAM, but it did not appear until several years later. When Dolly left Monument Records to sign with RCA, she left behind a number of unissued recordings. In 1970, Monument owner Fred Foster packaged some of these in an album he titled *As Long as I Love*. This topical song was among them.

As I look around the little house
We were so happy in,
I think of all the happy times
We'll never see again.
Then I break down and start to cry.
The children ask what for.
I can't find a way to tell them
That Daddy won't be home anymore.

Each night before they go to sleep,
They fold their little hands,
And say a prayer for Daddy
Fighting in that far-off land.
So tonight I'll help them say their prayers,
Like I've always done before.
God give me courage to tell them
That Daddy won't be home anymore.

But, honey, as for me,
There'll never be another man,
And I'll bring our children up
The best way that I can.
You died for what you thought was right,
That much I know for sure.
But the children just can't understand
Why Daddy won't be home anymore.

No, the children just don't understand
Why Daddy won't be home anymore.

In my songwriting, I've never shied away from what is going on in the world. I don't voice issues publicly, myself. But in my songs, I can write about whatever I feel. That's what I'm about. I can say what I need to say without having to march in the streets or make big public statements. I express in my own way what I believe other people need to hear and might not be able to write about their feelings.

"Daddy Won't Be Home Anymore" is about knowing that your husband or your father or your kids are out there in the war. They may not be coming home. Many people can relate to that.

The way the song is written, it's not saying war is wrong. It's saying, from a woman's point of view, how heartbreaking it is. I'm not making a political statement, I'm just saying it's tragic.

That's true in any war, and especially with the Vietnam War. The government sent our people to war. They had to fight, whether they believed in it or not. And the people left at home are feeling that sorrow and grief and fear and worry over never seeing someone again. As a songwriter, it's a wonderful thing to be able to do that, to be able to express things for other people.

They call the Grand Ole Opry "the show that made country music famous." It is every country performer's dream to become a member of its cast, and I was no exception. I celebrated my fiftieth anniversary as a member in 2019.

The Bridge 1968

THIS SUICIDE SONG WAS INCLUDED on Dolly's album *Just Because I'm a Woman*.

The bridge, so high. The bridge, so tall.
Here is where it started, on the bridge

The moon is big and yellow,
And the stars are all a-glow.
From the bridge, I see reflections
In the waters far below.
You kissed me for the first time here
And held me awful tight
And the bridge became our favorite place.
We came here often in the night.

One night while standing on the bridge,
Desire swept through us both.
Passion took us by the hand
And showed us where to go.
From the bridge we saw a meadow,
So we ran together there.
Where we found love together,
Our emotions filled the air.

The bridge, so wide. The bridge, so long.
Where once we stood together,
Tonight I stand alone.
Tonight, while standing on the bridge,
My heart is beating wild,
To think that you could leave me here
With our unborn child.

My feet are moving slowly,
Closer to the edge.
Here is where it started,
And here is where I'll end it . . .
On the bridge.

OPPOSITE PAGE: Signing autographs is a part of life for a country entertainer. In my early years in Nashville, I learned as much about country fans as I did about the country industry.

"The Bridge" is a song I wrote before I ever left school. I didn't put it out until much later. But I wrote it way before [Bobbie Gentry's 1967 hit] "Ode to Billie Joe." I had my own bridge, back home.

In "The Bridge," she is thinking, "There's no way out of this, so I'm just going to take that plunge and go." A lot of people go through that. I've had suicides in my own family. It's a horrible thing to have to deal with.

As a songwriter, I love to write those mournful things and put myself in those situations. It comes from those early days with all of the old songs I grew up with. I loved feeling all the sorrow in a song. In my early days, I just wrote about everything. I just wanted to write great stories, or write about situations that I could imagine myself in.

I wrote a lot of songs that people wouldn't play on the radio, but I didn't care. It bothered me at the time, but I never thought, "I shouldn't have done that." Whatever I write is just what comes out of me, and I refuse to be judged.

My Blue Ridge Mountain Boy 1969

THIS SONG MADE IT TO No. 45 on the country charts. It also served as the title tune of her 1969 LP. Her publicity-averse husband, Carl Dean, appears in the album's cover photo.

From a shack by a mountain stream
To a room in New Orleans,
So far from my Blue Ridge Mountain home.

The men I meet ain't warm and friendly,
Like the one in old Virginny.
Oh they ain't real, like my Blue Ridge Mountain boy.

I was just a little past eighteen
When I came to New Orleans
I'd never been beyond my home state line.

There was a boy who loved me dearly,
But I broke his heart severely,
When I left my Blue Ridge Mountain boy.

Life was dull in my hometown.
Lights were out when the sun went down.
And I thought that city life was more my style

But nights get lonely away from home,
And it's easy to go wrong.
The men ain't kind like my Blue Ridge Mountain boy.

New Orleans held things in store,
Things I'd never bargained for.
And every night a different man knocks on my door.

But late at night when all is still,
I can hear a whippoorwill,
As I cry for my Blue Ridge Mountain boy.

Oh, but I can't ever go back home,
Since the boy I love is gone.
He grew tired waiting for me to return.

They say he married last October,
But I never will get over
Oh the sweet love of my Blue Ridge Mountain boy.

Blue Ridge Mountain boy.

Carl Dean hates the spotlight and has always stayed away from my professional life. That has led a lot of people to believe that my husband doesn't exist, that I made him up. To this day, I don't share many of our private photos, but here are a few.

"My Blue Ridge Mountain Boy" is about a girl whose dream was to get out of the country. She didn't leave to become a prostitute, but that's what she wound up doing in order to make a living. She thinks she's going to go out and do so much with her life, but it doesn't work out. She keeps missing the boy she left behind, and it is too late to go back home.

This was during my early years in show business, and my goodness, I was writing about a girl becoming a prostitute. But I never shied away from any topic, whether it was suicide or prostitution or women's rights or whatever. I was always like that and still am. Whatever it is, I can say it in a song, in my own way.

A lot of people don't realize that I put my husband on the cover of the album. They say, "We've never seen your husband." I say, "Well, yes you have, if you've looked at the album *My Blue Ridge Mountain Boy*."

"A lot of people don't realize that I put my husband on the cover of the album. They say, 'We've never seen your husband.' I say, 'Well, yes you have, if you've looked at the album **My Blue Ridge Mountain Boy.'"**

Photographer Les Leverett specialized in "trick" pictures like this one of Carl and me "together" on the album jacket of *My Blue Ridge Mountain Boy*. He also did the "put together" photos on the covers of my *Bubbling Over* and *My Favorite Songwriter, Porter Wagoner* albums. Les also did the cover of Porter's *The Bottom of the Bottle*, where the "wino" is inside the booze bottle.

Just Because I'm a Woman 1968

IN THE FALL OF 1968, this proto-feminist anthem became a country hit for Dolly, reaching No. 17 on the charts. The song served as the title tune of her debut solo LP for RCA. No other performer at the time was addressing the issues that are raised in this lyric.

I can see you're disappointed
By the way you look at me.
And I'm sorry that I'm not the woman
You thought I'd be.
Yes, I've made my mistakes,
But listen and understand:
My mistakes are no worse than yours,
Just because I'm a woman.

So when you look at me
Don't feel sorry for yourself.
Just think of all the shame
You might have brought somebody else.
Just let me tell you this,
Then we'll both know where we stand.
My mistakes are no worse than yours,
Just because I'm a woman.

Now a man will take a good girl,
And he'll ruin her reputation.
But when he wants to marry,
Well, that's a different situation.
He'll just walk off and leave her
To do the best she can,
While he looks for an angel
To wear his wedding band.

Now I know that I'm no angel
If that's what you thought you'd found.
I was just the victim
Of a man that let me down.
Yes, I've made my mistakes,
But listen and understand:
My mistakes are no worse than yours,
Just because I'm a woman.

No, my mistakes are no worse than yours,
Just because I'm a woman

I look ready to greet the world on the cover of my first solo album for RCA Records. I wrote the title song for me, but lots of other women say they can relate to it.

This song came from a very personal experience. My husband, Carl, had never asked me if I'd ever been with anybody else, so I never said. I wasn't going to volunteer that kind of information. He hadn't been around all that much, either. But after we'd been married a few months, he asked me if I'd ever been with anybody else.

I thought, "Well, I don't want to start this marriage with a lie." But how do you tell someone something like that? So I just said, "Yeah, I have been." He was just crushed by that, and I was kind of an outcast for a little while there.

So I went and wrote this song: "My mistakes are no worse than yours, just because I'm a woman. I've made my mistakes, but listen and understand." It was about a man "ruining" a girl's reputation. And I addressed all these things. Like, "Who the Hell are you to think you deserve an angel?"

Anyhow, Carl got over it, and we got over it. So that's over, thank goodness.

The song became a huge hit, and stayed a hit for many years. It was even on the charts in South Africa [where it earned a Gold Record]. It was for all those women who had never been able to express this themselves.

It's a song that says a lot in a simple way. But it addresses an issue that's very important.

2
3
8

CHAPTER

3

PORTER WAYNE AND DOLLY REBECCA

COUNTRY SUPERSTAR PORTER WAGONER (1927–2007) HIRED DOLLY as the "girl singer" for his troupe in the summer of 1967. They began to record together that fall. She was twenty-one; he was forty. At the time, he'd had more than twenty-five hits, and she had two.

Porter Wagoner introduced such country standards as "A Satisfied Mind" (1955), "Misery Loves Company" (1962), and "Green, Green Grass of Home" (1965). He had a state-of-the-art road company that included dancing fiddler Mack Magaha, electric-banjo innovator Buck Trent, and hayseed comic Speck Rhodes. He also hosted country music's most widely seen syndicated weekly TV series, *The Porter Wagoner Show*.

The job was a stupendous opportunity for the still-green Dolly. Porter engineered her move from the independent Monument label to the powerhouse RCA Records. In 1969, he helped her become a member of the Grand Ole Opry cast.

He also took over her career, becoming her duet partner, teaching her showmanship, and mentoring all aspects of her professional development. As a result, her songwriting evolved in several directions.

Dolly's education under his tutelage was grueling. Between 1969 and 1974, the typical pattern was for her to write songs for two duet LPs and two solo LPs per year, tape the weekly TV shows, and perform more than two hundred concerts annually as a member of Wagoner's road company.

Porter Wayne Wagoner and Dolly Rebecca Parton became one of the most successful country duet teams of the era. They were named the Country Music Association's favorite vocal combo in 1968, 1970, and 1971. They scored Grammy Award nominations in 1969, 1970, 1971, and 1973.

These are the Dolly Parton songs that helped fuel their reign of fame, as well as some of the big solo hits she began to enjoy.

These were taken the day Porter gave me the gift of a Cadillac in 1973. I would have rather had a raise. Anyhow, I don't have the best history with cars: The back wall of the RCA studio on Music Row still shows the marks from where I crashed into it arriving at a recording session.

Tomorrow Is Forever

With Porter Wagoner 1970

PORTER WAGONER URGED DOLLY to stop writing so much about her poor-folks upbringing and to craft love songs instead. She responded with an outpouring of deeply romantic titles. This was the first of several to become a Top 10 hit for the team, reaching No. 9 in early 1970 and appearing on their LP *Porter Wayne & Dolly Rebecca*. Soul-music great Solomon Burke teamed with Dolly to revive this elegant lyric in 2006. The song is also in the repertoire of the Grateful Dead.

Take my hand and run with me out of the past called yesterday.
And walk with me into the future of tomorrow.
Yesterday must be forgot, no looking back no matter what.
There's nothing there, but mem'ries that bring sorrow.

Yesterday is gone, gone, but tomorrow is forever.
No more crying. Tears leave tracks, and mem'ries find their
way back.
Tomorrow's waiting. Let's journey there together.
Yesterday is gone, gone, but tomorrow is forever.

I care not for yesterday. I love you as you are today.
Yesterday just helped to pass the time while waiting.
We must forget the passing time. My love for you is the real kind.
The kind that won't hurt you, no, never.

Yesterday is gone, gone, but tomorrow is forever.
Yesterday is gone, gone, but tomorrow is forever.

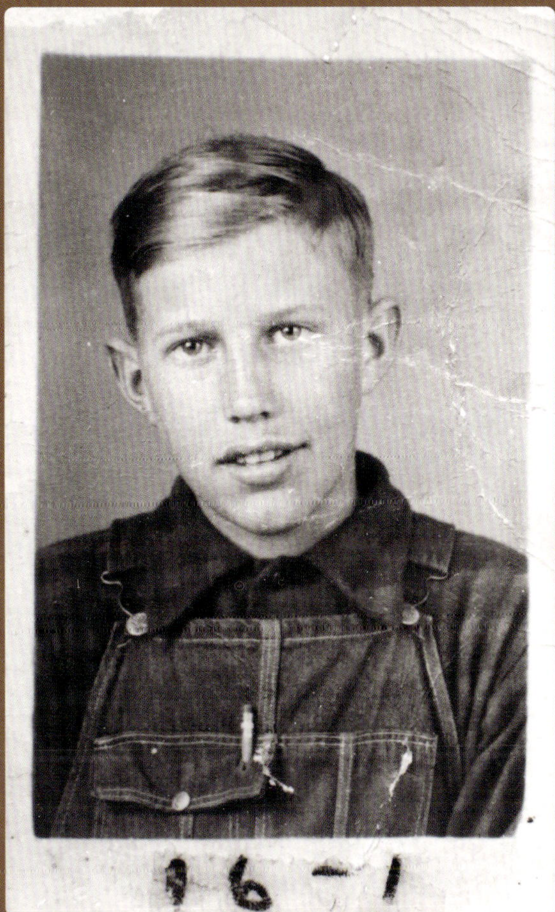

When I started with *The Porter Wagoner Show*, that was when I really became well known. It was a really huge break. At the time, Porter Wagoner was the head of the number one syndicated TV show. There was also *The Wilburn Brothers Show*, and that's the one Loretta Lynn started on. So I was the "girl singer" on *The Porter Wagoner Show*. Before that, he had Norma Jean as the "girl singer," but she was going to get married and move back to Oklahoma. Her spot opened, and Porter asked me. I was young. I was new.

I'd already been sending songs to Porter and to Norma Jean so when I got the call from Porter, I thought he wanted to record one of my songs. So I took my guitar down to his office, in case he wanted me to sing it. But when I got in there, he asked me if I'd become a member of his show.

I started writing songs for our duets, writing songs for my own albums, writing stuff for him, doing the show dates, and doing all that other stuff that we were doing. I look back at that time and think, "How in the world did I ever do all that?"

But I've always been like my daddy. I'm a working girl. I always say, "I may look like a show pony, but I'm a workhorse." You take it on, and you've gotta finish it. I'm still like that, today.

On top of all that, I was maintaining a home life. It's a good thing that my husband, Carl, has always been such a loner. You know, he don't want to be around anybody but me anyway, and he loves to be home. So that worked out fine.

"Tomorrow Is Forever" is one of my favorite love songs that Porter and I did. I was always writing love songs, but because we were doing duets we needed more of them. Porter encouraged me to write more love songs instead of story songs and songs about my home. So this was when I started expanding my songwriting.

These were the childhood photos that were put into antique frames for the cover of the album *Porter Wayne & Dolly Rebecca*.

Lost Forever in Your Kiss

With Porter Wagoner 1972

THIS HIT DUET REACHED NO. 9 on the country hit parade. The team included it on their LP *Together Always*.

This is not at all like me.
I never thought that I could be
So overcome by anyone like this.
But you caught me by surprise,
Caught me before I realized,
Now I am lost forever in your kiss.

CHORUS
So take me if you want me.
Love me if you will.
For you have all control of me.
And I am yours until
You say that you don't want me.
Oh, I hope that never will be.
For I am lost forever in your kiss.

You're on my mind constantly
Oh, this is all so new to me
And when you reach for me, I can't resist.
For I've become a part of you,
And I'll do anything you want me to,
For I am lost forever in your kiss

REPEAT CHORUS

Porter and I sang in perfect harmony on stage and on records. Off stage, things weren't always so harmonious between us.

With any romantic duet, people always think the singers are having an affair. Country fans especially assume that. And when you work that closely with someone, you do have a relationship. And it is based in passion. You have to experience emotions if you're going to sing a song like "Lost Forever in Your Kiss." You're living with these people, day in and day out.

But Porter and I fought like cats and dogs. My husband and I have never fought, and Porter and I did nothing but fight. So when I would write love songs, it wasn't so much about Porter. Some were. Some were based on love. But people always assume it. And you do have a love affair, of a sort.

But whether it's a love affair or not, you're all in, in the relationship. Whether it's sexual or whether it's just passionate, you are connected. It's a love-hate relationship. It is a marriage, of a sort. And if people think that you are "doing it," that helps sell the duets. So who's going to admit whether it's true or not?

The Last One to Touch Me

Recorded by Porter Wagoner 1971

THIS SONG BECAME A SOLO success for Porter Wagoner in the early weeks of 1971, reaching No. 18 on the charts. But Dolly's version on her *Joshua* LP that same year is even more moving. Others who have recorded this powerful message include George Jones, Kitty Wells, Nat Stuckey, and Conway Twitty.

If there ever was an angel, then surely you must be one.
If there ever was a perfect love, when I look at you I see one.
If there's Heaven on earth, then this must surely be.
I want you to be the last one to touch me.

The last thing I remember, before I go to sleep
Is the touch of your sweet lips softly kissing me.
And I go to sleep a-thinkin' how happy you make me.
I want you to be the last one to touch me.

And when it's time to lay me down for my eternal sleep
Once more, let your fingers softly touch my cheek.
If I know that you have touched me, oh then I can sleep in peace.
I want you to be the last one to touch me.

And when the night is over, and time will be no more,
They tell me we shall meet again upon the golden shore.
And so when I awaken from my eternal sleep,
I want you to be the first one to touch me.

I want you to be the first, the last, the only one to touch me.

The longer that Carl and I are together on our journey, the more the lyrics of "The Last One to Touch Me" mean to me. He is my home and my heart.

As far as I'm concerned, "The Last One to Touch Me" speaks to everyone who's truly in love, who is really there "'til death do us part." One of my favorite songs ever is the [1980] George Jones song, "He Stopped Loving Her Today," and to me, "The Last One to Touch Me" is kind of along those same lines. When I wrote it, I thought it spoke of true love that you want to last a lifetime. And true love that you hope will last even longer, that you'll meet and be together if there is such a thing as an afterlife. It's a wish to have a love that's that strong.

I can't even sing that song without crying, because I think about my husband. I'm sure that when I wrote it, I was thinking about Carl. You're together when you're in your young life. You're together through prosperity. You're together through sickness and health, through poverty and wealth, until death.

Most people don't get that far. Most people don't get through the rough times. Most people don't get through the poverty part. That's when things go out the window.

But this is about a love that lasts so long that on your deathbed you can say, "I want you to be the last one to touch me." Before the undertaker gets me, ha!

You know what I say . . . my songs can make you laugh or they can make you cry, myself included.

Jeannie's Afraid of the Dark

With Porter Wagoner 1968

THIS WAS THE FIRST SONG to make the country charts that Dolly wrote for her Porter Wagoner duets. It was the flip side of their Top 10 hit "We'll Get Ahead Someday" and only reached No. 51 on its own. Although not a big chart hit, it became the most-requested song at the team's concerts.

(Dolly sings)
Her two little feet would come running into
Our bedroom almost every night.
Her soft little face would be wet from her tears
And her little heart pounding with fright.
She'd hold out her arms, then she'd climb in beside us.
In a small voice, we'd hear her remark,
"Mommie and Daddy, can I sleep here with you
'Cause Jeannie's afraid of the dark?"

One day in the summer, we took some flowers
To place on some old family graves.
Jeannie said, "Mommie, ain't it dark in the ground.
Oh, Daddy, I'd be so afraid."
Then she looked up at her daddy and me
And said somethin' that broke both our hearts.
She said, "When I die, please don't bury me,
'Cause Jeannie's afraid of the dark."

(Porter recites)
Jeannie was always afraid of the dark
And we never could understand why.
'Cause we looked after Jeannie with the very best of care,
Because Jeannie was our only child.
Perhaps it was death that she was so afraid of,
'Cause it took her one dark stormy night.
I think we always knew that we'd never see Jeannie grown,
'Cause it seemed she was destined to die.
But on Jeannie's grave, we placed an eternal flame
That glows and never loses its spark.
And on the darkest night, there's always a light,
'Cause Jeannie's afraid of the dark.

(Dolly sings)
Our Jeannie's afraid of the dark.

One of the biggest duet favorites with the fans was a little song I wrote called "Jeannie's Afraid of the Dark." It's about a child who died. She was afraid of the dark. Because the little girl was afraid of the dark, they put an eternal flame on her grave. I kind of based it on the fact that I hate the dark and have ever since I was a child.

It wasn't that big of a hit, but if Porter and I didn't sing it during our shows, people were very disappointed. They wanted that song. Porter did the recitation, and I'd sing the lyric. We were good at that.

It addressed the fact that there are many children who do die. Everywhere, but especially in the mountains, where it's cold and they can't get medical care. Maybe they died of pneumonia, or maybe they're born with a condition. Sometimes it's something you don't even know about until the child is gone, like a hole in his heart.

I lost my little brother, Larry. Because there were so many of us, Mama would kind of assign each new baby to one of us, to look after. Like, "This is going to be your baby." Larry was going to be "my" baby. I had planned and worked so hard to be ready for him, to be his "little mama." Then when he died, it just absolutely crushed me, crushed me. I still start crying when I think about little Larry. I was at a very vulnerable age [Dolly was nine at the time]. It was like I'd lost a baby of my own.

Death was new to me at that time. I was trying so hard to deal with death, with sorrow, with grief. There was a little dead baby there. I remember seeing him in his little coffin, and I just couldn't connect all that. Sorry to get so emotional, but that's a really hard thing.

So now when I sing songs like "Jeannie's Afraid of the Dark" or "Me and Little Andy," I always think of Larry and of how he touched my life. I think people can relate to that.

J. J. Sneed

(Dorothy Jo Hope / Dolly Parton) 1971

THIS BONNIE-AND-CLYDE "OUTLAW" TALE was included on Dolly's *Joshua* solo album. Kitty Wells later recorded it. Its plot inspired a 2019 Netflix movie in an anthology series based on Dolly's songs.

At last I have caught up with you,
And you're a sight to see.
Could this really be my outlaw lover,
J. J. Sneed?
Could a woman with a painted face
And pretty sweet disguise
Turn your heart against me
With her evil cunning eyes, her evil
cunning eyes?

J. J., it's been you and me
Right from the very start.
And ever' job we ever pulled,
I always done my part.
We agreed we'd stick together
Until the bitter end,
And it was my understanding
We were whole lots more than friends, a whole
lot more than friends.

And it was me that kept you warm
When nights were dark and cold.
But I guess I didn't look like much
In these old ragged clothes.
But you said it didn't matter
'Cause you loved me that a-way.
You said that no one else
Could ever steal your heart away, steal your
heart away.

Do you recall the Union Bank
We robbed in Franklin Town?
And as we made our getaway,
The sheriff gunned you down.
And I doctored up your bullet wounds
And nursed you while you set.
But now you have betrayed me.
Is that the thanks I get; is that the thanks I get?

Oh yeah, J. J., I'm thinking now
Of how we'd all begun,
Of all the times we've robbed and killed
With our trustworthy gun.
Why we stood off a posse once,
J. J., just you and I.
But now you have betrayed me
And for that you're gonna die. Yeah, for that
you're gonna die.

The good old days are over
As we stand here in the rain.
J. J., I'm gonna shoot you now.
I hope you'll feel no pain.
I hear hoofbeats of the horses
The posse's on my trail.
I guess I'll join you soon,
But for now, J. J., farewell, for now, J. J.,
farewell.

People often ask me who my influences were. They think I'm going to say some big names, and there were a few "stars" I was impressed with. But my hero was my aunt Dorothy Jo, Mama's baby sister. She was not only an evangelist, she played banjo, she played guitar, and she wrote some great songs.

We were like the best of friends. I'm very much like her. I saw myself in her, and do to this day. I really related to her more than anybody else. In my young teenage years, we started writing songs together.

We wrote "J. J. Sneed" years ago. We thought, "There have always been men outlaws. Why don't we write something about girls?" I remember we had so much fun writing it, rhyming things, and coming up with the story. It was like writing a movie. And actually, it did become a movie.

We wrote several songs together. Some of the most joyous times I had were when I wrote songs with her.

Daddy Come and Get Me

(Dorothy Jo Hope / Dolly Parton) 1970

THIS STRIKING SONG MADE IT to No. 40 on the charts in the early weeks of 1970. Dolly introduced it on her 1969 LP *The Fairest of Them All.*

In this mental institution, looking out through these iron bars,
How could he put me in here, how could he go that far?

Yes I need help, but not this kind, he didn't love me from the start.
But it's not my mind that's broken, it's my heart.

Oh Daddy, come and get me, and take me home with you.
I'm depending on you, Daddy. There's nothing I can do.
And you said that I could come to you, if I ever was in need.
But Daddy I can't come to you. You'll have to come to me.

When he said he loved another, I was crazy with jealousy.
That's 'cause I was crazy over him, and I couldn't stand to set him free.

And I couldn't stand to lose him, and I cried and cried for days.
He said that I was crazy, but he just put me in here to get me out of his way.

Daddy, come and get me.

Oh Daddy, come and get me, and take me home with you.
I'm depending on you, Daddy, 'cause there's nothing else I can do.
And you said that I could come to you, if I ever was in need.
But Daddy I can't come to you. You'll have to come to me.

Oh Daddy, come and get me.

This is one of the saddest songs I've ever been a part of. I wrote it with my aunt Dorothy Jo. We both knew a story back home about a very nervous and emotional woman that some man had driven crazy. He was having an affair. And because this woman was so crushed and broken, he put her in a mental institution. We knew this woman, and she didn't have much family on her side to keep it from happening. He just put her in that institution to get her out of the way so he could go on with his life.

Later on, I knew someone in Nashville who had the same thing happen to her. It was a situation that nobody knew how to handle. This song was based on those stories.

We thought, how sad it must be to have to reach out to your father to say, "I'm in this mental institution looking out through these iron bars. How could he put me in here? How could he go that far?" She couldn't call on her husband, obviously. You can always count on your parents, although in the song, you can't tell if the daddy will rescue her or not.

We loved writing that song. During some of my happiest times, I've written some of my saddest songs, and vice versa.

This was the costume I wore on the cover of my album *The Fairest of Them All*. The photo showed me looking at my reflection like "Mirror, mirror on the wall."

Gypsy, Joe, and Me 1969

THIS MELODRAMA WAS INTRODUCED on the album *My Blue Ridge Mountain Boy*. Although it wasn't a hit single, Dolly also included it on her LP *The Best of Dolly Parton* in 1970.

We might have slept in the rail yard,
Or camped by the riverbank.
We fed ourselves from the fruit of the land
And quenched our thirst with rain.
We never did allow no roots
To grow beneath our feet,
Life just had no pattern for Gypsy, Joe,
and me

All we had was each other
And the rags upon our backs.
The closest thing to a home we knew
Was some abandoned shack.
But we had all we wanted,
And the rest we didn't need.
Life was free and simple for Gypsy, Joe,
and me.

Now Gypsy was my little dog
I found by the road in a ditch.
And so I named him Gypsy,
'Cause that name just seemed to fit.
Oh and Joe, he was my man,
The flower of my soul.
Though he never said he loved me,
I just always seemed to know.

While standin' by the highway,
A-thumbin' for a ride,
The speeding wheels of a passing car,
Took Gypsy's life.
I lost him where I found him,
And his loss was misery.
Now there's no more Gypsy. There's just Joe
and me.

Well the winter came, and the snow did fall,
And the night was cold and still.
The rags we wore were not enough.
Joe, he caught the chill.
And he told me how he loved me,
And in my arms he went to sleep
Now there's no more Gypsy, no more Joe;
there's just me.

While standin' here,
On the edge of this bridge,
Lookin' down, I see
The face of Joe and Gypsy, lookin' up at me.
Oh, and somewhere in the distance
I can hear them callin' me.
Tonight we'll be together again, Gypsy, Joe,
and me.

Yeah, tonight we'll be together again, Gypsy,
Joe, and me.

This song is about a guy and a girl and a dog. They're just out, roaming about. They sleep in the rail yard, and camp by the riverbank, and do all that. The guy gets pneumonia and dies. The dog gets run over and dies. Who wants to live without the people you love? So she gets on a bridge and jumps off.

I've killed a lot of puppies and kids and ladies in my songs. I've killed myself a few times. I don't want to do it in real life, but I can do it in a song. You're safe doing it that way.

I think sometimes I ought to get sued for writing such pitiful songs. Like I say, I write a lot of sad songs, and some of them are just plum pitiful.

During my seven years touring with Porter and the Wagonmasters, it wasn't unusual for us to play more than two hundred concerts a year. Add the days riding on the tour bus together between shows, and you can understand how your fellow band members become as close to you as family members.

Two Sides to Every Story

With Porter Wagoner (Dolly Parton / Bill Owens) 1968

ONE ASPECT OF COUNTRY MUSIC'S male-female duets is that they often portray "the battle of the sexes." Dolly joined that tradition with this tale, wherein the singers accuse each other of being boozy and floozy, respectively. It appears on their LP *Just between the Two of Us*. In real life, arguments between Porter and Dolly began within six months of her joining his show. Dolly's rebellious, independent spirit clashed instantly with Porter's obsessive need to control her.

DUET CHORUS

Two sides to every story, we can straighten
this out if we'll take time.
Two sides to every story, you tell yours
and I'll tell mine.

(Porter)
Well where were you last night when
I came home?
When I came in, you were out and gone.

(Dolly)
Well I waited up 'til after two, then I went
downtown to look for you.
So how's about tellin' me where you were at?

(Porter)
Well, me and the boys stopped off for a
drink or two.
(Dolly interjection)
Now ain't you a pretty thing?
(Porter)
Well we got to drinkin', and I guess that
time just flew.

(Dolly)
Well the time must've flown for you, alright,
'Cause I thought you were gonna stay
out all night
And I told myself I ain't a-puttin' up
with that.

REPEAT DUET CHORUS

(Porter)
You said you went downtown to look for me.
Did you have to dress up fancy as could be?

(Dolly)
You know I never leave the house, in old
tacky clothes lookin' like a slouch.
And I's downtown, just lookin' my best
for you.

(Porter)
Now I'm not accusin' you of doin' wrong.
But that's awful late for you to be out
and gone.

(Dolly)
Now look who's talkin' 'bout bein' late.
I wasn't about to sit and wait
While you were out there with no tellin' who.

REPEAT DUET CHORUS TWICE

In the 1960s, my show costumes were always pretty conservative. I was shy and modest, so most of them had high necklines and long sleeves.

Whether they are "country" or not, people fight all the time. For some people, that's the only excitement they have in their lives, is to fight. When Porter and I were doing duets, we tried to find colorful songs, with subjects that would relate to our audience, so bickering seemed like a good idea. Then there was the fact that Porter and I did fight all the time.

Carl and I have never fought. We might get a little pissy now and then, but we don't go back and forth. I never wanted to have anything like that between us. So we just sulk a little and go off by ourselves.

Run That by Me One More Time

With Porter Wagoner 1970

IN THIS ERA OF COUNTRY MUSIC, duet songs like this were called "funny fight" numbers. This cute, husband-and-wife spat from the *Porter Wayne & Dolly Rebecca* album is one of Dolly's best "funny fight" songs. Behind the scenes, she and Porter argued strenuously over songs, over show jokes, over record production, over her vocals, and over a myriad of other tensions.

DUET CHORUS
Run that by me one more time,
To make sure that I heard you right.
I hope you don't expect me to believe that line.
I might be crazy, but I ain't dumb.
And I know a lie, when I hear one.
Would you run that by me one more time?

(Dolly)
Well, you're late again, I see.
What's your excuse this time?
Don't you try to kiss and make up
When you smell so strong from wine.

(Porter)
Well, I'm not late, the clock is wrong.
You need to wind Big Ben.
Honey, that's not wine you smell,
That's aftershave for men

(Dolly)
Would you run that by me one more time?

REPEAT DUET CHORUS

(Porter)
What happened to the money
I gave you to pay the rent?
The rent is overdue,
And we ain't got one red cent.

(Dolly)
Well I put it in the cookie jar
That day you brought it home.
One day when I came back from town,
I looked, and I'll be dogged, if that money wasn't gone.

(Porter)
Would you run that by me one more time?

REPEAT DUET CHORUS

(Dolly)
You keep drinkin' that aftershave, it's gonna kill you if I'm lucky.
(Porter)
You spent that money didn't you?
(Dolly)
I didn't spend that money,
(Porter)
I oughta box your jaws.
(Dolly)
Oh you'd hit your mom before you'd hit me.
(Porter)
You just talkin' to hear your head roll.
(Porter)
Would you run that by me one more time?
(Dolly)
I don't want to run that by you one more time.
(Porter)
Shut your mouth.
(Dolly)
I don't have to. You ain't my boss.

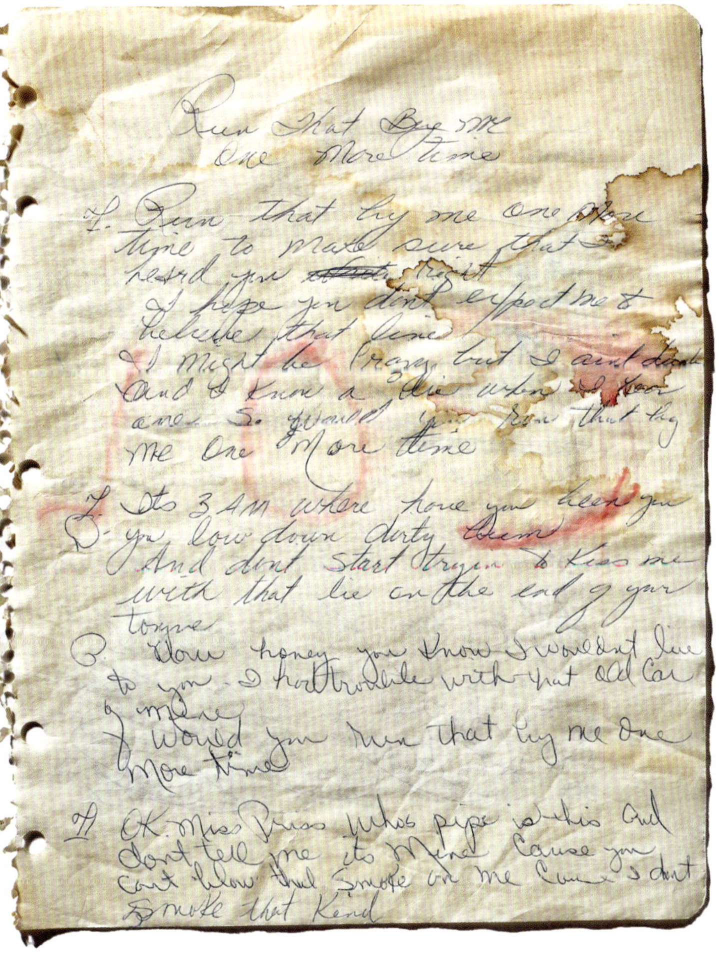

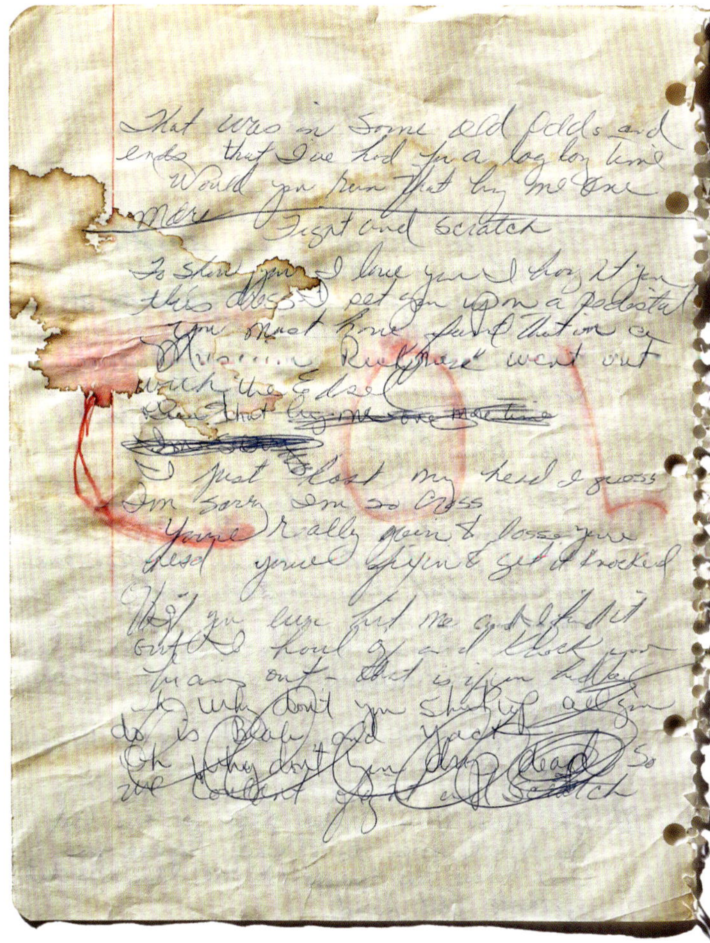

Well, I'm clever and witty, and I liked to write funny stuff. Porter and I were famous for our ad-libs. After this song had finished, we'd keep bickering back and forth, just throwing lines at each other. We weren't literally fighting in front of the audience, but we came up with some of the funniest things in the fade-outs of those songs.

Everybody fights. Some people just irk you, and you just can't keep from getting back at them. Then if you're smart, you can come up with clever lines. To put it in a song was a better way for us to fight. It was healthier and smarter than the way things really were.

LEFT: To the fans, it must have looked like it was all fun and games between Porter and me. It wasn't.

Curse of the Wild Weed Flower

With Porter Wagoner (Dolly Parton / Louis Owens) 1971

THIS SONG APPEARED ON THE duo's *Two of a Kind* album. Dolly's co-writer on it was Louis Owens (1933–2014), another of Avie Lee Parton's brothers. Louis wrote songs, but his main job in Dolly's early career was running Owepar Publishing. The company was founded by Dolly and her uncle Bill in 1967, just before she joined Porter Wagoner's troupe. Also working at Owepar was Dolly's confidante Judy Ogle, her best friend since the two girls were seven years old. Later, Louis was put in charge of Dolly's merchandise, and Judy became Dolly's right arm and personal assistant.

Their thoughts are all mingled, their dreams
all confused.
Their minds and their bodies, how they
abuse,
Searching for answers that doesn't grow
there,
Bound by the curse of the wild weed flower.

Their plans, their desires, and all of their
hopes
Wither and die as they go up in smoke.
Sharp as a needle, and filled with despair
Such is the curse of the wild weed flower.

From a moment of joy to a lifetime of sorrow,
For one day of pleasure they trade their
tomorrows.
Lost in a garden where bulbs all grow
With blossoms of heartaches and petals
of woe.

Eyes full of emptiness just stand and stare,
Bound by the curse of the wild weed flower
Bound by the curse of the wild weed flower
Bound by the curse of the wild weed flower

I knew early on that I wanted to have my own company and publish my own songs. While I was writing with Uncle Bill, we were trying to work on the business end of things, too. We started a company called Owepar Publishing, which is "Owens-Parton." Bill's brother was in Nashville, and we brought him on board.

Uncle Louis was also a singer-songwriter, and he was a guitar player. He sometimes played bass in our little trio that I had backing me with Uncle Henry playing drums, Uncle Bill playing guitar, Uncle Louis playing bass, and me singing and playing my guitar.

Louis taught me a lot in those early days, and I loved him. He bought me instruments. I think it was his little Martin guitar that was given to me as a child. We even wrote some songs together.

Louis was smarter than some of us, as far as paperwork was concerned, so he came to run the publishing company. He worked there for many, many years.

My uncle Lester gave us some of the money to start the publishing company. He was a truck driver. A lot of people don't know about him, but he afforded some of us to make music. Even back in the Cas Walker days, he'd send me money to buy clothes. All my mom's brothers were involved in my career, in one way or another.

One of the songs Uncle Louis and I wrote was this one, about marijuana. That was back when we thought anything to do with any kind of drugs was scary. So the song was about this girl who was strung out on drugs and stuff. I still think it's a great title, "The Curse of the Wild Weed Flower," because we were playing off of Mother Maybelle Carter's [1928] classic "Wildwood Flower." We wrote it back in the early 1960s, long before it actually came out as a duet with Porter.

Please Don't Stop Loving Me

With Porter Wagoner (Dolly Parton / Porter Wagoner) 1974

BY THE TIME THE DUO released this song on the *Porter 'n' Dolly* LP, Dolly had called it quits with Porter. Ironically, it is the only No. 1 hit they ever had as duet partners. And perhaps equally ironically, they had written it together.

DUET CHORUS

Please, please, don't stop loving me,
For I couldn't live with you gone.
Please, please, don't stop loving me,
For I couldn't make it alone.

(Dolly)

You bring me the sunshine when none is in sight.
And when I'm in darkness, you bring me the light.
You opened my eyes when I couldn't see,
So please, oh please, don't stop loving me.

(Porter)

You're my inspiration, my purpose in life.
When things go all wrong, you make them alright.
I would be useless if you ever leave,
So please, oh please, don't stop loving me.

REPEAT DUET CHORUS

Please, please, don't stop loving me.

Porter and I used to write together. Sometimes it was easy, sometimes not. We were both very bullheaded. Maybe we were too much alike, or maybe we were too different, I never quite figured that one out.

When I met him, Porter was not known as a writer. I kind of helped him get into that. I was writing so much and getting a lot of attention, so I started helping him with his writing.

Porter had a great ear for music, and he did write some great songs. I helped with a lot of them that don't have my name on them. But I was happy to do it, because he had done so many things for me. When we wrote together, sometimes it was fun and sometimes it would be based on whether or not we were fighting.

We had our ups and downs, like all writers do. I usually don't write with other people if it's not fun. In fact, I haven't co-written with many people at all.

"Please Don't Stop Loving Me" is one that Porter and I wrote together, and it's a very commercial song. All of the things that he and I wrote together were bits and pieces of what our relationship had been—the good, the bad, the indifferent, and the different. That one happened to be the very last thing we did together, and it was the one that went to No. 1. That's kind of ironic, ain't it?

OPPOSITE PAGE: That's me with Uncle Louis. We sometimes wrote songs together, and he was a help to me when I was first starting to figure out the "business" part of the music business.

Together Always

With Porter Wagoner 1972

THIS UP-TEMPO SINGLE SERVED AS THE TITLE SONG of one of Porter and Dolly's thirteen duet albums. It reached No. 14 on the charts. In gratitude for all he'd done for her, Dolly gave Porter the half of Owepar Publishing that Uncle Bill relinquished in 1969.

(Porter)
You and I have been together for a long,
long time.
And we vowed that we would stay together
always.

(Dolly)
Life at times has been unpleasant,
Down the trails where fate has led us.
But we pray that God will let us
Be together always.

DUET CHORUS
Together together
Together always you and me
Forever and ever
Together always you and me

(Porter)
Through the years our love will multiply
and be divided
By the children added to enrich our lives.

(Dolly)
God's been good to you and I.
And in Heaven, there's eternal life,
Beyond this world where you and I
Will be together always.

REPEAT DUET CHORUS TWICE

I've Been Married Just as Long as You Have

With Porter Wagoner (Dolly Parton / Porter Wagoner) 1973

THIS DOMESTIC SPARRING MATCH is another of the duo's "funny fight" numbers. In real life, Dolly and Porter were butting heads constantly by 1973. She had intended to stay with him for five years, and now it was approaching seven. The song appears on their album *We Found It*. Its cover illustration pictures Dolly wearing the most elaborate, towering wig of her career thus far.

(Dolly)
Last night you went out again
With what you said was your best friend.
You say you need some time away from me.
The sun was high when you got in,
But not as high as you had been.
And I wonder how you would act
If I done just the way I please.

DUET CHORUS
I've been married just as long as you have
And I get tired of the same old things just the
same as you have

(Dolly)
Well let me tell you this, big boy,
When you go out for a night of joy
You better start takin' me along
Or you'll be singin' a different song.
For I've been married just as long as
you have.

(Porter)
While I'm workin' hard all day
You run around and spend my pay.
You entertain your friends at my expense.
But you cry and carry on
When I do somethin' on my own.
And you accuse with lack of evidence.

REPEAT DUET CHORUS

(Porter)
So let me tell you this sweetheart,
I figure I've done my part.
So don't get cute and get so smart.
I'll tell you this before you start,
I've been married just as long as you have

(Porter)
And that's a pretty good while
(Dolly)
Honey, you're the cat I've spent nine
lives with.
(Porter)
I know you have, you ain't spent no time
at home.
You're running around all over town.
You're here there and everywhere.
(Dolly)
Well if I could stand you long enough,
I might stay at home a little more.
(Porter)
You move so fast an umbrella would be
in your way,
Honey, if it was a-rainin'.
(Dolly)
Oh boy, now ain't that cute.
If your heart was as big as your mouth,
You'd give everything we own away.
(Porter)
But I love you, you little devil.
So don't you ever take off and leave me, now,
here to myself.
I'll hit you right in the . . .

(Dolly)
I wouldn't. I wouldn't trust you with
yourself.
(Porter)
I'll hit you right in the mouth with my
mouth, honey,
And it'll go . . . (kissing sounds)
(Dolly)
You will? Golly.
(Porter)
One day, you'll look like you'd had the
mumps,
When I get done with you.
(Dolly)
Why don't you do it now?
(Porter)
I ain't had the . . . Here I go . . .
(kissing sounds)
(Dolly, in a witch's voice)
I'll get you in my next brew, ah-ha-ha.
(Porter)
You're killin' me, but I love every minute
of it.

The funny songs were based on a truth, and that was that Porter had a great sense of humor. He was a prankster, he was a jokester, and he had great stories. He just loved to do things to make me laugh. When he was at his best, there was no one more fun to be around.

Porter had a lot of friends. He had a lot of golfing buddies and a lot of fishing buddies, and they loved being with him.

It was only when we would clash over business things that we would have our rows. He had a bad temper, and when it flared, it flared. But when he was in good spirits, he was a joy.

There was a lot of joy and a lot of fun on the bus. He had wonderful band, and they had a good time with him. They played golf together all the time. I'd often go with them and ride around on the golf cart just to see how much fun they were having.

Porter and the boys were more into their western suits, but I didn't want that look. I just wanted my stuff to be shiny, flashy, and colorful, and I still do. I feel like a butterfly when I am in all of my colors. I can't get enough rhinestones, enough color, enough gaud, because it fits my personality.

When I started with Porter's show, I started having my clothes custom-made. It's hard to fit me. I'm little in places and big in others, you know? It's hard to find stuff off the rack that fits, so my clothes have to be tailor-made. I'm only big on top; I'm a tiny little person. But I wear my high heels and my hair as high as I can get it.

I always wore my hair all teased up. Whenever that style started, I was the first to get my hair all poofy. Then as soon as I could buy those hairpieces and wigs, I wanted them. For one thing, they were so handy. Plus, my hair would never do exactly what I wanted it to do. So the wigs became kind of my trademark.

When I was on *The Porter Wagoner Show*, we had makeup girls. They would do their basics, and then I would add on to that. I was always into makeup, but I never could stand anybody else's version of me. No matter who I paid to do the makeup for album covers or shows, I'd go right in there and start adding more to my eyes or to my lips. I just have to kind of enhance things.

The more I grew in the business and the more confident I became in the world, the more I wanted to look like the pictures I saw as a teenager in the Frederick's of Hollywood catalogs. I wanted to feel like the way I thought all the movie stars in Hollywood did.

When Possession Gets Too Strong

(Dolly Parton / Louis Owens) 1969

THIS SONG WAS WRITTEN with Dolly's uncle Louis. He and Uncle Bill (not to mention Fred Foster of Monument Records) were pushed aside by Porter Wagoner as he maneuvered for greater dominance over Dolly.

I can't live with you if you try to own me,
Though you may give me love like I have never known.
But if you try to control me, then you won't ever know me.
And I'll be movin' on, when possession gets too strong.

So love me just for what I am. Don't try to change a thing.
And I'll take you, just like you are, and I expect the same.
So if you want to love me, you must understand all of me,
Or I'll be movin' on, when possession gets too strong.

CHORUS
And I have no control over what I feel inside.
And I can't change the way I am, and you must be satisfied.
So if you think you can't be without placin' chains on me,
Then I'll be movin' on, when possession gets too strong.

REPEAT CHORUS

I'll be movin' on when possession gets too strong.

"When Possession Gets Too Strong" was written a long time ago, but it kind of describes the relationship I eventually had with Porter. Porter was a very controlling person, but that had served him well. That's how he became a star. When it's your show, you have to feel like you're in control of it. I completely understood that with Porter. He had to be the boss of everything.

And that was one of the reasons we fought so much. Because I have to be the boss of me. I can't be bossed.

Porter was very aggressive in his temperament, and he kind of tried to frighten me. I think a lot of times, he did. But I had a father and six brothers and many uncles. I was used to men. I didn't fold like some women, which is why I would just fight back.

Porter didn't want anybody else to have anything to do with me. Porter insisted I leave Monument Records. He tried to get me away from Bill and get me away from my uncle Louis. He thought those people were not good for me. In all truth, they were not good for him.

So then our fights became more intense: He was not going to push me around, just because I'm a girl. I am not the kind of person to be pushed around. That is not my nature.

Porter is not here to defend himself. So I'll have to defend him, in my way. I'm sure all of his intentions were good, even if some of them were self-serving. But ain't we all guilty of that sometimes?

I look back on all that now, and I realize this helped to build my character. It helped me build my own strength. So even the bad times were good. There were good times as well as bad times. But that's how memories are made, and that's why I'm sitting here today.

So, yes, I had to move along. And, yes, possession did get too strong.

If You Go, I'll Follow You

With Porter Wagoner (Dolly Parton / Porter Wagoner) 1981

PORTER WAGONER SUED DOLLY PARTON after she left him. The case dragged on for many months. When it was finally resolved, she got her Owepar songs back. He got their Fireside recording studio, which Owepar's income had subsidized, and a cash settlement. In addition, Porter won the right to release *Porter & Dolly* as their final duet LP, which had been "in the can" ever since Dolly's departure. On it was this enduring-love composition, which went to No. 12 and became their final hit together.

DUET CHORUS
If you go, I'll follow you.
You can't leave my love behind.
If you go, I'll follow you.
Even death could never end this love of mine.

(Dolly)
I have loved you for so long,
With a love both true and strong.
You are all I've ever had,
And I love you, good or bad.

(Porter)
Where you go, I'll go with you,
No matter where you take me to.
I'd go to Hell and back again.
I'll be with you until the end.

REPEAT DUET CHORUS

If you go, I'll follow you.

I Will Always Love You 1974

A NO. 1 COUNTRY SMASH from the *Jolene* album, this song is in the Grammy Hall of Fame. Dolly re-recorded it for the soundtrack of her 1982 movie with Burt Reynolds, *The Best Little Whorehouse in Texas*. Ten years later, Kevin Costner suggested it to Whitney Houston for the soundtrack of their movie, *The Bodyguard*. It became one of the biggest pop hits in history and has been recorded by dozens of other greats since. Dolly originally wrote it about trying to obtain her freedom from Porter. Despite many prior attempts, he'd always refused to let her go. Her last date with Porter's road show was reportedly April 21, 1974, although he continued to produce her records for two more years.

If I should stay,
I would only be in your way.
So I'll go, but I know
I'll think of you each step of the way.

And I will always love you.
I will always love you.

Bittersweet memories
That is all I'm taking with me.
Goodbye. Please, don't cry.
We both know I'm not what you, you need.

And I will always love you
I will always love you.

I hope life treats you kind,
And I hope you have all that you ever dreamed of.
And I wish you joy and happiness,
But above all this, I wish you love.

And I will always love you.
I will always love you.

WSM
GRAND
OLE

"I Will Always Love You" came from a whole lot of places, for a whole lot of reasons, over a long period of time. I had always dreamed of being my own star, having my own band, and doing my own thing. But working with Porter was such a good opportunity. In the beginning, I told Porter that I would stay for five years.

But when we started having hit duets and his show became a bigger success, a lot of it was beginning to be because of me. I was getting a following, and he didn't like that too much.

I wanted to get on with my life. I didn't want to be known as the "girl singer" in someone else's band. I said to Porter, "I've got to go. I want to start my own show."

He'd say, "You can't go. You can't do that to me, because of all I've done for you." That whole kind of thing. Or he would try to win the argument by being mean and hateful. Or by trying to pull a guilt trip on me. Eventually, I thought, "There's no way I'm ever going to win an argument with this man. He's not going to listen to me. He's just going to fight and fight. But I am going to go, one way or another."

I thought, "Well, why don't you do what you do best? Why don't you write it in a song?" So I went home and wrote this song about bittersweet memories. I said, "If I should stay, I would only be in your way." But I should have said, "You'd only be in *my* way." Ha-ha. Really, we were in each other's way. He was trying to control something that's not controllable, and that was making him miserable and me miserable.

The song came straight from the bottom of my heart. All of those feelings, all of those thoughts, all of those things we had been through, all the things we had been to each other, all of the things we had done to each other, all of that was in one song. I was so emotional I was crying when I was writing it.

I went into his office and said, "Porter, sit down. I want to sing you a song I wrote." When I started to sing the song, he started to cry. He knew that I had been crying when I wrote it. He got it. He said, "That's the best song you ever wrote. And you can go, if I can produce that song." I said, "It's a deal!"

It changed our relationship, even though we worked together a little while longer. It broke the tension. Of course, later it flared up again. But nothing's ever easy.

Elvis loved the song and wanted to record it. But his manager demanded half of my publishing rights. It broke my heart, but I couldn't give up my copyright. I cried my eyes out, because I could just hear Elvis singing it. But sometimes you just have to stand your ground. Priscilla [Presley] told me years later that it was the song he sang to her when they were leaving the divorce courtroom. So that touched me even more.

I wrote a song later called "I Dreamed about Elvis" and had an Elvis soundalike come in and sing it. It was about dreaming of him singing my song.

Years later, Kevin Costner's office contacted our office and said, "Can we get a copy of Dolly's song 'I Will Always Love You'?" He said that [producer] David Foster was going to be doing the music for this movie. That sounded good to me, because I had worked with David.

But that was the last I'd heard of it. Then one day I was driving my Cadillac back home to Brentwood from my office. I had the radio on, and all of a sudden I heard this spoken voice say, "If I should stay. . . ." It caught my ear, but I didn't recognize it. Then, when it went into the music, I thought I was going to wreck the car. I have never had such an overwhelming feeling. I had to pull off to the side of the road, because it just got bigger and bigger and better and better. I have never experienced a greater feeling in my life than hearing Whitney Houston sing that song for the first time.

I had already taken it to No. 1 twice by then. But she took that little simple heartbroken song of mine and took it worldwide. For what she did with that, I will always love you, Whitney Houston.

Now the song is going to live forever. I thank Porter for that song. I think of him every time I sing it. If it hadn't been for him, I'd never have written that song.

OPPOSITE PAGE: Some songs come and go in your set lists. But "I Will Always Love You" has been a part of my concerts for every show in every year for the past five decades. It has to be, because it's been a hit five times. I had a country hit with it twice before Whitney Houston made it a pop smash. Then Vince Gill and I won awards with it as a duet. The CMA chose it as the finale song of "Forever Country" to celebrate the organization's fiftieth anniversary, and it was a big hit again.

CHAPTER 4

PUTTING WINGS ON MY DREAMS

IN RETROSPECT, DOLLY'S LEAVING *THE PORTER WAGONER SHOW* seems inevitable. Between 1971 and 1975, Dolly Parton had five solo No. 1 hits. Porter Wagoner had none. His last Top 10 success on the charts as a solo artist was in early 1972. By mid-1975, she had ten of them.

During her seven-year tenure with Porter, Dolly was an employee making $200 to $350 per concert. His package show's booking fees went steadily upward, but her salary did not.

His weekly television show was the most successful in country music, airing in eighty-six markets. Although her solo and duet appearances on it increasingly became highlights, she was only paid union scale, like the rest of the band members.

Meanwhile, on Music Row, the country industry was becoming increasingly aware of her songwriting prowess. The sheer diversity of her lyrics was startling, as she addressed suicide, adultery, insanity, drugs, illegitimacy, poverty, death, and more. Her songs have been populated by orphans, alcoholics, prostitutes, preachers, vagabonds, widows, gamblers, ghosts, moonshiners, senior citizens, outlaws, hermits, and many other assorted characters.

She has also been more than capable of crafting a meaningful love song, which is the enduring staple of all genres in American popular music. Several of Dolly's love songs became huge hits, beginning in the early 1970s.

She fulfilled a childhood dream by becoming a member of the Grand Ole Opry cast on New Year's Day 1969. She scored the first of her Grammy Award nominations in 1970, for her exuberant, feminized reworking of the 1930 Jimmie Rodgers classic "Mule Skinner Blues." This was a harbinger of her increasing prominence as that decade unfolded.

Dolly rose to solo country stardom on the strength of these widely respected compositions of 1968 to 1974. They laid the groundwork for her gaining independence. Or as she put it, "putting wings on my dreams."

The late Nashville photographer Hope Powell took hundreds of color portraits of me like this one. Hope later sang in the Christ Church Choir that backed me on "He's Alive" in 1989.

Mommie, Ain't That Daddy?

With Porter Wagoner 1968

THIS ANTI-ALCOHOL SONG is on the Porter and Dolly duet album *Just between the Two of Us*.

(Dolly)
The snow was falling swiftly, and
It mounted on the street.
Little footprints in the snow
Made by our children's feet,
As I walked them to the Goodwill store
To get some clothes to wear.
As we turned around the corner,
I saw you standing there.

I tried to turn the children
And walk the other way.
I prayed they hadn't seen you,
Then I heard the baby say,
"Mama, ain't that Daddy
Holding out his hand,
Begging for money
From that other man?"

They asked me "Ain't that Daddy?"
And "Yes" I had to say.
And I wondered if I'd failed you,
And made you turn this way.

(Porter, spoken)
No, you didn't fail me.
My weakness was just too strong.
Because, you see, I thought more of the bottle
Than our family and our home.
No, you didn't fail me, Sweetheart.
You loved me all you could.
You had my babies and you loved me like
No other woman ever would

You know, I guess I'd be better off dead
Than in the awful shape I'm in.
But death just don't seem to have a place for
those
That stay drunk on whiskey, wine, and gin.
You see, I die a constant death
Over and over every day.
If I could change, you know I'd do it for you,
The babies and our home.

But you might as well forget me,
For I'm just too far gone.
But I wish you would do me one last favor,
And do it just for me.

When they ask you, "Mama, ain't that
Daddy?"
Just say "It used to be."

Alcohol is the number one killer. A lot of people don't realize that it's like a drug you can become addicted to. It's so easy to get, and it seems so innocent to have a beer or a cocktail. If you have a weakness for it, before you know it you can become an alcoholic. I've seen a lot of sorrows, because alcoholism runs on both sides of my family. An alcoholic might say, "Well, it ain't hurting nobody but me." That's a crock. It hurts everybody and you.

Porter did not drink at all, nor did he allow his musicians to drink when they were on a job. I have never had a drug nor alcohol problem, thank God. I never wanted anything to mess with my mind. I want to use my brains for something more productive.

Porter was also very dramatic. He loved recitations. He loved dressing up and being an actor for album covers and publicity shots. He would dress up like a wino, put on dark makeup, and lay in the alley with ragged clothes to play a part. So I wrote songs for him to fit that, like "Mommie, Ain't That Daddy?" and "Wino."

The Party

With Porter Wagoner 1968

A LURID LYRIC LIKE THIS ONE is like a modern reinterpretation of the emotions in the tragic Anglo-American ballads of Dolly's youth. Similar to such classic folk songs, it is also a mini morality play. It appears on the Porter and Dolly duet album *Just the Two of Us*.

(Dolly)
As we were dressing to go out,
Our little girl and boy
Came in and asked
If they could go this time.

We told them little girls and boys
Don't belong at parties
And that they should be in bed
Asleep by nine.

The babysitter came in then,
And we kissed the kids goodbye.
And told them that we'd be home soon,
And told them not to cry.

(Porter, spoken)
Then we left for the party,
Like we'd so often done,
Thinkin' only of ourselves
And not our little ones.

The party started out wild, and it grew wilder
As the night wore on,
With drinkin', laughin', tellin' dirty jokes,
Nobody thinkin' of home.

Then the strangest feelin' came over me,
And it chilled me to the bone.
And I told my wife that we'd better leave
the party,
'Cause I felt that we were needed at home.

As we rode along, I got to thinkin' of how the
kids that mornin'
Had asked if we would take them to church
the next day.
And how I'd put 'em off, like I'd so often
done,
By sayin' we'd probably get home too late.

Then my thoughts were interrupted by the
sound of sirens
As they cut through the still night air.
Then we turned down our street. That's when
we saw the fire.
The rest was like a nightmare.

We took their little bodies
To church the next day.
Though we'd left the party early,
We still got home too late.

Little Bird 1969

DOLLY INTRODUCED THIS POETIC LYRIC on her 1969 LP *In the Good Old Days (When Times Were Bad)*. Porter released his rendition of it on the flip side of his 1972 hit single "What Ain't to Be Just Might Happen."

Beauty is a rare perfume,
Precious, yet doesn't last long.
Youth is but a playful breeze
That blows our way once, then moves on.
Love is a hidden treasure
Some never find where it lies.
And memory is a little bird,
Flies through life, lives, and dies.

CHORUS
Little bird, take me aboard your beautiful wings
And let me fly.
Fly me away back to yesterday,
And drop me off there awhile.

Let me smell the rare perfume
Of the sweet flower of beauty again.
Let me run in the playful breeze
Of youth long gone with the wind.
Let me sit for a while by the place
Where I found the treasure of love.
Then sing me a song as you fly me along
On our long last journey above.

I love to write poetic songs and sing flowery words. I like to make you see something visually, so I want to paint a picture. And I love to come up with clever lines, not just like a songwriter, but like a poet.

I do write a lot of poetry, and sometimes I think the poems are so good that I say, "I've got to put a tune to that," rather than leave it as a poem. So I kind of go back and tear them apart and rework them. And that was the case with "Little Bird."

Down from Dover 1969

THIS SONG IS ON DOLLY'S *Fairest of Them All* album. Artists as diverse as Nancy Sinatra, Kate Campbell, and Marianne Faithfull later recorded it, and Dolly, herself, revisited it on her 2001 *Little Sparrow* CD.

I know this dress I'm wearing doesn't hide
The secret I have tried concealing.
When he left, he promised me that
he'd be back
By the time it was revealing.
The sun behind a cloud just cast a
crawling shadow
O'er the fields of clover.
And time is running out for me.
I wish that he
Would hurry down from Dover.

He's been gone so long, when he left
The snow was deep upon the ground.
And I have seen a spring and summer pass,
And now the leaves are turnin' brown.
At any time a tiny face will show itself
'Cause waiting's almost over.
But I won't have a name to give it
If he doesn't hurry down from Dover.

My folks weren't understanding. When they
found out,
They sent me from the home place.
My daddy said if folks found out,
He'd be ashamed to ever show his face.
My mama said I was a fool.
She did not believe it when I told her
That everything would be all right, 'cause
soon he would
Be comin' down from Dover.

(I found a place to stay out on a farm
Takin' care of that old lady.
She never asked me nuthin', so I never talked
To her about my baby.
I sent a message to my mom with
a name and address
Of Miz ol' Grover,
And to make sure he got that information
When he came down from Dover.) *

I loved him more than anything, and I could
not refuse him
When he needed me.
He was the only one I'd loved, and I just can't
believe
That he was usin' me.
He couldn't leave me here like this.
I know it can't be so, it can't be over.
He wouldn't make me go through this alone,
Oh, he'll be comin' down from Dover.

My body aches. The time is here.
It's lonely in this place where I'm lying.
Our baby has been born, but something's
wrong.
It's much too still, I hear no crying.
I guess in some strange way she knew
She'd never have a father's arms to hold her.
And dying was her way of tellin' me
he wasn't
Comin' down from Dover, from Dover,
from Dover.

* This verse was edited out of Dolly's original recorded version of the song.

"Down from Dover" is a fan favorite. It couldn't be released as a single because of its subject. Disc jockeys weren't interested in it; it was too controversial. Even to this day, people don't talk about this, and they especially didn't back then.

Back when I wrote it, if you got pregnant out of wedlock, you were either going to have to get rid of the baby, have it adopted, or you just had to leave home altogether.

I remember that I started writing it on Porter Wagoner's tour bus. We rode past Dover, Tennessee, and my mind started going. It was a beautiful day, and the wind was blowing. There was this field of clover waving in the wind. So there we were, Dover-clover, and that started me off: "The sun behind a cloud just cast a crawling shadow o'er the fields of clover. And time is running out for me. I wish that he would hurry down from Dover."

The song was big in England, so everybody over there thinks it is about Dover, England. And Dover, Delaware, claims it, too. We used that city as the backdrop for the [2019] Netflix movie about "Down from Dover." But it was inspired by Dover, Tennessee.

In the song, the parents turned against the girl. They sent her out, so she found a place out on a farm with an old lady, and the baby died. Lord, I just can't get depressing enough, can I?

When you tell these stories, you have to have a beginning, a middle, and an end. So I just keep writing along. I never know, myself, how I'm going to end it, until I get close to the end.

Only when I start talking about it or thinking about it do I realize how morbid I really am. People always say, "You just seem so happy." I say, "Yeah, but I can certainly write you a morbid song!" But this is still one of my favorites.

I can write a song anytime, anyplace, anywhere. That's why I always keep a guitar and a piece of paper handy at all times. This photo was taken during a moment alone at Fireside Studio.

Joshua 1971

THIS BECAME DOLLY'S FIRST NO. 1 HIT. It was also the first of her songs to make an appearance on the pop charts, even though it was only at No. 108. Her performance of "Joshua," complete with its celebratory finale yodel, was nominated for a Grammy Award. As a measure of her growing respect in the music industry, in that same year her gospel LP was also nominated for a Grammy, as was her duet work with Porter Wagoner.

Well a good ways down the railroad track
There was this little old rundown shack,
And in it lived a man I'd never seen.

Folks said he was a mean and a vicious man.
And "You better not set foot on his land."
But I didn't think nobody could be
that mean.

So I took me out walking down the
railroad track.
I was a-gonna go down to that little old shack,
And just find out if all them things I'd heard
was true.

There was a big black dog laying out in
the yard.
And it growled at me, and I swallowed hard.
And I heard somebody say, "Well, who
are you?"

Oh and there he stood in the door of
that shack.
His beard and his hair was long and black.
And he was the biggest man I'd ever seen.

When he spoke, his voice was low and deep,
But he just didn't frighten me.
'Cause somehow I just knew he wasn't mean.

He said, "What you doing, snooping 'round
my place?"
And I saw a smile come across his face,
So I smiled back, and I told him who I was.

He said, "Come on in and pull you up a chair.
You might as well, since you already here."
And he said, "You can call me Joshua."

Joshua, Joshua,
Whatcha doing living here all alone?
Joshua, Joshua,
Ain't you got nobody to call your own?
No, no, no, no.

We talked 'til the sun was clean out of sight,
And we still talking when it come daylight.
And there was just so much we had to
say, hey.

I'd spent my life in an orphan's home.
And just like him, I was all alone.
So I said, "Yeah," when he asked if I'd stay.

Oh we grew closer as time went on,
And that little old shack, it was a happy
home.
And we just couldn't help but fall in love.

That big black dog and little old shack
Sitting down by the railroad track,
It's plenty good enough for me and Joshua.

Joshua, Joshua,
Why, you're just what I've been looking for.
Joshua, Joshua,
You ain't gonna be lonesome anymore.
No, no.

Yodelay-he-ho, lay-he, he-he-he-he
Papa-pa-pa-pa-pa-pa-pa

Me and Joshua
Me and Joshua
Me and Joshua, yeah
Me and Joshua

Nineteen seventy-one was a good year, wasn't it? But you only realize it when you think back about different points in your life and about how your career grows. Three Grammy nominations for three different songs in the same year, that's something.

I love the story of this song. But I also love its little musical arrangement. The record sounded really good.

I based the character on two or three mountain men I knew as a kid, reclusive people who lived alone way back in the mountains. I just kind of built the story around them.

In my show, I don't include a lot of my old songs anymore. But this is one that people sometimes ask me to sing when I'm on tour. I think it's because it set a lot of things in motion for me. It's always been a real favorite with the fans.

Since it was my first No. 1 hit, you could say that "Joshua" sent me off on a lifetime of touring. These well-worn road cases tell the tale.

JOLENE

By DOLLY PARTON

3. You could have your choice of men, but I could never love again.
He's the only one for me, JOLENE.
I had to have this talk with you,
My happiness depends on you
And whatever you decide to do, JOLENE.

CHORUS: JOLENE, JOLENE, JOLENE, JOLENE,
I'm begging of you, please don't take my man.
JOLENE, JOLENE, JOLENE, JOLENE,
Please don't take him even though you can.

TAG: JOLENE, JOLENE, please don't take my man, JOLENE,
JOLENE, my happiness depends on you, JOLENE.

Jolene 1973

THIS IS THE DOLLY PARTON SONG that is most performed by others, from bluegrass acts to alternative-rock bands. "Jolene" was a No. 1 country smash and marked Dolly's first appearance on the adult contemporary (easy listening) hit parade. The song was nominated for Grammy Awards in 1974 and 1975. Dolly finally won a Grammy for "Jolene" in 2017 via a collaboration with the *a cappella* pop group Pentatonix. Her original recording is now in the Grammy Hall of Fame. In 2019, it inspired a Netflix movie.

CHORUS
Jolene, Jolene, Jolene, Jolene,
I'm begging of you, please don't take my man.
Jolene, Jolene, Jolene, Jolene,
Please don't take him just because you can.

Your beauty is beyond compare
With flaming locks of auburn hair,
With ivory skin and eyes of emerald green.
Your smile is like a breath of spring.
Your voice is soft like summer rain.
And I cannot compete with you, Jolene.

He talks about you in his sleep.
And there's nothing I can do to keep
From crying when he calls your name, Jolene.
And I can easily understand
How you could easily take my man,
But you don't know what he means to me, Jolene.

REPEAT CHORUS

You could have your choice of men,
But I could never love again.
He's the only one for me, Jolene.
I had to have this talk with you.
My happiness depends on you,
And whatever you decide to do, Jolene.

REPEAT CHORUS

"Jolene" is my most recorded song. Worldwide, through the years, they say it has been recorded four-hundred-and-some times. Whether it's in another language or whether it's a garage band, everybody seems to love that song. I guess every band can sing it, and every woman can relate to it.

It's just so simple, that chorus over and over, "Jolene, Jolene, Jolene, Jolene, don't take my man." Little bitty kids sing it, even though they don't know what "take my man" means. I don't know what the reason is, but people go right to that one. That makes me happy, because I love it, too. I never get tired of singing that song.

There was a little girl at one of the shows when I was touring with Porter. We used to sign autographs after the shows. She came up to the stage and said, "Would you sign this 'To Jolene'?" I said, "Jolene, that's a beautiful name. I bet you're named after your daddy. Is his name Joe?" She said, "No, it's just Jolene." I said, "Well, I love that name, and if you ever hear a song with it, you'll know it's about you."

So I just kept it in my mind. To remember the name, I went "Jolene, Jolene, Jolene, Jolene" until I could get back to the bus and write it down. Which is when I thought, "I'll just start the song like that, because that's how I remembered the

PAGE 116: This is the "lead sheet" for my 1973 song "Jolene."

BELOW: You can view the costume I wore on the cover of *Jolene* in my museum at Dollywood.

name, and I'll add to that." So then I came up with a story that I knew women could relate to.

Of course, then I thought of a story loosely based on Carl flirting with a girl down at the bank, which was true. I went down there, and she *was* pretty. And he *was* flirting. And I made the whole thing into my song's lyric.

I got a letter not long ago from a girl who did have that red hair and all. But her name was Jolie-ann or something. Yet I distinctly remembered it being "Jolene." It might have been her, but I'm not certain. I don't really know where she is to this day.

It's possible that "Jolene" and "I Will Always Love You" were written on the same day. When we were going through all my old tapes to put my songs on hard drives, we found that "I Will Always Love You" and "Jolene" were on the same cassette tape, back-to-back. I don't know; I might have written "Jolene" later that night.

When you write so much, you lose track of time, and I wrote so much back then. So it had to have been written during that same time frame. Otherwise, I would have gone onto another cassette, or there would have been other things on it. It very well could have been on the same day.

"It's possible that 'Jolene' and 'I Will Always Love You' were written on the same day. When we were going through all my old tapes to put my songs on hard drives, we found that 'I Will Always Love You' and 'Jolene' were on the same cassette tape, back-to-back. I don't know, I might have written 'Jolene' later that night."

Like Willie Nelson, I've really worked my guitar hard, as you can see. And I'd like to think that we both have a lot of soul. This is one of my favorite old Martins.

Daddy 1969

THIS SONG REACHED NO. 40 on the charts. It was included on Dolly's LP *My Blue Ridge Mountain Boy*.

Daddy I feel that I must talk to you.
Are you sure this is what you want to do?
Now it's not for us kids that I beg you to stay.
Please don't just walk out on Mama this way.

She's mothered your children, she's spent her whole life
Trying to be a good mother and wife.
And she stood by you when the rest let you down.
Daddy, how can you walk out on her now?

I'm your oldest daughter, my age twenty-three.
Your new love is even younger than me.
She's young, she's pretty, her hands soft as dew,
While Mama's are withered from working for you.

Mom's not young anymore, like your new love.
But your new love won't love you like my mama does.
You've taken her best years, so don't leave her now.
Please, Daddy, say that you won't let her down.

"Daddy" is nothing but the truth. When I wrote it, I knew that so many men want to go chasing younger women. My mama used to say, "They are just chasing their youth." And I think that's true. They can't bear the fact that they are getting older.

That song relates to so many things I've seen within my own family and amongst my friends. I wrote it from a child's standpoint: "After all that Mama's been to you, how can you do this, just throw her over for a younger girl?" Addressing it from a child's point of view works because everybody suffers when there is an affair or a divorce.

There is something of me in everything I write. I have to know my own emotional self, but I have to write about other people's feelings, too. A lot of times, people can't express themselves in the same way that I can. I try to become them. I suffer for them, because I care for them. That's what I did in that song.

Mama, Say a Prayer 1969

IN THIS TUNE from her *In the Good Old Days* album, Dolly sings from the point of view of a prostitute far from home. In reality, young Dolly didn't really know much about such women. This became clear during one of her early Christmas seasons in Nashville, when Dolly decorated with a red light above her front door.

The bright lights of the city are a pretty sight to see.
Perhaps they're extra pretty to a country girl like me.
Temptation waits at every turn, and it won't let me be.
So, Mama when you pray tonight,
Say a special prayer for me.

CHORUS
I miss your tender goodnight kiss of love and understanding.
The goodnight kisses I get now are cruel and so demanding.
So, Mama when you pray tonight, and while you're on your knees,
Mama, say a special prayer for me.

The nights get cold and lonely when you're far away from home.
And lonely makes it easy for a good girl to go wrong.
Evil eyes search through the night for lonely girls like me.
So Mama when you pray tonight,
Say a special prayer for me.

REPEAT CHORUS

"Mama, Say a Prayer" was another song about being a prostitute. I wrote a lot about that kind of stuff.

It was Christmastime, and I was kind of new in Nashville. I was living in this old trailer of Uncle Bill's out on Murfreesboro Road. I felt like decorating so I put a big red light over the door. No other Christmas lights, just a big red light on the door, ha!

I didn't realize that prostitutes put a red light over their door! I guess in the old days, that's how you would know that was a house to stop at for that. But I was young; I didn't know.

Uncle Bill was in and out, working on the road, and I was dating Carl at that time. Well, both Carl and Uncle Bill came home, right after each other, bam-bam. They were always scared to have me living by myself, anyway.

When they both saw that light, they were horrified. They went, "You've got to take that down right away! People are going to come here with the wrong idea." I thought about saying, "How do you know it's the wrong idea? Maybe you don't know what I'm all about." But I didn't, and I had to take it down.

You're the One That Taught Me How to Swing 1974

THIS SONG CAN BE FOUND on the Dolly album *Love Is Like a Butterfly*.

You were not content with me
When I was like I used to be.
I was too old fashioned, too simple, and too plain.

And so you took this country girl,
Taught me all about the world.
Yes, you're the one that taught me how to swing.

I used to never drink or smoke
I'd even blush at dirty jokes
I never wanted to take part in all those worldly games.

But you dressed me up in sexy clothes,
Took me where the swingers go.
Yes, you're the one that taught me how to swing.

CHORUS
But you don't want me swingin' now,
But you're the one that taught me how.
It was you that wanted me to change.
I'm only what you've made of me.
Your mistake was changin' me.
Yes, you're the one that taught me how to swing.

You want me like I was before,
But I'm not like that anymore.
This plain old simple country girl won't ever be the same.

So don't expect me to go back,
'Cause it's a bit too late for that.
And you're the one that taught me how to swing.

REPEAT CHORUS

Yes, you're the one that taught me how to swing,
Taught me how to swing.

"You're the One That Taught Me How to Swing" is very much in keeping with [Tammy Wynette's hit] "Your Good Girl's Gonna Go Bad." I don't know exactly when I wrote it, but it might have been around that time [1967].

It goes back to all of those women's songs that I write so well, like "Just Because I'm a Woman." It's about, "Who do you think you are to condemn me? You're the one who taught me how to swing, and now you don't want me swinging? You wanted me to be all this, and now you want me to be a perfect little housewife? Well, that ain't happening."

A Little at a Time 1972

DOLLY SINGS THIS WORKING-GIRL SONG on her 1972 LP *Touch Your Woman*.

Well, the lady said "Will this be cash?"
And I thought, "Boy if that ain't a laugh."
Why, I don't carry money of that kind.
Just put it on my charge account.
On account of, I can't pay you now.
I'll pay for it a little at a time.

I'm just an average working girl
Trying to get along in this ol' world,
Looking for that rich man I might find.
But up 'til now, the times are hard.
I'm a-livin' on my credit card,
And paying for life a little at a time.

CHORUS
A little at a time, that's how I pay my bills.
That's the story of the working girl.
Always going overboard,
Buying things I can't afford.
In this charge-account, credit-card,
Pay-for-it-a-little-at-a-time world.

My weekly check don't amount to a lot,
But I'm making payments on what I got.
At the end of the month, I ain't got one thin
dime.
And this old car I bought brand new.
But I'm still payin' on it, too.
I've been payin' for it a little at a time.

Got a new apartment. I just moved in,
And I'll do well to pay the rent.
It's unfurnished, so a bargain I must find.
I saw a sign in a store downtown,
"House goods for nothing down.
Pay for it a little at a time."

REPEAT CHORUS

I want to pay on my layaway:
Here's a dollar on my mink collar . . .

I love to write about working people. This one is about a working girl who's on the job and trying to make ends meet. It reminds me a little of "9 to 5."

The saleslady says, "Will this be cash?" And I say, "Boy, if that ain't a laugh. I don't carry money of that kind. Just put it on the credit card. I can't pay you now. I'll pay for it a little at a time."

A little at a time is how you live your life. The song has things in it that everybody goes through, every single day. People go in debt for the things they want. It's about people just trying to get by, every day. I love my working-girl songs.

Cracker Jack 1974

IN 2019, "CRACKER JACK" inspired a Netflix movie. It originally appeared as a bonus track on Dolly's *Jolene* album.

Once I had a little dog. I called him
Cracker Jack.
He had a spot around one eye that looked just
like a patch.
His legs were way too long, and he was
awkward as could be.
He wasn't much to look at, but he looked
alright to me.

I found him by the riverbank, just wandering
about.
He was cold and hungry, and his ribs were
sticking out.
I snapped my fingers, whistled. When he
came, I picked him up.
I was just a kid, and Cracker Jack was just
a pup

I took him home and fed him 'til he couldn't
eat no more.
I took him to my room, and put a blanket on
the floor.
After that, beside my bed, is where he'd
always sleep.
Each night in my prayers, I'd pray the Lord
his soul to keep.

CHORUS
Cracker Jack.
The best friend that I ever had was
Cracker Jack,
But he was more than that,
A playmate, a companion
He was love and understanding
That was Cracker Jack.
The best friend that I ever had was
Cracker Jack,
But he was more than that
Everything a kid could want,
I had in Cracker Jack

Cracker Jack would run to meet me after
school each day.
He'd jump and wag his tail, and look at me
as if to say,
"I love you, and I've missed you, and I'm
glad you're home again."
I knew just how he felt, 'cause me and
Cracker Jack was friends.

Through the woods and fields, we would
often roam about.
And when we got in trouble, we would help
each other out.
I could run almost as fast as Cracker Jack
could run.
We had a lot in common, and we had
a lot of fun

He was always with me when I was
growing up
We shared each other's good times, and
we shared each other's love.
He only lives in memories now, but often
I think back
To the days of childhood, the days of
Cracker Jack

REPEAT CHORUS

Here I am with Popeye. I have always loved dogs. The saddest thing about it is that they don't live as long as people do. They come into your life, you love them, and then they have to go.

I love dogs. I love all animals, and I write a lot of songs about them. "Cracker Jack" is based on different family members who had dogs and lost them. Your dog always lives in memory. Even though they don't live as long as people, dogs leave lasting memories. You might get another dog with a different name, but you'll always remember that other dog, especially if it was your first one.

And like Cracker Jack, your first dog in your childhood can help you through a lot of problems. Cracker Jack only lives in memories now, but he was the best friend I ever had; more than that, he was a playmate, a companion with love and understanding. That's what pets are. They have that unconditional love. You can tell them anything, and they accept it. And they won't tell anyone your secrets.

We always have pets. My husband and I had a little dog named Popeye, a little Boston terrier. When he passed away, it was like losing a kid. We never had children, but we were so attached to that little dog. That's the way you get with your pets. Some people don't understand that. But we grieved and cried over that dog.

Evening Shade 1969

THIS MEMORABLE SAGA appears on Dolly's collection *My Blue Ridge Mountain Boy.*

My train of thought was broken by a sudden
burst of laughter,
Something badly needed to lighten up the
chores.
Seemed old Mrs. Bailey had accidentally fell
In the water being used to scrub the floors.

Now Mrs. Bailey was the meanest matron
at the home.
She believed in lots of work with little play.
And we laughed 'til we bent double, though
we knew we'd get in trouble.
But trouble's all we had at Evening Shade.

Now Evening Shade was where they claim to
teach you understanding,
Teach you love, and keep you off the streets.
And all the kids that live there are said to be
a problem,
Juvenile delinquents, so to speak.

But understanding isn't learned from
punishment and anger.
An iron hand has no gentle touch. Love ain't
learned from hate.
The reason we were there is 'cause we had no
one to care.
But they cared even less at Evening Shade.

Little Susan Bradley, one night had wet
her bed.
Mrs. Bailey took the razor strap, and beat
her half to death.
And I knew that something must be done
to put an end to this.
And so I started talkin' plans with the
older kids.

Plans were that Joe Johnson would steal
the kerosene,
And I would get some matches when
nobody seen.
Beckie Adams would make sure the kids
were all outside.
Billy Watson would look out for the Evil Eye.

Now, Mrs. Bailey took a nap at three o'clock
each day.
We knew that she'd be a-sleepin' as the plans
got underway.
Now that it's all over, and the sun is goin'
down,
There's no Evening Shade, because we
burned it to the ground.

Evening Shade was burning, just like the Hell
it was.

I wrote "Evening Shade" thirty or forty years ago. It's about children who have been placed in a correctional home called Evening Shade. They've got problems, but they are basically good kids. The facility treats them terribly. They punish and mistreat this one little girl, because she peed in the bed.

I put myself in the song as one of the children. We all kind of get together and rebel against the whole system. We burn the whole place down: "Evening Shade was burning, just like the Hell it was."

Now I'm not advocating violence of any kind. It's just a song. And I can get away with that in a song.

I have often thought about this song becoming a movie sometime. Because it's got all those dramatic issues—young kids, mistreating adults, violence.

Even though Porter took a lot of credit for my success, and deserved a lot of credit, I'd like to think I would have made it on my own. But you never know. I will always be grateful to Porter, and I will always love him.

Love Is Like a Butterfly 1974

THIS SONG HIT NO. 1 on the country charts, No. 38 on the adult contemporary charts, and No. 105 on the pop charts. Butterflies fascinated Dolly as a child, and the butterfly has long been Dolly's "symbol." Fans continually send her trinkets, figurines, and artwork with the image. In 1976 to 1977, this song introduced each episode of her *Dolly* syndicated TV series. The series was discontinued, but not before featuring three people who later became highly successful collaborators with her—Kenny Rogers, Linda Ronstadt, and Emmylou Harris.

CHORUS
Love is like a butterfly,
As soft and gentle as a sigh.
The multicolored moods of love
Are like its satin wings.
Love makes your heart feel strange inside.
It flutters like soft wings in flight.
Love is like a butterfly,
A rare and gentle thing.

I feel it when you're with me.
It happens when you kiss me,
That rare and gentle feeling
That I feel inside.
Your touch is soft and gentle.
Your kiss is warm and tender
Whenever I am with you,
I think of butterflies.

REPEAT CHORUS

Your laughter brings me sunshine.
Every day is spring time.
And I am only happy
When you are by my side.
How precious is this love we share,
How very precious, sweet, and rare.
Together we belong,
Like daffodils and butterflies.

REPEAT CHORUS

I think "Love Is Like a Butterfly" is a very poetic, very descriptive, very innocent, and very flowery song. It talks about being soft and gentle as a sigh, just like it feels when you are newly in love.

I have loved butterflies from the time I was very little. I used to get lost in the woods, chasing them. I was not afraid of them, because they were so gentle. I knew they weren't going to bite me or sting me. They were beautiful and colorful, and they were doing something, being productive and being harmless.

There were so many different kinds where we grew up. So I would just find one and chase it, follow it as long as I could. I loved the butterflies, because they just pulsated with light and color. I also loved the fireflies at night in summer, the lightning bugs, as we called them.

"Love Is Like a Butterfly" became a really big song in France, where they called it "The Papillon." It was so sweet, the way that singer sang my song.

When I did my earliest TV show, at the beginning of every show, I would open with "Love Is Like a Butterfly." I would come down from above on a swing decorated with flowers and butterflies all over its ropes.

So the butterfly became my symbol. When we created Dollywood, the "W" in the Dollywood sign became a butterfly. That's how much I love the butterflies.

Dolly

CHAPTER 5

GOLDEN STREETS OF GLORY

THROUGHOUT HER CAREER, DOLLY PARTON HAS REPEATEDLY returned to gospel themes in her songwriting. Many of her secular albums contain gospel songs, and she is one of the few artists who has had major hits with gospel singles on mainstream country charts.

Dolly's grandfather Jake Owens (1899–1992) was an evangelist, as was her aunt Dorothy Jo Owens Hope (1929–2008). Both were also multi-instrumentalists who influenced her melody making as well as her lyrics.

Jake played fiddle, guitar, piano, and just about any other instrument he touched. He was also a songwriter. Kitty Wells recorded his "Singing His Praise," and Dolly recorded his "Book of Life."

Dorothy Jo was proficient on guitar, banjo, and other instruments. She and Dolly were frequent song collaborators during Dolly's youth.

In addition to her own songs "The Seeker" (1975) and "Daddy Was an Old Time Preacher Man" (1970), Dolly has scored major successes singing others' gospel songs. She won a CMA Award with Brad Paisley by performing on his song "When I Get Where I'm Going" (2005) and earned a Grammy Award by collaborating with For King & Country on that group's song "God Only Knows" (2019).

Her Dollywood theme park is the home of the Southern Gospel Hall of Fame, which honors the white gospel quartets that have flourished in Dixie since the 1940s. The genre has spawned such notables as the Oak Ridge Boys ("Elvira"), the Statler Brothers ("Flowers on the Wall"), Elvis Presley's backup vocalists the Jordanaires, and the famed Blackwood Brothers, who earned three Grammy Awards via recordings with Porter Wagoner.

In 2009, Dolly Parton was elected to the national Gospel Music Hall of Fame, which is headquartered in Nashville. These are the songs that helped get her there.

This is me on stage in one of my "angel" dresses. When I'd [illegible] would spread out like wings.

God's Coloring Book 1977

THIS SONG HAS MEMORABLE RECORDINGS by Bluegrass Hall of Fame members the Country Gentlemen and by Country Music Hall of Fame superstar Charley Pride. Dolly's version is on her million-selling LP *Here You Come Again*.

Today as I was walking
In the fields just down the way,
I sat down on a fallen log
To pass the time away.

CHORUS
And as I looked around me,
The more that I did look,
The more I realize that I was viewing
God's coloring book.

I saw a golden ray of sunlight,
A silver drop of dew,
The soft white floating clouds
Sailing across a sky of blue.

A yellow dandelion,
A pretty evergreen
And some red and orange flowers
Growing wild along the stream.

REPEAT CHORUS

The grayness in an old man's hair,
The pink in babies' cheeks,
The blackness in a stormy sky,
The brown in fallen leaves,

And the multicolored rainbow
Stretched out across the sky,
And the purple haze at sunset
Just before the night.

REPEAT CHORUS

Then I turn my face toward the sky,
And say a silent prayer.
Though God doesn't speak to me,
I see Him everywhere.

He is all around me.
He's everywhere I look.
And each new day is but a new page
In God's coloring book.

Each new day is but a new page
In God's coloring book.

OPPOSITE PAGE: The bugle beads below the waist, the sequins on the sleeves, the gathered drapes, and the silver appliqués are some of the details that make this "angel" dress so beautiful . . . and heavier than you can imagine. No wonder I'm so short.

"God's Coloring Book" is about how God talks to me. A lot of people think that because I look so artificial, I never spend time outside. But I would never live anywhere but on a farm.

I love to be out in nature. I have to smell the flowers. I have to touch the trees and the leaves. I sit under trees to write songs. I listen to God's voice through the wind. I have to have that. I have to be part of that, and I am.

Growing up in the mountains, like we did, we were a part of the birds and the bees and the trees and the flowers.

"God's Coloring Book" expresses my spirituality and explains my connection with God. When I see nature's colors, that's when I am closest to Him. I think that I am at my best when I write songs that are connected to God, as I see Him.

The Master's Hand 1971

THIS TAMBOURINE-THUMPING SONG later became a bluegrass favorite, thanks to versions by the New Coon Creek Girls and Dale Ann Bradley, among others. It was introduced on Dolly's debut gospel LP *Golden Streets of Glory*.

In the days before the flood
The world grew wicked and corrupt.
But Noah was a good man,
And the Lord unto him came.

And He said to Noah, "Go build an ark."
Noah did, and the sky got dark,
And a great flood destroyed everything.

Except for Noah and his wife
And their three sons and their wives
And a pair of every kind of creature
Walkin' in the land.

And the people mocked.
And they made fun.
But ol' Noah worked 'til it was done,
'Cause he was holding to the Master's hand.

CHORUS
The Master's hand is always held out to us.
And it will lead us to the Promised Land.
And the evil of this world cannot outdo us
If we are holdin' to the Master's hand.

Three Hebrew children in days of old
Were marched into the fiery coals,
'Cause they would not deny the Lord,
Would not obey command.

And the furnace roared like a mighty storm,
But the Hebrew children saw no harm.
The flame was smothered by the Master's hand.

The Hebrew children loved their God,
And with them in the flames He trod
To show the world that He was King
And ruler over man.

Shadrach, Meshach, and Abednego
Had no fear of the fiery coals,
'Cause they were holdin' to the Master's hand.

REPEAT CHORUS

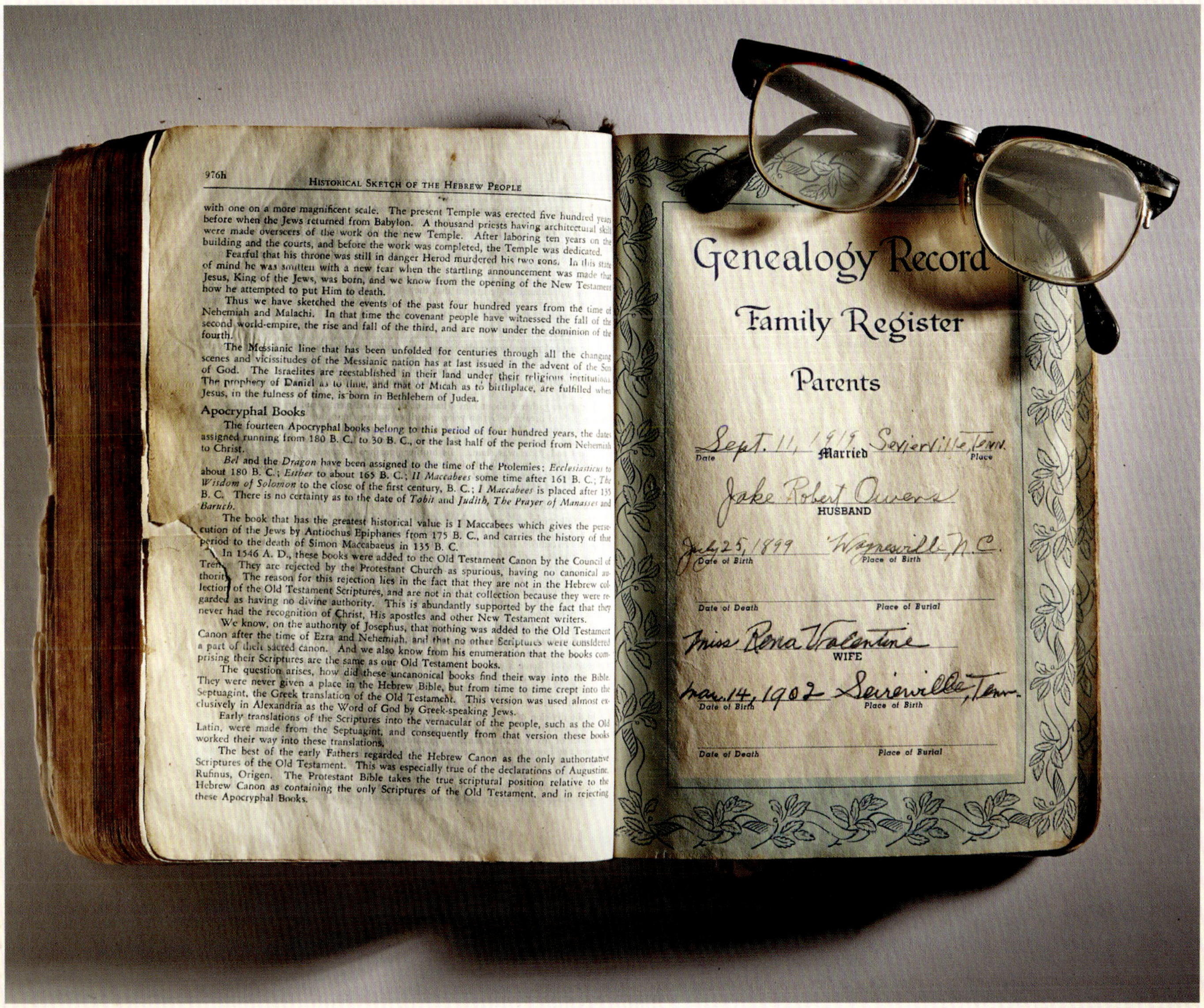

I'm not that religious, but I'm very, very spiritual. I grew up in very religious surroundings. I grew up with a Bible background, and I'm glad I did. I know my Bible stories, like the ones I mention in this song.

I'm glad I've been everywhere, done everything, and been exposed to other people's beliefs. I "get" all of it. And I don't condemn the sincerity of anybody's faith.

Grandpa Jake's Bible records his marriage to Grandma Rena. He always wore his glasses when he preached from it.

Golden Streets of Glory 1971

IN 1971, THIS WAS THE TITLE TUNE of Dolly's debut religious LP. The album was nominated for a Grammy Award in the Sacred Performance category.

Glory to His name, oh, holy, holy.

There's a city where the streets are paved in
gold,
A land where the milk and the honey flow.
And a mansion waits for me,
Because my Bible tells the story.
I just hope my feet are clean enough
To walk upon the golden streets of glory.

Green meadows where the little children play,
No sorrow there, just one long happy day.
And none will linger there, except the pure
and the holy.
I just hope my feet are clean enough
To walk upon the golden streets of glory.

REFRAIN
And when I've reached my journey's end,
And if I'm worthy to go in,
Golden streets of glory, I'll walk on.
And the golden streets of my new home
Will lead me up to the Master's throne.
With the angel band I'll sing,

CHORUS
"Glory to His name, oh, holy, holy."
I just hope my feet are clean enough
To walk upon the golden streets of glory.
Hallelujah.
I just hope my feet are clean enough
To walk upon the golden streets of glory.

REPEAT REFRAIN AND CHORUS

This song talks about when I get to the "Golden Streets of Glory." I hope that when my journey ends, that's where I will end up. But you have to be good enough during your life to get there. If I am, I'll be able to walk those golden streets.

The song goes back to my growing up in the church. It was influenced by the songs that I used to sing at Rev. Jake's House of Prayer. It's a real good, up-tempo thing.

One special thing about this song is that Connie Smith recorded it. She has been one of my favorite singers since she opened her mouth. Ever since I first heard her at the Grand Ole Opry, I have loved her. I'm prouder of her record of the song than I am of my own. [Connie Smith was inducted into the Country Music Hall of Fame in 2012.]

OPPOSITE PAGE: That's Reverend Jake Owens in the door of his little House of Prayer church. He was highly musical and could play just about any instrument he laid his hands on when it came time to praise the Lord in song.

Sacred Memories 1974

DOLLY SANG THIS ON HER LP *Love Is Like a Butterfly*, which rose to No. 7 on the charts. The song has entered the bluegrass repertoire via versions by the popular bands Joe Mullins & the Radio Ramblers and the Forbes Family.

Sacred mem'ries often take me to the place where I grew up,
And that little country church that I love so much.
I used to go there every time that old church bell would ring.
And I remember how I love the songs we used to sing.

Like, oh Lord you know, I have no friend like you.
If Heaven's not my home, then Lord what will I do?
The angels beckon me from Heaven's open door,
And I can't feel at home in this world anymore.

They were singing "Lord I'm Coming Home" when I got
saved,
And when I got baptized they sang "Amazing Grace."
And oh how sweet the sound when everybody would join in
And sang my favorite song, "If We Never Meet Again."

Where the charming roses bloom forever,
And where separation comes no more,
If we never meet again this side of Heaven,
I will meet you on that beautiful shore.

My mama loved to sing, and she sang clear and loud.
I can close my eyes, and I hear Mama now.
I recall the song my mama always loved so much
She always sang the loudest singin' "Power in the Blood."

Oh there's power, power, wonder-working power
In the blood of the lamb.
There is power, power, wonder-working power
In the precious blood of the lamb.
Sacred mem'ries.

This song draws from my memories of my childhood, because it talks a lot about the church. It even uses lines from a lot of the old gospel songs that we used to sing in my grandpa's church. The music that was born out of that church kind of shaped and molded my whole career—sometimes in ways that I don't even understand.

I often talk about my grandpa, the Reverend Jake Owens, "Brother Jake." He was a Pentecostal, "Holy Roller" preacher, and allowed us to express ourselves, to make that "Joyful Noise," as he called it. We would sing gospel songs, but he didn't require us to.

If I'd written a song with my guitar, I could get up and sing that. We even had a little band in our church, made up of our family members. You were allowed to get up and just express your gifts. If my grandpa thought you had a gift that was God-given, it didn't have to be just a sacred song.

I loved the freedom of that church. And it was a good thing, too, because people went to our church for recreation and entertainment. We had little else to do.

One time, we sang in a church that drew out sin by handling snakes. We didn't have that in our church. When those snakes came out, my daddy came running down the aisle, cussing the preacher in the middle of that church. He wanted his kids out of there. He was scared to death of snakes, and he didn't believe in that kind of worship.

I don't follow any traditions. I don't think I have to, because I believe my church is in my heart. God is right there. But those gospel songs are so embedded in me. That music means so much to me, to this day.

Country people all over the South sang from little songbooks like these. They are where you'll find "Power in the Blood," "Lord I'm Coming Home," "Amazing Grace," and the other lyrics I quote in my song "Sacred Memories."

There 1977

DOLLY RECORDED THIS SONG on *New Harvest First Gathering*, the album she created to celebrate her musical independence. The collection marked the true launch of her solo career and of her artistic freedom.

There is a place where the sun's always glowing.
Take me there, won't you take me there?
Meadows grow green near the streams gently flowing.
Take me there, won't you take me there?

A city of riches beyond comprehension.
Take me there, won't you take me there?
Streets are of gold, gates of pearl, brilliant mansions.
Take me there, won't you take me there?

CHORUS
Take me and show me this rare place you speak of.
Take me there, won't you take me there?
To this land of plenty, where there is complete love.
Take me there, won't you take me there?

At the foot of the throne, the kingdom rejoices.
Take me there, won't you take me there?
The angels are singing His praise with their voices.
Hallelujah, hallelujah, take me there.

Peace, joy, and love linger on through the ages.
Take me there, won't you take me there?
Lambs lay with lions and lions with babies.
Take me there, won't you take me there?

REPEAT CHORUS, WITH A LYRIC CHANGE IN THE LAST LINE
Take me there. I can't take you there.

But there is a church where they teach all about it.
Take me there. I will walk with you there.
There is a book. We must not be without it.
Take me there. I will read with you there.

There is an altar where sins are forgiven.
Take me there. Yes, I'll kneel with you there.
We'll find there the God of eternal living.
Take me there. He will take you there.

There is no sorrow and no heartache there.
There is no crying and no dying there.
Won't you take me there? Won't you take me there?
Hallelujah, won't you take me there?

Lord Hold My Hand

(Dolly Parton / Ginny Dean) 1971

THIS SONG APPEARS ON THE LP *Golden Streets of Glory*. Dolly's song collaborator here is her mother-in-law. Virginia Dean (1920–1991) died too soon from cancer, but Dolly thinks her husband, Carl, will always be a "mama's boy."

CHORUS
Hold my hand, lest I lose my way.
Hold my hand, and lead me home.
Guide each step that I might take.
Hold my hand, and keep me strong.

And let the path I walk be straight.
Let the deeds I do be kind.
Let me never hesitate
To help my brother walking blind.

REPEAT CHORUS

And let my words have meaning, Lord,
Anything that I might speak.
If you see me leaning on,
Just hold my hand and strengthen me.

REPEAT CHORUS

Amen.

Carl's parents were Virginia and E. H. Dean. His name was Edgar Henry, but everybody called him Big Ed.

A lot of people say, "I don't like my in-laws." Well, I loved mine. I loved my husband's mother. She was very sweet, and we were like best friends. Her name was Virginia, but everybody called her Ginny. Carl's mother was very religious. She was in church every Wednesday night and every Sunday morning.

The Deans were Church of Christ people. They don't believe in having any instruments in their church; they just use their voices. Ginny had this big, beautiful "church" kind of voice. Very proper. It sounded totally different from our "Holy Roller" church back home.

Anyhow, she was writing this song called "God Hold My Hand." I loved her to death, and she knew I was in the music business. I thought, "This would be a good way for the two of us to get together. We can write this song, and I can put it on an album."

I wanted to do it for Carl. I wanted to do it for all of the Deans, so that they could feel proud of it. The fact that I have a song with Ginny Dean, my mother-in-law, makes me feel good. She's long passed away now, but I got to pay tribute to her with that.

He's Everything

With Queen Latifah 2012

DOLLY WROTE THIS SONG for the soundtrack of her 2012 movie *Joyful Noise* and recorded it with her costar Queen Latifah.

I see Him when the children are at play.
I hear Him when the church bells ring on
wedding days.
I feel Him when the breezes blow,
Adore Him where the flowers grow,
Revere Him when the oceans roll.
He's everything.

Ah, ah, ah, ah, ah.
He's everything.

We're born, we live, we die, and life goes on.
We love, we laugh, we cry, so forth, so on.
And we're a part of His creation,
Every person, every nation.
He's in every situation.
He's everything.

Let's lift Him up.
Through everything, He's loving us.
Is it asking all that much
That we should do the same?

So let us sing and raise our voice.
Let us make a joyful noise.
Let us praise His holy name.
Rejoice, His joy remains.
He's everything.

In everything, He plays a part.
In everything, He leaves His mark.
Restores our lives, our broken hearts,
The God of hope and change.

So let us sing and raise our voice.
Let us make a joyful noise.
Rejoice and praise His name.
Rejoice, sing it again.
Rejoice, His joy remains.
He's everything.

Ah, ah, ah, ah, ah.
He's everything.

Rejoice and praise His holy name.
He's everything.
He's always lovin' us.
We should show a little love
In everything, everything.

He's the God of hope and change.
He's the cure for hurt and pain.
You know He loves us all the same.
'Cause He's everything.

Ah, ah, ah, ah, ah.
He's everything. He's everything.

In everything, He plays a part.
Heals and mends our broken hearts,
Restores us when we fall apart,
'Cause He's everything.

So lift Him up, rejoice, rejoice.
Let us sing and raise our voice.
And let us make a joyful noise.
He is everything.

One of my favorites of the movies I've made is *Joyful Noise*. I loved being in Atlanta to film it, loved the singers in the choir, and loved working with Queen Latifah.

I think this is one of my better songs. I love to write songs that are simple but have a feeling in them that allows them to grow big, with an orchestra or a choir.

I remember filming *Joyful Noise* in that church that day. They had a lot of extras and a lot of people there. I remember being so touched that the song moved so many of them. They weren't told to cry. They weren't told to react in any certain way. They were just being part of the movie. But I saw that they were really moved. That made me just want to "high-five" God for giving me the inspiration to write something like that.

Every day, I ask God to let me uplift people, to glorify Him. I want people to feel and see Him through me. I saw that in my song on that day, and I felt really humbled by that.

Raven Dove 2002

THIS UTOPIAN VISION WAS INTRODUCED on Dolly's CD *Halos & Horns*.

There will come a day when sorrow
fades away,
And anguish and heartache shall ease,
No mothers cryin', no soldiers dyin',
And turmoil and misery shall cease.

The hungry shall be fed. The aimless shall
be led.
And sad eyes will no longer weep.
The last shall be first. Through Heaven
He'll burst
With His heavenly host from the East.

Weapons to plowshares, hate turns to love,
Descending from Heaven, He'll sweep down
to us
In radiant splendor, oh, won't it be sweet
When the raven of darkness turns into a
white dove of peace?

Raven Dove.

Oh, there will come a day when I'll fly away
Forever to be in His keep.
Eternal life in the sweet By-and-By
When Raven Dove, Raven Dove speaks.

When lambs walk with lions, a child tames
the beast.
Nations shall gather and bow at His feet.
And loved ones shall rise up from their
earthly sleep
And He'll separate all the chaff from
the wheat.

Hallelujah, hallelujah, hallelujah, how sweet
When the raven of darkness turns into a
white dove of peace.

Raven Dove.

Behold He cometh in the clouds.
And every eye shall see Him:
Sweet bird, sweet bird of peace,

Raven Dove.

"Raven Dove" sort of goes back to my poetic self. I felt really inspired to write that song; it kind of came to me. It's about those feelings you have about the mystical part of faith and religion. Everything seems mysterious about that song, the melody, the way I sang it, the way I felt it, and the way I wrote it.

The symbols in the lyric are haunting, too. We always think about the raven being the dark side and the dove being the white side. The song has those symbols kind of merging. It's like a battery that has to have a positive and a negative. One doesn't work without the other. You've gotta have the good and the bad in order to know what's right, and in order to know what's real and what ain't.

Circle of Love

Recorded by Jennifer Nettles 2016

IT'S HARD TO WRITE a new Christmas song, but "Circle of Love" gets the job done by joyously revisiting the biblical noel story. Jennifer Nettles introduced this when she portrayed Dolly's mother in the Emmy-nominated 2016 NBC-TV movie *Christmas of Many Colors*. She also included it on her holiday album *To Celebrate Christmas*. At the 2019 CMA Awards, Nettles wore a "protest" ensemble, calling out country radio's blatant gender discrimination. Dolly co-hosted that gala, which defiantly celebrated country's women. She released her version of "Circle of Love" on her 2020 Christmas album.

CHORUS
Circle of love, halo of light,
When Jesus was born, on that Christmas
night.
And oh what a night that holy night was
When Bethlehem glowed in a circle of love.

God sent his Son, His great gift to us.
Salvation for all, He loved us that much.
We honor and praise, that gift from above.
He holds all of us, in a circle of love.

REPEAT CHORUS

Happy birthday to You, we praise and
we sing.
We celebrate You. We're so glad You came.
Happy birthday dear Jesus. Let us lift You up.
How thankful we are, for all of Your love.

So Jesus was born,
Wore a crown of thorns.
Gave it all up,
Just to save us.

REPEAT CHORUS

Circle of love
In a circle of love

"Circle of Love" came from a very special place. The movie *Christmas of Many Colors: Circle of Love* told a true story about my mother's wedding ring. Mom and Daddy had been married for many years, but he had never been able to afford a ring for her. So all of us kids saved up money to buy Mama a wedding ring. So that was the "circle" of our family, and the basis for the movie's story.

Then the song also became about the "circle" that was the Father/Son/Holy Ghost. That little song just kept winding itself around to where it became very inspired. It was very emotional to me when I wrote it. When I was finished, I thought, "Oh, I love this." I was so proud of how it all happened.

Jennifer Nettles sang the song in my movie *Christmas of Many Colors: Circle of Love*, and I sang it to introduce that show. Then she did it on her Christmas album. We sang it together that year on the season finale of *The Voice*.

I hope and believe that someday it could become a Christmas classic. I get people all the time asking me for the sheet music, and a lot of churches are singing it. I hope a lot of other people record it. I've already recorded it for a new Christmas album I'm planning to do.

My parents, Robert Lee Parton and Avie Lee Owens Parton, were a "circle of love."

Once upon a Christmas

With Kenny Rogers 1984

THIS IS THE TITLE TUNE of Dolly's million-selling holiday-duets collection with Kenny Rogers. It is Dolly's version of the Christmas story, complete with her inventive semi-rhymes for "Bethlehem."

(Kenny)
Once upon a Christmas far away in Bethlehem,
Mary being great with child had no place to lie down.
So Joseph found a stable in which Mary had her child.
Once upon a Christmas was the birth of Jesus Christ.

(Dolly)
Once upon a Christmas in a manger far away
A King was born. His palace was a manger filled with hay.
His royal robe was swaddling cloth. A halo was His crown,
Once upon a Christmas, away in Bethlehem.

DUET CHORUS
And all the world rejoiced because the King was born at last.
A savior had been promised. Now it had come to pass.
And the joyful news that He was born spread quickly far and wide,
Once upon a Christmas was the birth of Jesus Christ.

(Kenny)
Once upon a Christmas from the Far East, wise men came,
With gold and myrrh and frankincense to praise the newborn King.
(Dolly)
And shepherds left their flocks and came to see and worship Him,
Once upon a Christmas away in Bethlehem.

REPEAT DUET CHORUS TWICE

(Dolly)
Once upon a Christmas far away in Bethlehem.

I always kid that I'm the one who turned Kenny's hair and beard gray. We loved each other like a brother and a sister.

I wrote "Once upon a Christmas" about forty-five years ago. In 1973, Carl and I were building our home [on seventy acres in the tony Nashville suburb of Brentwood]. They were working on the basement. My best friend, Judy, and I would go over there, and I would write. I loved the wonderful echo in this basement.

I didn't have an instrument with me. I just started singing, and it was like I was in Bethlehem when I would hear that echo. We all know the story of Christmas. It's been written a thousand times. But the song just started coming to me, the birth of Christ and the whole thing with the Wise Men. It just kept on coming: "And all the world rejoiced because the King was born." The bigger I sounded with that echo, the louder I sang and the more I'd get inspired. Before I knew it, I had written the whole Christmas story.

When I recorded it with Kenny [Rogers], I said to [producer] David Foster, "Let's try to get that echo sound," because that's kind of what "sold" the song to me. I had the cassette of me singing it in the basement, and I still have it.

Daddy Was an Old Time Preacher Man

With Porter Wagoner (Dolly Parton / Dorothy Jo Hope) 1970

THIS TOE-TAPPER WAS CO-WRITTEN with Dolly's evangelist aunt, Dorothy Jo Hope. A No. 7 hit duet for Porter and Dolly, it was drawn from their *Once More* LP. The song tells the story of a pure-of-heart, self-sacrificing man of God. To be clear, it was Dorothy Jo's father, Dolly's grandfather, who was a preacher. Dolly's dad wasn't even much of a church-goer.

DUET CHORUS
Daddy was an old time preacher man.
He preached the word of God throughout
the land.
He preached so plain a child could
understand.
Yes, Daddy was an old time preacher man.

(Dolly)
He told the people of the need to pray.
He talked about God's wrath and
Judgment Day.
He preached about that great eternity.
He preached Hell so hot that you could feel
the heat.

(Duet)
Daddy was an old time preacher man.
Aunt Leona would get up to testify,
As we'd sing, "In the Sweet By-and-By."
Then we'd sing, "I'm on My Way to
Canaan's Land."
Yes, Daddy was an old time preacher man.

(Porter)
Revivals and camp meetin's went for weeks.
Folks came from all around to hear
him preach.
Daddy said, "If one is saved, it's worth it all."
But the aisles were always filled at altar calls.

REPEAT DUET CHORUS

(Duet)
Daddy worked for God, but asked for no pay.
For he believed that God provides a way.
We never had a lot, but we got by.
Guess it's 'cause the Lord was on my
daddy's side.

Yes, Daddy was an old time preacher man.
"In the sweet By-and-By,
We shall meet on the beautiful shore."
"I'm on My Way to Canaan's Land."
Yes, Daddy was an old time preacher man.

"In the sweet By-and-By,
We shall meet on the beautiful shore."
"I'm on My Way to Canaan's Land."
Yes, Daddy was an old time preacher man.

"In the sweet By-and-By,
We shall meet on the beautiful shore."
"I'm on My Way to Canaan's Land."
Yes, Daddy was an old time preacher man.

Grandpa Jake inspired "Daddy Was an Old Time Preacher Man."

OPPOSITE PAGE, TOP: When the song became a hit, I brought him onto the set of *The Porter Wagoner Show*.

OPPOSITE PAGE, BOTTOM: His daughter, my aunt Dorothy Jo, was one of the greatest influences on me as a songwriter.

Jake Owens was Mama's daddy, and Aunt Dorothy Jo's daddy, and Aunt Estelle's daddy. One night, Dorothy Jo and I were writing, and we were talking about Jake, my grandpa, and about him being a preacher. I said, "Let's write a song about him," and that became "Daddy Was an Old Time Preacher Man." It's about her daddy, my granddaddy.

Here again, in the lyrics we used a lot of those old songs that we used to sing in Grandpa's church. Because I love doing that, finding a way to include and incorporate a lot of public-domain songs that everybody knows. It had some really good lines in it.

The story is basically about him. He preached about Hell so hot that you could feel the heat. We had fun writing it, knowing that it was about Grandpa. We figured it was going to memorialize him forever.

It turned out that it was one of mine and Porter's most successful duets. It was a big record, and a lot of people loved it.

While Grandpa Jake was still alive, he started to get childish in his older years. He'd just walk up to people and say, "You know that song 'Daddy Was an Old Time Preacher Man'? That's about me!" It was just so cute and childlike. He'd just walk up to anyone, saying, "That's about me!" And I loved that.

Shine On 1998

THIS DOLLY PARTON LYRIC is sung to the melody of "Amazing Grace" (1779). The melody is so old that nobody has a copyright on it; it's a "public domain" tune. Dolly introduced the song by performing it at the funeral of her friend and fellow country superstar Tammy Wynette (1942–1998). This was four months before it was released on Dolly's *Hungry Again* CD.

CHORUS
The greatest gift, the gift of life,
The gift of love divine.
God gave us all a special gift.
He meant for it to shine.
He meant for it to shine.

The darkest night can be made light,
By one bright word or smile.
If we'd put on our neighbor's shoes,
And choose to walk a mile.

God gave us all our own free will
To choose the paths we take.
No greater deed could e'er be done
Than for another's sake.

REPEAT CHORUS

Shine on, shine on, for all to see,
God's light inside your soul.
Shine on, shine on, let love flow free.
Warm others in its glow.

Shine on, shine on, shine on.
So hide it not, or it will fade.
Shine on, shine on, shine on.
Shine on, shine on, shine on.

REPEAT CHORUS

Tammy Wynette, at right, sang with me and Loretta Lynn on our album *Honky Tonk Angels*. When she died, I wrote "Shine On" for her funeral service at the Ryman Auditorium in Nashville.

"Amazing Grace" is the greatest melody, ever. That's why so many people try to use it, and I've always loved that melody myself. A lot of songs have been based on it. "Delta Dawn" is based loosely on it, but a lot of people don't realize it. If it has new words, you might not recognize that it's the same tune, or similar. On this particular song, I used it purposefully.

When Tammy [Wynette] died, they asked me to sing a song at her service. I felt like I should write something especially for it. I lost my voice that day, because I was so emotional. I couldn't hardly even sing it. But I felt I owed it to her.

I wrote "Shine On" using "Amazing Grace" because I love that melody. And also because I knew it would sound like church.

To make the record of it, I went back to Grandpa Jake's House of Prayer church and asked its congregation to sing it with me. [Siblings David, Bobby, Rachel, Randy, Cassie, and Willadeene are pictured with songbooks in the album's photos next to the lyrics of "Shine On," as are her father, aunt Dorothy Jo, and uncles Bill, John Henry, and Louis.] I love going back to the old church that I grew up in, when I can. If I'm doing a gospel song, like "Shine On," I like to record the singing of the people that I know and love.

The Seeker 1975

THIS QUESTING, SEARCHING, YEARNING LYRIC manages to be profoundly devout and inspirational without ever mentioning Jesus or God by name. To date, it is Dolly's biggest gospel composition, reaching No. 2 on the charts. It is also the standout song on her 1975 album *Dolly*.

REFRAIN

I am a seeker, a poor sinful creature,
There is no weaker than I am.
I am a seeker, and you are a teacher.
You are a reacher, so reach down.

CHORUS

Reach out and lead me. Guide me and
keep me
In the shelter of your care each day.
'Cause I am a seeker, and you are a keeper.
You are a leader. Won't you show me
the way?

I am a vessel that's empty and useless.
I am a bad seed that fell by the way.
I am a loser that wants to be a winner.
You are my last hope.
Don't turn me away.

REPEAT REFRAIN AND CHORUS

Oh, you are a mountain from which there
flows a fountain.
Let its water wash my sins away.
'Cause I am a seeker, and you are a keeper.
You are a teacher.
Won't you teach me the way?

REPEAT CHORUS

This song is for those people who are struggling for some kind of truth. It could even be about people who are not religious. People look for whatever that meaning of life is, whether you call it science or whether you call it "higher knowing," or whether it's just seeking that better part of you.

As for me, it came to me at a time when I was going through a lot. I felt like I wasn't being as good a Christian as I should have been. Not that I have ever been, but I believe that I do my best.

I'm just a seeker. I'm weak. I'm no saint, that's for sure. I'm no angel, and that's for sure, too. I'd love to be, and maybe if I ever get There, I can be. But I don't claim to be. I'm doing my best, but I need a little help. So if there's something out there to help me, please help me.

If this song is just about seeking a higher power, however you define it, then it's everyone's song. I didn't even realize that I hadn't mentioned Jesus or God in the lyrics until some years later, when somebody pointed it out to me. That's when I thought that it really is for everybody. I think it was God's will for me to write that song.

I love singing "The Seeker," because it gives you a lot of space as a vocalist. You can be very gospel-y and put some soul into it.

I don't think the song is done yet. I just have a feeling that somebody else is going to record it and maybe make it an even bigger hit. I think it could even be a good dance song.

OPPOSITE PAGE: Whenever I sing a gospel song on TV, I try to always wear something white. It's a very inspiring feeling when you're performing religious music with a choir.

CHAPTER

6

BUBBLING OVER

JUST AFTER SHE LAUNCHED HER SOLO TOURING CAREER, DOLLY Parton was named the Country Music Association's Female Vocalist of the Year in 1975 and 1976. These accolades cemented her status as an undisputed star in her own right.

At the time, Nashville was promoting its new style of music, dubbed "countrypolitan." This style introduced pop instrumental elements to the country sound and updated the production of the genre's records. Previously identified as a hard-core country artist, Dolly demonstrated that she could easily adapt to this new reality. Whether on ballads such as "We Used To" or boppers like "Bubbling Over," Dolly kept pace with the times.

Although she had left his show in 1974, Porter Wagoner continued to produce her records through 1976. So inevitably, their fights and musical disagreements continued during this period.

In 1976, Dolly traveled to New York to negotiate with the top national RCA Records executives. She did not include Porter. She was in search of greater autonomy.

By then, she had steadily built her solo career. From 1974 to 1976, her concert booking fees more than quintupled. By capitalizing on her hit records, Dolly was earning $100,000 a year by 1977, nearly double what she'd made as a Porter Wagoner employee.

Her freedom and independence came with a cost. The acrimonious split with Porter drained her emotionally, financially, legally, and spiritually. But Dolly pressed onward.

She might have first attracted attention with her voluptuous beauty, flamboyant fashion sense, and one-of-a-kind mountain soprano, but the Nashville music community is built on songwriting. And it was her gift of song that truly made her a country superstar of the 1970s.

The leopard-print accents on this gown might mean I was feeling fierce and wild about my new independence as an artist in the mid 1970s. Or maybe I thought they were just fashionable at the time.

The Man 1978

THIS SONG WAS INTRODUCED on the *Heartbreaker* album, which went to No. 1 on the charts.

I don't know why I like him, I just only know
I do.
I don't know why I trust him, I just know his
heart is true.
I don't know why he's more a man than any
man I know.
I don't know how I know the man's for real,
but I still know.

The man is more than what meets the eye.
He is worn and weary from life.
He is rugged, but he's got style.
The man has got what matters inside.

Weary, yes, he must get weary, but he
doesn't say.
But you can read between the lines that wind
along his face.
The man has got his memories that he hides
inside his mind.
And you can see the sadness in the eyes they
hide behind.

The man is more than what meets the eye.
He is worn and weary from life.
He is rugged, but he's got style.
The man has got what matters inside.

Love him, yes, I've always loved him, and I
always will.
He holds a place in my heart no one else could
ever fill.
He's always been my hero, the best friend I've
ever had.
The man is something special, and I'm proud
that he's my dad.

The man is more than what meets the eye.
He is worn and weary from life.
He is rugged, but he's got style.
The man has got what matters inside.

The song "The Man" is really about all the precious men in my life, including my dad. It's about Carl, too. He puts up with me and accepts me. He's not weak. He has all the confidence in the world. Despite all my years with Porter, Carl never felt threatened by him. Because he knew I was always coming home, and he knew our strength as a couple.

He is just such a good man, not only to me, but to all the other people around him. But this particular song is about all good men.

The Bargain Store 1975

WITH ITS REFERENCES TO "PURCHASING MERCHANDISE," "come inside," and "completely satisfied," this song's lyric was apparently a little too strongly worded for some conservative country radio broadcasters. They felt it could be construed as "dirty" and initially resisted playing it. Nevertheless, it eventually climbed to No. 1, became a No. 35 adult contemporary success, and served as the title tune of a hit album.

My life is likened to a bargain store,
And I may have just what you're looking for,
If you don't mind the fact that all the merchandise is used,
But with a little mending it could be as good as new.

Why you take, for instance, this old broken heart.
If you will just replace the missing part,
You would be surprised to find how good it really is.
Take it and you never will be sorry that you did.

CHORUS
The bargain store is open, come inside.
You can easily afford the price.
Love is all you need to purchase all the merchandise,
And I can guarantee you'll be completely satisfied.

Take these old used memories from the past,
And these broken dreams and plans that didn't last.
I'll trade them for a future. I can't use them anymore.
I've wasted love, but I still have some more.

REPEAT CHORUS

My life is likened to a bargain store,
And I may have just what you're looking for,
If you don't mind the fact that all the merchandise is used,
But with a little mending it could be as good as new.

The bargain store is open, come inside.
The bargain store is open, come inside.

When I wrote "The Bargain Store," I swear on my life that I was never thinking about love in any vulgar way. I was using the "bargain" as it related to a broken relationship. But every man I know thinks it's dirty. Somehow, this lyric is a dirty thing to a man. But I never saw it that way.

All I was thinking of was the heart: "If you don't mind the merchandise is slightly used, with a little mending it can be good as new." I was saying that you'll be surprised at how good this broken heart is. Just take it. You'll never be sorry that you did. Just come inside, come inside my heart. The words just meant that I've had relationships: I've been through stuff; I'm not new at this.

I thought for sure that I had written a hit song. And then the disc jockeys wouldn't play it, because they thought it was suggestive. At that time, they were so difficult. Now you can show something much stronger on TV, and people don't think a thing about it.

Daddy's Moonshine Still 1971

ALTHOUGH DOLLY'S RELATIVES, INCLUDING HER FATHER, did make moonshine, this song depicts the still as an evil force that kills both parents and destroys the family. It was introduced on her *Joshua* LP.

Folks say my daddy wasn't much of a man
For disobeying the laws of the land.
Folks say that my daddy wasn't fit to kill.
Oh, and I know it was true what the
people said,
'Cause we'd all have been better off dead
Than to live a life of shame and strife
'Cause of Daddy's moonshine still.

My mama was always sweet and kind,
But she grew old before her time
Worryin' about the way we had to live.
Yeah, my daddy put the wrinkles in my
mama's face.
He drunk his share of all he made
And just one more reason I grew to hate
My daddy's moonshine still.

CHORUS
Daddy's moonshine still was good for nothin'
But to break Mama's heart
And to tear our home apart
Make our lives a livin' Hell.

Them old mason jars that Daddy made
us wash
And set 'em out to sun on our back porch
'Til he got ready to take 'em up on the hill.
When Daddy got word of the Revenue
He made us kids help hide his brew,
Made us swear that we never knew
About Daddy's moonshine still.

Yeah, and two of my brothers drove across
the state line
Once a week with a load of moonshine.
And the wounds that came from that won't
ever heal.
'Cause on a moonshine run one rainy night
My two brothers lost their lives
And oh my God, how I despise
My daddy's moonshine still.

REPEAT CHORUS

Well, it broke Mama's heart, but she
understood
The day that I left home for good.
But I had to find me another way to live.
Well, I sent Mama money nearly every day,
And how I made it, well, I'd rather not say.
But at least it took me far away
From Daddy's moonshine still.

My bootlegging daddy was known quite well,
And he made our home a livin' Hell.
And I ain't forgot it, and I knew that I
never will.
My mama finally died. She just gave up.
And Daddy finally died from drinkin'
that stuff.
And bad memories haunt the rest of us
From Daddy's moonshine still.

REPEAT CHORUS

My daddy made moonshine for a while, and Mama didn't like that. He didn't really want to do it, but people make moonshine in the mountains because they need the income. So Daddy did that for a time, and so did a lot of my relatives.

It broke a lot of hearts, because not only did they make it, they drank it. Then they began mistreating their families—their wives and their kids. I take poetic license in most everything I write, but I could base the song loosely on things that have happened in my life.

I love the song's story. I think it would make a good movie. Years ago, there was a song and a movie called *Thunder Road*, with Robert Mitchum. The movie was about moonshine runners. It was playing at a drive-in theater, and everybody said, "That's about us, down on Kingston Pike." We had never been to the movies, but we piled into somebody's old car or truck and went to see it. So if that story made a good movie, I figure "Daddy's Moonshine Still" would, too.

This is Daddy sitting at the foot of his and Mama's bed. I had just been sitting on the bed singing "Daddy's Moonshine Still," which is why my guitar is still there. The song became one of his favorites, and I had to sing it every time I went home.

I Get Lonesome by Myself

With Porter Wagoner 1973

THIS SONG WAS RECORDED for the Porter Wagoner and Dolly Parton duet album *Love and Music*. The biggest hit single from that collection was "If Teardrops Were Pennies," written by Dolly's old Knoxville booster, Carl Butler.

(Porter, spoken)
In a dingy upstairs room in a dirty part
of town,
A little girl stood waving from a window.
She was calling to me.
I was standing down below.
And I heard her small voice sayin',

(Dolly, spoken in a child's voice)
Hey Mister, won't you to come up here and
talk to me
If you ain't got no other place to go?
I can't come outside and play 'cause I ain't
got no friends.
I can't come outside no way 'cause my mom
is gone and locked me in.
But there is the key outside the door.
It's layin' on the shelf.
Won't you to come up here and talk to me,
'Cause I get lonesome by myself?

(Porter, spoken)
I was feelin' lonesome too,
And I knew just how she felt.
And I knew just what she meant
When she said she got lonesome by herself.
She kept callin' to me, and I thought, "Well,
since her mama's gone
I'll go up and talk to her awhile since we're
both alone."
We got to talkin', and I asked her why she
was there by herself.

(Dolly, spoken in a child's voice)
Well my mommy never used to leave me by
myself at night
But mommy says I'm a big girl now. I'm not,
but that's alright.
I don't go to school 'cause I'm not old
enough, right yet.
But I can go to school next year 'cause next
year I'm gonna be six.

I used to have a daddy, but he left a long
time ago.
I asked my mommy why he left.
But my mommy says she don't know.
I know she loves my daddy, 'cause sometimes
when I smile,
Mommy says I look just like him.
Then these tears get in my mommy's eyes.

My mommy drinks. I know she does,
'Cause I can smell it on her breath.
Mommy never used to drink, so I know it's
'cause my daddy's gone.
And my mommy, she just gets lonesome
by herself.
I sure get lonesome by myself.

(Porter, spoken)
How she talked about her daddy, it reminded
me of me,
How I'd walked out on my own little girl,
And a woman that really loved me.
As I was thinkin' of them, she said,

(Dolly, spoken in a child's voice)
Have you got a little girl that's about the size
of me?
Have you got a picture of her I can see?

(Porter, spoken)
I took a picture from my wallet and handed
it to her.
When she saw the picture, I couldn't believe
her words.

(Dolly, spoken in a child's voice)
Hey that's my mommy in that picture!
And that baby, well, that baby must be me!
And you must be my daddy, then.

(Porter, spoken)
Then the tears rolled down my face like
they never had before.
I just couldn't believe it as I held her in
my arms.
And I said, "I'll wait here until your
mama comes.
And I'll tell her that I still love her, and I'm
sorry that I ever left.
And I'd like to stay if she'll let me,
'Cause I sure get lonesome all by myself."

(Dolly, spoken in a child's voice)
Well, you won't be lonesome now, 'cause I
love you.

I have always loved recitations. Red Sovine, Hank Williams, Red Foley, and a lot of other people would "talk" country songs, and I always thought that was so effective. You need to have a flair for drama to pull it off and stay in the emotion.

I don't do it a lot, but I did the last verse of "I Will Always Love You" as a recitation. Sometimes on stage, I will talk portions of "Coat of Many Colors" to make a point. To me, sometimes it seems appropriate to talk certain things, because it carries the story.

Porter was a master at recitations, so I wrote songs like "I Get Lonesome by Myself" so that he could do them. This time, I did one, too, talking in the voice of the little girl.

But by the time we recorded it, I was wanting to leave. People don't realize that when you work with a band on the road you are bonded like a family. And we were on the road so much.

It's just like when you're with your own family. When you're with somebody all the time, you love them one day, and you want to kill them the next. Because they get on your last nerve, and I'm sure you get on theirs, too. But you do get to know exactly who they are.

Those seven years of being with Porter, it was damn near like being married to him. In fact, you're closer in some ways to your working partner than you are to your spouse. You're working together and putting in your creative self, putting in every emotion that you have. It all goes into that relationship.

After I left and started doing well, Porter sued me for $1 million, and that was money that I didn't have. I had to pay that over a long period of time.

But you have to forgive and forget. He gave me great opportunities, and I did appreciate him. Later on, we got back together and he said he was sorry about all of that. So I forgave him, and I asked him to forgive me. I'm sure I was a pain in the ass to him. I was, because I believed in what I believed in, and I was going to fight for it. There's truth on either side.

Poor Folks Town 1972

THIS SONG DEBUTED on the Porter and Dolly duet LP *Together Always* in 1972. Dolly's solo version was recorded for her 1980 LP *9 to 5 and Odd Jobs.*

The work is hard, and the hours are long.
The money ain't much, but we get along.
We're rich in things that life can give
That can't be bought with a dollar bill.

CHORUS
So, come on down.
Have a look around.
At rich folks livin' in a poor folks town.
We got no money, but we're rich in love.
And that's one thing that we've got
a-plenty of.

So come on down. Have a look around
At rich folks livin' in a poor folks town

We got no carpets on the floor.
We've got wall-to-wall love. Who could ask
for more?
We got no big fine things to show,
Just a place to watch our children grow.

We got no big fine car to drive
And no fancy clothes to keep in style.
What we've got we're payin' on,
But it's mostly love that we're livin' on.

REPEAT CHORUS

So come on down. Have a look around
At rich folks livin' in a poor folks town.

We've got a little simple church nearby,
And the promise of a mansion in the sky,
A heart of gold, a million-dollar smile,
And a one way ticket to Paradise.

REPEAT CHORUS

So come on down. Have a look around
At rich folks livin' in a poor folks town.

REPEAT CHORUS

So come on down. Have a look around
At rich folks livin' in a poor folks town.

I have always believed that "Poor Folks Town" could be a big hit record for somebody. To me, it's kind of like a gospel song.

It's really about just regular, everyday, working people: "We got no money, but we're rich in love, and that's one thing that we got plenty of." It talks about the home. It talks about the church. It talks about the community. And it talks about all the stuff that—if you're lucky enough—you will get when you get to Heaven.

It kind of sums up my whole life. It's one of those special songs that came from my early days. Everybody in the community stuck together. Nobody had any money, but our lives weren't based on money. We needed just enough to get by.

It's true that money can't buy love. And I'm not all about money. It isn't everything, but we all need it. Money can buy a lot of stuff you want and need. This song just tells it like it is, in the best way possible. I think it's one of my best written songs, ever.

Beneath the Sweet Magnolia Tree

With Porter Wagoner 1980

AS DOLLY'S STAR ROSE HIGHER in the 1970s, Porter Wagoner became increasingly resentful. He sued her to claim a portion of her dramatically increased income. As part of the legal negotiations, he got the right to release their long-shelved final duets LP. It revealed that some fine Dolly compositions had been left behind. This love lyric is one of them.

A hint of autumn was in the air.
Grass was turning a soft shade of brown.
Petals were falling from withering flowers.
Amber leaves were flowing around.

There, beneath the sweet magnolia
In each other's arms, we lay hidden away.
Our needs grew stronger as our hearts
grew closer.
Autumn winds blew, and the magnolia
swayed.

CHORUS
Beneath the sweet magnolia tree,
We found love we knew was for keeps.
We made love and sweet memories
Beneath the sweet magnolia tree.

Through the years we live over and over
The time and the place it started for us.
There, beneath the sweet magnolia.
That long-ago autumn when we fell in love.

REPEAT CHORUS

We made love and sweet memories
Beneath the sweet magnolia tree.

After leaving Porter, I realized there were a lot of things left "in the can," meaning songs we recorded that didn't make it onto our albums.

So Porter thought, "Well, she's doing so well. We should put out some more duets." I didn't see it that way. I was having hits of my own and didn't need something coming out like that. I thought there would be a better place and time, later on. But he insisted that we put this out.

It did turn out to be a good album, and I have some good songs on it. In fact, "Beneath the Sweet Magnolia Tree" is one of my favorite songs that I wrote in those Porter days. It has a beautiful melody, and we did sing it so well together.

That whole period of time was so convoluted. I thought I had moved past everything and that we had leveled out. Then, here it all comes again, stirring things up as if nothing had ever changed.

But that's part of life, and it's bound to happen. I understand it all now. It was all meant to be, and I don't regret any of it. I honestly don't. Because it took every single thing that happened in my life to put me here, right now. To change one thing would change everything.

It was painful and confusing at the time. But I'm sure he was doing the best he could. And I know I was doing the best I could. So it all worked out okay. You have to accept, and you have to grow.

Touch Your Woman 1972

THIS WAS ANOTHER OF DOLLY'S SONGS that some country stations resisted playing because they found it too sexual. But the overall message is that love has the power to overcome both tumultuous times in a relationship and the tribulations of everyday life. The year after Dolly made it a No. 6 country hit, "Touch Your Woman" was recorded by the highly regarded soul-music stylist Margie Joseph.

We can't always both be right.
We sometimes disagree.
But you've got the right to speak your mind,
And it's the same with me.
When the anger's at an end.
And you want inside my arms again,
All you have to do to make it right is just

Touch your woman.

CHORUS
Touch your woman.
Everything's gonna be alright.
Touch your woman.
Touch your woman.
Let me know, let me know, everything's alright.

There are times when I should be strong
When I'm awfully weak.
When the sudden blows of life have brought me to my knees.
Woman needs a helpin' hand,
Needs someone to understand,
Needs the man she loves to help her stand, so

Touch your woman.

REPEAT CHORUS

And when the busy day is done,
And you lay by my side,
You know exactly what it takes to keep me satisfied.
You know exactly what I need, and I always go to sleep in peace,
Thanking God that you belong to me, so

Touch your woman.

REPEAT CHORUS

I think this is a very sweet song, and a really good love song. It talks about the couple's sensuous, sexual, tender relationship. But it also says, "We're bound to fight." When it is all said and done, all you gotta do is just touch your woman, and let me know that everything's gonna be okay.

It's sexy, and it's intimate. But it is also innocent and pure. It's "just let me know you love me." Touch me, and let's get back to where we've been and how we got together to start with. We can't let some little upset make us get bitter and calloused. Let our love build and grow. Just touch me, tell me that you're sorry, or let me say that I'm sorry. Whoever is sorry, let's just do it and touch again.

We Used To 1975

DOLLY'S ROMANTIC HISTORY has always been relatively happy. Yet she writes many heartache songs. This one became her tenth Top 10 solo chart success, reaching No. 9 in the fall of 1975. Its "parent" album was titled, simply, *Dolly*.

We used to walk through fields of green.
We used to sit by clear blue streams.
We used to be so happy, me and you.
We used to do such silly things.
We used to make love in the rain.
We used to
Yes, we used to

CHORUS
Then you went away,
Leaving me with the mem'ries we made.
Memories of those sweet yesterdays
Spent with you, spent with you
And even though you're gone,
I still think so often of you,
And the things that we no longer do.
Like we used to
Oh we used to

We used to be so much in love.
We used to kiss and hold and touch.
We used to find so many things to do.
We used to laugh and plan and dream.
We used to own the world it seemed.
We used to
Yes, we used to

REPEAT CHORUS

I write a lot of love songs. I write so many of them that people say, "You have to have had affairs." I say, "Well, I don't admit or deny anything." I have been everywhere, and I have felt everything. I'm a very passionate person, and I feel everything to the nth degree

But the truth is that I can draw from other people's sorrows, as well as my own. It's easy for me to write about heartaches. Hurt is hurt, whoever you are.

Hell, I had boyfriends from the time I was three years old. I have always loved boys. I've had my sweethearts. I'm like Will Rogers, "I've never met a man I didn't like."

I was writing heartache songs from the time I was a little kid. Whether it's young love, new love, or first love, it's as real as anything you're going to feel when you're older.

"We Used To" can be a heartache song that fits someone of any age. Love is love. Feelings are feelings. Life is life. Whatever the feeling is, as a songwriter you just go there.

Bubbling Over 1973

DESPITE BEING THE TITLE of a hit album, this effervescent song was never released as a single.

You're the one that puts the sparkle in my eyes.
You're the one that puts the laughter in my smile.
You're the one that puts the meaning in my life.
And I'm bubblin' over, bubblin' over, bubblin' over
'Cause you are mine.

CHORUS
Bubblin' over with the joy that only love can bring.
Bubblin' over with the song you taught my heart to sing.
Oh and I'm so happy lovin' you, anyone could see
That I'm bubblin' over, bubblin' over, bubblin' over
'Cause you love me.

I have never known a love that felt like this
You're the one I want to share my lovin' with.
Your gentle way of lovin' me and your thoughtfulness
Keeps me bubblin' over, bubblin' over, bubblin' over with happiness.

REPEAT CHORUS

Yes, I'm bubblin' over, I'm bubblin' over, I'm bubblin' over
'Cause you love me.

This is just a cute, upbeat, happy little song, and people are always saying that about me. But I'm not happy all the time. I don't deserve to be happy all the time. And I don't want to be because if I was, I couldn't write some of the stuff I do. I make a joke out of it. When people say, "Oh, you always look so happy," I say, "Well, that's the Botox." But it is true that if I'm happy, I'm happy all over.

"Bubbling Over" was a song that named an album. For the album cover, we tried to use the fountain at the old Country Music Hall of Fame. It's an awful picture of me. We kept working and working on that picture, trying to make it look right. We needed that fountain, and we kept trying to superimpose my face on it. It's just one of those mistakes you make. [Nonetheless, *Billboard* magazine gave photographer Les Leverett its award for the best country album cover of the year.]

CHAPTER 7

THEY'RE SINGING MY SONGS

DOLLY PARTON HAS WRITTEN ROUGHLY THREE THOUSAND SONGS. Approximately 450 of them have been recorded, though not always by Dolly. There are more than two hundred versions of her songs by other artists. She began her career in Nashville by writing for others, and her works have exhibited enduring appeal for her fellow recording artists ever since.

Porter Wagoner championed her songwriting talent from the very start of their association. He began the stampede of Dolly-song seekers by recording more than a dozen of her works in the early 1970s.

Others soon scurried to scour her songwriting catalog. Porter was joined by many other country artists during the 1970s, as well as by pop superstars such as Linda Ronstadt and Tina Turner.

Glen Campbell, Reba McEntire, Buck Owens, Kris Kristofferson, and Willie Nelson recorded Dolly Parton songs in the 1980s. In the 1990s, they were joined by an increasingly diverse group, everyone from RuPaul to Whitney Houston, not to mention Tom Jones, Randy Travis, Take 6, and LeAnn Rimes.

By the dawn of the new millennium, it seemed that the entire music world had become aware of her songwriting. The White Stripes, Norah Jones, Sinéad O'Connor, Jimmy Sturr & His Orchestra, Meshell Ndegeocello, Joan Osborne, and Bettye LaVette were just some of the artists who recorded Dolly songs in the early 2000s. The superstar's country peers also continued to mine her catalog—Shania Twain, Loretta Lynn, Patty Loveless, and Alison Krauss.

During the 2010s, these names have been joined by Michael Bolton, Il Divo, Rhiannon Giddens, the Oak Ridge Boys, and Kristin Chenoweth, among others.

The Dolly songs that these artists record are not just her existing hits. Several stars recorded songs that the prolific Dolly has never recorded herself. Here are some highlights.

Merle Haggard was one of the greatest singers, songwriters, and bandleaders of them all. I was deeply flattered and honored that he recorded songs of mine.

Wino

Recorded by Porter Wagoner (Dolly Parton / Porter Wagoner) 1968

PORTER WAGONER RECORDED MANY SONGS about alcoholics. He even devoted three concept albums to the subject—*Confessions of a Broken Man* (1966), *The Bottom of the Bottle* (1968), and *Skid Row Joe Down in the Alley* (1970).

The clatter of the garbage cans
In a dark and lonely alley,
Searching for a bottle with a drop or two
of wine.
The wino makes his rounds from garbage
cans to gutters
Runnin' like a wild man to every bottle that
he finds.

The wine makes him happy for a little while,
But his world of fantasy don't last long.
Then his frail, lonely body seeks refuge,
But he's lost in a world of his own.

What would cause a man
To give up everything life has to offer
And end up with no family, no home,
no nothin'.
Sleepin' on the ground in some filthy alley,
Holdin' tight in his hand an empty wine
bottle?

In his eyes a look of sadness,
As though he'd just seen the gates of Hell.
Could it be that he loved and lost?
Or could it be that he was lost and unloved?
Whatever it might be, it's a pitiful sight to see

A man known only as a wino.

I become whatever I'm writing about. If I'm writing about a wino, I am one. I throw myself right into that street. I get myself right in that bottle and try to think about how it would feel to be in that position. When I write songs like this one, I am an actress.

When I wrote songs for a Broadway musical [2009's *9 to 5*], I had to write for every single character. There are good characters, and they've got their stories to tell. But you've gotta write about the ones who are awful, too. In order to write from their point of view, you've gotta become them. And I love doing that.

One of the reasons I love being a songwriter is because I become all of these characters I write about. It satisfies my restless soul and keeps me out of trouble. Because I can just be whatever I want to be.

Steady as the Rain

Recorded by Stella Parton 1979

DOLLY'S YOUNGER SISTER STELLA PARTON launched her own recording career in 1975. Dolly gave her this tune, which became a Top 30 chart success for Stella four years later. Dolly revived the song as a bluegrass number on her 1999 CD *The Grass Is Blue.*

Raindrops tumble to the ground
Making puddles all around.
Drops of rain that look like tears
Fall on my window pane.

Raindrops seem to harmonize
With teardrops falling from my eyes.
And my tears keep falling down
As steady as the rain.

CHORUS
Steady as the rain they fall,
Tears that just won't dry at all,
Tears that cannot wash away the pain.
Sometimes without knowing it,
I touch my face and find it wet.
And my tears keep falling down
As steady as the rain.

I can't face the fact that I
Am not important in your life.
Once you lived for only me,
And then your feelings changed.

There's just no gettin' over you.
I try so hard, but it's no use.
And my tears keep falling down
As steady as the rain.

Raindrops just keep falling down
Beatin' out their rhythmic sounds,
Dancin' as they play their sweet refrain.
Mem'ries of you cloud my mind,
Cloud my eyes and I start cryin'.
And my tears keep falling down
As steady as the rain.

As steady as the rain

REPEAT CHORUS

As steady as the rain

When songwriters do things with teardrops and rain, it's really easy. I've always written about window panes and tears. Those are great images to pull lyrics from.

This is another song I wrote in the basement when my house was being built forty years ago. I wrote the song in that old basement before it even had a top on it.

I remember when I was singing it, my sister Stella said, "Oh, I love that song. I'm gonna record that someday." And, sure enough, she did. And she had a hit with it. I was really proud of her record of that song.

Then I recorded it later as a bluegrass tune. It lends itself well to bluegrass harmonies and bluegrass mandolins and fiddles. But it kind of lends itself to any style of production that you might want to do on it. It has a good up-tempo tune and a really good arrangement.

Stella is the sister who is closest to me in age. I'm especially proud of her because she has had a successful Nashville music career on her own.

House of Shame

Recorded by Porter Wagoner 1969

PORTER RELEASED THIS SONG as a single in 1969, but it did not make the charts. He had better luck with Dolly's song "Carolina Moonshiner," which became a Top 20 hit for him in 1975.

There's nothin' unusual about the way my day begins,
As I walk up and down the streets with my mail pouch in my hands.
I've run this route for years. Everybody knows my name,
Especially at the old-folks home, which I call the House of Shame.

The old-folks home is my last stop. That's where I end my daily route.
And my mail pouch is usually empty by then. Not always, but just about.
Except for an occasional letter and they all wait anxiously
With sad eyes that ask the question, "Is there anything for me?"

And I hear their trembling voices as they talk back and forth,
"I guess the children're just too busy to write.
They've got a lot of things to do, of course."
And I try to cheer 'em up, and say things to make 'em feel better.
And I think to myself just how little effort it takes to write a letter.

Their old and wrinkled faces and hair as white as snow
And memories locked up in their minds that only they could know.
I spend many hours there at the end of each day's run,
Tryin' in some way to fill the place of a daughter or a son.

And I listen as they tell me of their families of days gone by.
And the sadness there at times is so great, I can't help but cry.
And though it's reality, it seems more like a dream,
That some of them have grandchildren that they've never even seen.

And I think it's such a shame that children they have raised
Would put 'em in this House of Shame to spend their latter days.
So there they sit just waitin'. Waitin' for letters they never get.
Waitin' for children that never come by. Waitin', just waitin' to die.

You see, my folks are old now, too,
And we've put 'em in a home.
But the difference is they live with us,
And they'll never be alone.

Porter and I often agreed on songs. He liked dramatic, storytelling lyrics as much as I do.

Who writes about old-folks homes? Well, I do because I can relate to that situation. I see what it's like for older people. You hope that the people you love are always going to be taken care of, but it doesn't always happen that way.

And now I'm old enough to be in one! Maybe I was thinking ahead when I was writing this back then.

But I write about everything. Is there anything in the world that I haven't written about? I don't think so, and if there is, I'm going to!

Just the Way I Am

Recorded by Skeeter Davis 1972

IN 1972, DOLLY'S FELLOW OPRY CAST MEMBER SKEETER DAVIS (1931–2004) became the first vocalist to devote an entire album to Dolly's songs. Dolly says that this is one of her favorites on that record, *Skeeter Sings Dolly*. It might have been Skeeter singing, but the character in this lyric is all Dolly, a free-spirited soul. Dolly's version was on her 1969 LP *The Fairest of Them All*.

If you hear me crying in the night,
Pretend that you don't hear me. It's alright.
Don't ask me why I'm crying. Please don't make a sound.
I don't know why, it's just the way I am.

And if you think I act a little strange,
And you don't understand when I do things
Like running through the fields while the rain is pouring down.
I don't know why, it's just the way I am.

And even though you may not understand me,
I hope that you'll accept me like I am.
For there are many sides of me. My mind and spirit must be free.
And I might smile when other folks would frown.
I don't know why, it's just the way I am.

I might go out chasing butterflies.
And if I fail to catch one, I might cry.
And if you want me, you might find me in the meadow walkin' 'round.
I don't know why, it's just the way I am.

I might be home and busy cleaning house.
And in the middle of my work, I might go out
And go play games with children at the playground.
It makes me happy, and that's just the way I am.

And even though you may not understand me,
I hope that you'll accept me like I am.
For there are childish sides of me. My mind and spirit must be free.
And I might smile when you think I should frown.
I don't know why, it's just the way I am.

"Just the Way I Am" describes the personality that I've had ever since I was the fresh-faced teenager in this photo. I was always a "different" kind of kid, a dreamer with her head in the clouds.

I wrote "Just the Way I Am" in the late 1960s. This song is like some of my other "nature" songs that I write where I connect myself to the more spiritual element of things, and explain how my personality is.

I might wake up crying in the night. Then I might laugh about something else, and I don't know why. Sometimes I cry for no reason. I don't know why—it's just the way I am. It's like I can get touched by the darndest things out in the middle of nowhere. Something might just move me to tears. So that particular song describes my tender heart and, I think, just my general nature.

I was just so excited about *Skeeter Sings Dolly*. I wrote the liner notes for the album. Here's a little bit of what I said, and it's as true today as it was then:

"When Skeeter decided to include me in her world and do an album of just my songs, I was touched beyond words. . . . In doing this album, she has paid me the greatest compliment anyone could ever pay a songwriter.

"My songs to me are like children. I know this has been said by other songwriters, but it really is true. . . . My songs are part of me, my mind, body and soul. And that's why this album means so much to me."

To Daddy

Recorded by Emmylou Harris 1975

IN 1975, EMMYLOU HARRIS BECAME the first of her generation to score a major hit with a Dolly Parton song. It was this feminist saga, which Emmylou took to No. 3 on the charts. The two women would eventually become disc collaborators.

Mama never seemed to miss the finer things in life.
If she did, she never did say so to Daddy.
She never wanted to be more than mother and a wife.
If she did, she never did say so to Daddy.

The only thing that seemed to be important in her life
Was to make our house a home and make us happy.
Mama never wanted any more than what she had.
If she did, she never did say so to Daddy.

He often left her all alone, but she didn't mind the stayin' home.
If she did, she never did say so to Daddy.
And she never missed the flowers and the cards he never sent her.
If she did, she never did say so to Daddy.

Being took for granted was a thing that she accepted
And she didn't need those things to make her happy.
She didn't seem to notice that he didn't kiss and hold her.
If she did, she never did say so to Daddy.

One morning we awoke, just to find the note
That Mama carefully wrote and left to Daddy.
And as he began to read it, our ears could not believe it,
The words that she had written there to Daddy.

She said, "The kids are old enough and they don't need me very much.
So I've gone in search for the love I need so badly.
I have needed you so long, but I just can't keep holdin' on."
She never meant to come back home.
If she did, she never did say so to Daddy.

Goodbye to Daddy.

There's a big story behind this record. I had gotten to know Emmylou a little bit before that happened. Then I heard that she was visiting in Nashville.

Porter and I had just recorded a bunch of songs, and we were about to put "To Daddy" out as a single for me. Porter always wanted everyone in town to hear everything we'd done. So he called Emmylou and said, "Come on over to the studio. We'll play you some songs, some of Dolly's stuff." So she came over to listen to what we'd done.

When we got to the song "To Daddy," she said, "Oh, you've got to let me have that song, because I'm about to put out an album." Porter said, "No, you can't have that song." She said, "I *have* to have that song!" Now, this is how serious I am as a songwriter. I said, "Okay," and let her have the song.

That's one of the biggest fights that Porter and I ever had. After everybody left, he said, "What the Hell do you think you're doing? You can't give her that song." I said, "Yes I can, because it's my song, and because I'm trying to build myself up as a songwriter."

We fought that out. She got the song, and it went to the top of the charts. And I'm as proud of that as I am of anything I've ever done.

It's also one of the best versions of one of my songs that anybody has ever recorded. I think she did a beautiful job with it.

That was one of the most emotional decisions I'd had to make. I had never faced anything like that as a writer. I don't know, I probably could have had a No. 1 hit with it. But Emmylou was getting to be so big at that time. Plus, I believed in her and loved her work so much.

So that's when I realized how serious I am as a songwriter. I let her have it, in spite of everything else.

A lot of stars had recorded my songs before Emmylou Harris did. But her version of "To Daddy" meant more to me than any of them. We have been friends ever since.

Kentucky Gambler

Recorded by Merle Haggard 1975

PORTER WAGONER WASN'T THE ONLY male star smitten with Dolly. Merle Haggard (1937–2016) carried a torch for her, wrote "Always Wanting You" about his unrequited passion, and displayed her portrait on his tour bus for decades. She wrote this for him, and he topped the charts with it. Her version is on *The Bargain Store*. In 1976, Dolly wrote "My Love Affair with Trains" as the title tune for Haggard's concept album about railroads. He was inducted into the Country Music Hall of Fame in 1994.

I wanted more from life, than four kids and a wife
And a job in a dark Kentucky mine.
A twenty-acre farm, with a shack-y house and barn
That's all I had and all I left behind.

But at gambling, I was lucky, and so I left Kentucky,
And left behind my woman and my kids.
Into the gay casino, in Nevada's town of Reno,
This Kentucky gambler planned to get rich quick.

Kentucky Gambler, who's gonna love your woman in Kentucky?
Yeah, and who's going to be the one to give her everything she needs?
Kentucky Gambler, who's going to raise your children in Kentucky?
And who's going to keep them fed and keep them shoes on their feet?

There at the Gambler's Paradise, Lady Luck was on my side,
And this Kentucky gambler played just right.
Hey, I won at everything I played. I really thought I had it made.
But I should have quit and gone on home that night.

But when you love the green-backed dollar, sorrow's always bound to follow
And Reno's dreams fade into neon amber.
And Lady Luck, she'll lead you on.
She'll stay awhile, and then she's gone.

You better go on home, Kentucky Gambler.

But a gambler never seems to stop, 'til he loses all he's got.
And with a money-hungry fever, I played on.
I played 'til I'd lost all I'd won. I was right back where I'd started from.
Then I started wanting to go home.

Kentucky Gambler, there ain't nobody waitin' in Kentucky.
When I run out, somebody else walked in.
Kentucky Gambler, looks like you ain't really very lucky.
And it seems to me a gambler loses much more than he wins.

Much more than he wins.

People have told me that this is the portrait of me that Merle displayed on his bus for decades.

Merle Haggard was a special, special person. I heard he had a crush on me. All I knew was that we had a great relationship. When I was on the road with Porter's show, we traveled some together. Merle would ride on my bus sometimes, and we'd play card games together. We just had a really good time. But I honestly never thought about him romantically.

We never had an affair or anything like that. We were just buddies, as far as I was concerned. He reminded me of my brother Denver, so I really related to him. We had a good time, and we loved each other's music.

He wrote a song about me called "Always Wanting You." And he sang it to me. I took it as a great compliment, just as a fellow songwriter would. I didn't connect it to anything any bigger. I didn't know it was that big of a deal.

Later, at a BMI banquet, Merle's wife, Bonnie, said to me, "Well, you know Merle's in love with you." And I said, "Well, I love him, too." She said, "I'm not talking about that. I'm talking about real love." I said, "Well, I can't help what he feels. I love him to death, but there's nothing going on between us, and there never was." I'm honored and flattered that he had a crush. But I'm sorry if it caused any problem.

I thought then, and I still think, that he is one of the greatest songwriters and one of the greatest singers, ever. He recorded a song of mine called "Kentucky Gambler" and had a No. 1 hit with it. It was a big, big record. I was very honored that he would even want to record that. It was another of my story songs, and he did a great job of it.

I love to write songs for men. And it's a good thing I do because back then, there weren't that many women in the country-music business to write songs for. Especially ones who weren't writing their own songs, like Loretta Lynn was. I didn't have a lot of space to write songs for women so I purposefully tried to write songs that men could record. Or songs that could go either way.

What Do You Think about Lovin'

With Brenda Lee (Dolly Parton / Bill Earl Owens) 1982

WITH HITS LIKE "I'M SORRY," "Rockin' around the Christmas Tree," and "Break It to Me Gently," Rock & Roll Hall of Fame member Brenda Lee was the biggest female pop star of the 1960s. Recording in seven languages, she was also the first global pop phenomenon. Known as "Little Miss Dynamite," Brenda became a recording artist when she was still a child and thus was a role model for Dolly as a youngster. Dolly's bopping pop ditty was perfect for their two sprightly voices.

(Together, in unison)
Well, loving, loving, loving,
Woh-oh woh-oh.

(Dolly)
Well, what do you think about loving, baby?
(It's alright)
Well, what do you think about loving, baby?
(It's alright)
I said, what do you think about loving, baby?
(It's alright)
In the morning, in the evening, yeah, and
In the night
Wo-oh wo-oh.

(Brenda)
Well, it's alright in the morning,
To start today out right.

(Dolly)
And it's alright in the evening,
To have somebody to hold you tight.

(Brenda)
And it's alright in the nighttime,
Especially in the night.

(Together, in unison)
Baby, any time, any way,
Loving's just alright.
Woh-oh woh-oh.

Well, loving, loving, loving,
Woh-oh woh-oh.

(Brenda)
Well, what do you think about hugging,
baby?
(It's alright)
Well, what do you think about kissing, baby?
(It's alright)
Just what do you think about loving, baby?
(It's alright)
In the morning, in the evening, yeah, and
In the night
Woh-oh woh-oh.

(Dolly)
And it's alright in the morning
To start today out right

(Brenda)
And it's alright in the evening
To have somebody to hold you tight
And it's alright in the night time
Especially in the night

(Together, in unison)
Baby, any time, any way,
Loving's just alright.
Woh-oh woh-oh.

Well, loving, loving, loving
Woh-oh alright
Woh-oh alright
Woh-oh alright

When I was a kid, Brenda Lee was already on the scene. She was a kid at the time, too. I always thought, "Oh, I could never sing like that." My older sister Willadeene said, "Oh, you're better than Brenda Lee." She might have been just saying that just because she loved me, but of course, I knew it was a lie. It did make me feel special to have my sister think I was that good. Because we all loved Brenda.

Then after I came to Nashville, Brenda and I met a few times and became friends. It turned out that Brenda's husband and mine went to Central High School together and were friends. And that gave us something to talk about. In my early days in Nashville, we visited together as couples—Ronnie Shacklett and Carl Dean, the high-school buddies, and Brenda and me. We'd go to each other's houses to eat or play cards or do whatever.

Brenda and I have always loved each other. We both love music, and we are both very short. [Brenda is 4'9" and Dolly is 5'1".] We'd joke about that. I'd say, "Hell, anybody is bigger than me." But she'd say, "No, you are taller than me." So I'd say, "Well then, you're the only person I know who I'm bigger than." So we've always had that "little" kidding thing going on.

When we got together to sing "What Do You Think about Lovin'," it was a pure joy for me. I was singing with my little childhood idol.

It is always a treat when you find out that your heroes are even nicer than you dreamed they might be. I idolized Brenda Lee when I was a kid and tried to sing like her. I adored her even more when I met her and we became buddies. Then when we sang together, it really was a dream come true.

Waltz Me to Heaven

Recorded by Waylon Jennings 1985

WAYLON JENNINGS (1937–2002) led country music's "outlaw" movement in the 1970s. This was during the period when Dolly Parton was seeking greater artistic independence. The two were label-mates at RCA Records for twenty years. "Waltz Me to Heaven" became a Top 10 hit for Waylon. Dolly's version of the song appears on the soundtrack of her movie *Rhinestone*.

It's been a long time
Since I've had a good time,
And I think it's high time I did.

Could I have this dance?
It feels like romance,
And it's good to be feeling like this.

The lights are down low.
The band's playin' slow
To the beautiful "Tennessee Waltz."

How many love songs
And how many dance floors
Have lovers like us waltzed across?

So waltz me to Heaven tonight,
To "The Waltz of the Angels," we'll blissfully glide
On past the Milky Way to Paradise.

Won't you waltz me to Heaven tonight?

Waltz me to Heaven tonight.
Honky tonk angels in heavenly flight
With the moon as our halo and the stars in our eyes,

Won't you waltz me to Heaven tonight?

Waltz me to Heaven tonight.
Hold your heavenly body against mine so tight,
As the band softly plays on this magical night,

We'll dance past the Milky Way to Paradise
With the moon as our halo and the stars in our eyes
Won't you waltz me to Heaven tonight?

Won't you waltz me to Heaven tonight?

As far as singers being originals and not sounding like somebody else, probably the two best are George Jones and Waylon Jennings. To this day, Waylon is honestly one of my favorite singers. I just love his voice.

So when he sang my song "Waltz Me to Heaven" and did such a great job on it, I was very, very proud. Not only that, it was a big hit record.

A lot of people thought the song was a bit out of character for him. They thought he was a mean ol' macho outlaw. But I knew him as a very sweet, tender guy.

I'm a Drifter

Recorded by Johnny Cash 2003

JOHNNY CASH (1932–2003) RANGED FAR and wide in the repertoires for his career-finale Grammy-winning "victory lap" albums with producer Rick Rubin. He recorded everything from folk songs to alternative-rock tunes. Many of Johnny's selections revealed his deep appreciation of classic country music. One example of that was his nod to this little-known Dolly "rambling man" composition from her 1976 LP *All I Can Do*.

I'm a drifter, a driftin' drifter.
Got no place to call my home no more.
I'm a wanderer, a wanderin' wanderer.
Got no one to call my own no more.

Got no strings to tie me down.
Got no cause to hang around.
What difference does it make
Which way I go?

Got an empty feelin' down inside.
Still I need to stay alive.
And who can tell
What waits beyond this road?

I'm a drifter, a driftin' drifter.
Got no one to call my own no more.

Got no strings to tie me down.
Got no cause to hang around.
What difference does it make
Which way I go?

Got an empty feelin' deep inside.
Still I need to stay alive.
Who can tell
What waits beyond this road?

I'm a drifter, a driftin' drifter.
Got no one to call my own no more.
Got no place to call my home no more.

Johnny Cash is one of my heroes. To me, he's like the John Wayne of country music. I just love his voice and his whole presence. You believe in anything he sings. It's every songwriter's dream to have a Johnny Cash cut. So I was so excited when I found out that he liked "I'm a Drifter" and had recorded it.

It's kind of like a cowboy song, so it did fit his image. It's just a simple thing about drifting along. It don't say all that much. It doesn't have a bunch of words. So it was easy for him to sing, especially in those last days of his life.

Around this same time, a lot of young people were discovering my music. I'm always shocked when they come up to me and say, "I love you," or "Will you sing with me?" [Jessica Simpson, Kesha, Jewel, and Galantis are among them.]

One of my favorites is a song I recorded with Miley Cyrus, my goddaughter. Billy Ray, her dad, opened shows for me in the days of his hit "Achy Breaky Heart," and that's when Miley was born. We were such good friends by then that I said, "Well, I've gotta be her godmother, or at least her Fairy Godmother."

Through the years, I became Aunt Dolly to her. When she was doing her *Hannah Montana* TV series, she wanted me to be on it as Aunt Dolly. We became very close, but she and I had never recorded anything together.

She had started to write this song called "Rainbowland." I didn't relate the rainbow to the gay community, although that is the symbol, and I do have a very huge gay following. I'm very supportive of that community. But the song is really about a whole lot of other feelings, too. She asked me if I would work on it with her, so we wrote and sang it together [in 2017].

So many young artists search me out and say that I've been an inspiration. That's a great compliment, a great honor, and a very humbling thing. I've been blessed, and I'm grateful. Hopefully, I'll be around forever! Maybe even after I'm gone, people will still be finding my songs.

Like millions of fans all over the world, I was struck by the charisma of Johnny Cash. As a kid, I used to sing "I Love a Tall Man," and Johnny certainly fit the bill.

CHAPTER 8

LIGHT OF A CLEAR BLUE MORNING

IMMEDIATELY AFTER LEAVING PORTER WAGONER AS A MEMBER OF his road show and TV cast in 1974, Dolly began to build her own career's infrastructure.

She formed Velvet Apple Music as her exclusive publishing company, instantly transferring the songs in her Owepar music catalog into the new entity. She has maintained ownership of her songs ever since.

As she had long dreamed, she became a solo touring attraction. From 1974 through 1977, she performed concerts with her own group, the Traveling Family Band. At various times, this act included her siblings Randy, Freida, Floyd, and Rachel Parton. After that, she formed another band to accompany her on the road, Gypsy Fever.

In 1976, she launched her own weekly television series. When it aired in syndication in 1976 to 1977, she became the first country-music woman in history to have her own TV program.

Porter continued to produce her records until 1977. She broke this final tie with him by producing her own album that year.

In 1978, Dolly Parton was named the Country Music Association's Entertainer of the Year. She became the second female artist to earn this honor, following Loretta Lynn's win in 1972.

Next, she took aim at the pop music hit parade and hired Los Angeles managers to guide her career. This ruffled feathers in Nashville. People in the country industry accused her of abandoning both country music and the community that created it. She answered her critics by saying, "I'm not leaving country music, I'm taking it with me."

Her new team successfully campaigned to expand her fame beyond country's borders. During the late 1970s, she attracted the attention of the mainstream show-biz world. Her wits and her glitz made her a huge favorite on the national TV talk-show circuit. Print interviewers were equally charmed, and she began appearing in the pages of *Rolling Stone*, *Time*, *People*, and *Good Housekeeping*, as well as on the cover of *Playboy*.

By the end of the decade, Dolly had transcended country stardom to become a pop-music presence. These songs chronicle that evolution.

By the time I got my own TV series in 1976,
I was "going for the gold" as a solo star.

All I Can Do 1976

JUST AFTER DOLLY SCORED A No. 3 country smash with this up-tempo tune, actress Mary Kay Place (TV's *Mary Hartman, Mary Hartman*, cinema's *The Big Chill*, etc.) issued her bouncy version of it. The song was the title tune of an album that earned Dolly a Grammy Award nomination.

CHORUS
It's all I can do to keep from falling in love with you,
All I can do to keep from letting it show.
Yeah it's all I can do to keep from falling in love with you
All I can do to keep from telling you so.

I wasn't looking for love when I found you
Just someone to be with and have a good time,
But I get these strange funny feelings around you.
When you're not with me, you're still on my mind.

REPEAT CHORUS

I had intended to wait for a long time.
I thought that love would just mess up my plans.
'Cause I had big plans for a bright, shining future.
Could this be my future that's holding my hand?

REPEAT CHORUS

I need to tell you how I feel about you,
But I'm so afraid that you don't feel the same.
But if I don't tell you how I feel about you,
I just might lose you, can I take that chance?

REPEAT CHORUS

I remember writing this one because I thought it was such a cute idea. I wrote it on this funky little guitar that has all those decals on it that are so cheap looking. I remember banging on the guitar with my thumb and beating out that rhythm. I was just bopping along with "It's all I can do, it's all I can do." I kept on playing that little riff until my thumb got sore. But I played it through, until I got the song wrote.

I wrote so many songs on that guitar with the butterflies all over it. It's now in the museum at Dollywood.

Hey Lucky Lady 1976

THE SECOND SINGLE RELEASED from the *All I Can Do* album reached No. 19 on the country charts. The album was her last to be produced by Porter Wagoner. When the final break came, Porter's longtime steel guitarist and harmony singer, Don Warden (1929–2017), left with her. Don became Dolly's manager. Her steadfast best friend, Judy Ogle, was by her side as well.

Lucky lady, lucky lady,
I was once the lucky lady.
I was happy with my baby.
I was such a lucky lady.

CHORUS
Hey, lucky lady, lucky lady,
You are now the lucky lady.
Are you happy with my baby?
You know you're a lucky lady, you lucky lady.

Lucky lady, that's what I was,
I was lucky to have his love
All a woman could wish for,
He was that and so much more

He was mine and how I loved him
Before your hands ever touched him
Long before your tempting eyes
Lured my baby from my life.

REPEAT CHORUS

Lucky lady, lucky lady,
I was once the lucky lady.
I was happy with my baby.
You know you're a lucky lady, you lucky lady.

Is it love or is it pleasure?
Do you know you've found a treasure?
Are you only having fun?
Do you know the prize you've won?

If you don't want something lasting,
If it's just the time you're passing,
Lucky lady, give him up,
'Cause I do love him very much.
Lucky lady, lucky lady,
I was once the lucky lady.
I was happy with my baby.
I was such a lucky lady.

REPEAT CHORUS TWICE

Talk about a "Lucky Lady," I certainly was one to have these two in my life. I have always thought that Judy Ogle and Don Warden were like angels who were sent to watch over me. But they should have kept me away from that food!

Somebody once said to me, "That is my least favorite of all your songs. I counted how many times you said 'Lucky Lady,' and it was an ungodly amount." I never thought about that. It was just that the phrase kept going around and around in my head. So I guess I did sing that a lot, but that's what the song seemed to want to say.

The song is on the *All I Can Do* album. I don't know that I knew at the time that this was going to be the last album with Porter [producing]. I thought our relationship was going to end years before it did. I just knew I needed to ride that horse until I got him back to home base and I could have a new beginning.

I left knowing that I had Don [Warden] and Judy [Ogle] with me. And Carl. Don and I were very, very close. He was there for me like a father. When Porter and I were fighting, he would comfort me when I was feeling down.

Don Warden had grown up with Porter in West Plains, Missouri. He was Porter's manager, steel guitarist, and high-harmony singer. He bought the buses, drove the buses, decorated the buses. He was a carpenter, he was a mechanic, he was the show promoter who'd get the [concert] money.

He went with me when I left Porter. He did everything for me, and he was still working for me when he passed away [in 2017]. When I lost him, it broke my heart. I didn't grieve any harder for my own dad than I did for Don.

My friend Judy Ogle was always there for me, too. She always helped me keep everything together. She did all the typing at Owepar Publishing. She was with me when I wrote so many of my songs. When I was writing all night, she was the one to make the coffee and was the first person I'd sing my songs to.

Our friendship and our devotion have always been so great. There are those angels in your life, and Judy was one of them.

And Carl has always been there for me. Even though he don't get involved in show business, every now and then he will say just the right thing. I always thought that God spoke to me through Carl. And still does. I'll have something on my mind, and Carl will say something that answers it without even knowing what I was thinking. It's amazing.

So I had a support structure. I had Don and Judy when I went out on my own. They were a blessing and a strength. It was just one of those wonderful things to happen to me, to have these good people in my life.

Everything's Beautiful (in Its Own Way)

With Willie Nelson 1982

BY THE LATE 1970S, Fred Foster had run into financial difficulties. Dolly and Willie Nelson (who'd also once been on Fred's Monument Records label) volunteered to make a record that would save him from bankruptcy. So did Kris Kristofferson and Brenda Lee, who also did duets with Dolly on the resulting album, *The Winning Hand*. Willie's duet became the collection's biggest hit, a No. 7 country smash and a Top 20 hit on the adult contemporary charts.

(Dolly)
When I look out over a green field of clover
Or watch the sunset at the end of the day,
I get kind of moody when I see such beauty,
And everything's beautiful in it's own way.

(Willie)
When I see a fountain flow from a mountain
Or see April showers bring flowers to May,
I can't help but ponder, life is such a wonder,
And everything's beautiful in it's own way.

DUET CHORUS
Words can't describe what I feel inside
When I see the beauty in each coming day.
What my eyes behold can't be bought or sold,
And everything's beautiful in it's own way.

(Dolly)
When I see the clouds form a black summer windstorm
That uproots the harvest and hurls it away,
In the midst of such anger, destruction, and danger,
The storm's even beautiful in it's own way.

(Willie)
When I see the leaves drop from off of the treetops
Or see the snow fall on a cold winter's day,
My thoughts seem to wander into the blue yonder.
God made all things beautiful in their own way.

REPEAT CHORUS

"I met Willie when I first came to Nashville. He was writing for Combine Music, and so was I. We kind of wove in and out of each other's lives and liked each other a lot. So anytime I get to do anything with Willie, I'll do it."

I wrote "Everything's Beautiful" before I ever left home. When I came to Nashville, I sat with my guitar and played it for Fred [Foster] in his office in 1966. He loved it. He said, "That's a beautiful, beautiful song." When Porter called me down to his office [in 1967], that's the song I thought he was calling me about. I still think it's a good song, one that gives people a little insight into who I am.

Ray Stevens produced the record for Monument. Years later, he had a hit of his own with [almost] the same title [1970's "Everything Is Beautiful"]. I always wondered if he remembered mine. Anyhow, I never got a big record out of it until Willie and I got to do it on our *Winning Hand* album.

I met Willie when I first came to Nashville. He was writing for Combine Music, and so was I. Fred Foster had his office out in Hendersonville. His office was on top, and there was a driveway around back to the basement. All the writers would go down there to write, and that's when I first met Willie. Later, we were both on RCA, so we kind of wove in and out of each other's lives and liked each other a lot.

So anytime I get to do anything with Willie, I'll do it. And anything I've ever asked him to do for me, he did. Fred Foster nurtured both of us and helped us both in our early days. We would have done anything for him, and that's how *The Winning Hand* album came about.

Fred Foster coaches me during one of my early recording sessions for his Monument label in the 1960s. When Fred and Monument ran into financial difficulties in the 1980s, we made *The Winning Hand* album to raise money for him. The icing on the cake for me was getting to work with Willie and Kris and Brenda on that record and its TV special.

Never try to teach a pig to sing.
It wastes your time and annoys the pig.

A Christmas to Remember

With Kenny Rogers 1984

ALTHOUGH SHE HAD MORE THAN A DOZEN HITS with Porter Wagoner, Dolly's most celebrated duet partner remains Kenny Rogers (1938–2020). Their "Islands in the Stream" was a monumental pop hit in 1983, yet they never recorded a mainstream collection together. Instead, they issued the holiday duets LP *Once upon a Christmas* the following year. Dolly wrote several songs for it, including this one.

(Duet)
You've made this a Christmas to remember,
Springtime feelings in the middle of
December.
Strangers meet and willingly surrender.
Oh! What a Christmas to remember.

(Kenny)
Almost went to Aspen but something
told me no.
I considered Mammoth, but there wasn't
enough snow.
And I even thought of Gatlinburg,
but seemed so far to go.
So I headed up to Tahoe for a Christmas
on the slopes.

(Dolly)
And I had fantasized about Christmas
in this way,
Curled up by a fireplace in a Tahoe ski chalet,
With a fast-talking lover, with some
slow-burning wood,
But even in my wildest dreams it never got
this good.

(Duet)
You've made this a Christmas to remember,
Springtime feelings in the middle of
December.
Change the radio, and I'll turn the lights
down dimmer.
Oh! What a Christmas to remember.

Strangers when we met, lovers as we leave,
Christmas to remember, too good to believe.
Don't know how or when, but I know we'll
meet again,
Blowin' back to somewhere like some wild
restless winter's wind.

And you've made this a Christmas to
remember,
Springtime feelings in the middle of
December.
'Neath the mistletoe you kissed me warm
and tender.
Oh! What a Christmas to remember.

(Dolly)
We loved and laughed and played and joked
Sang Christmas songs and talked to folks
Sleighed the fields and skied the slopes.
Then to the lodge for dinner. Now it's time
for us to go.

As our hearts melt like chimney snow,
There's just one thing I want to know.
Can we do this next winter?
Oh! What a Christmas to remember.

(Duet)
You've made this a Christmas to remember,
Springtime feelings in the middle of
December.
Though the fire is hot, we'll just have to let
it simmer.
Oh! What a Christmas to remember.

You've made this a Christmas to remember,
Springtime feelings in the middle of
December.
Though it's cold outside, we'll just stoke
the burning embers.
Oh! What a Christmas to remember.

I met Kenny when I was doing my TV variety show in Nashville [in 1976]. He was nice enough to come and do my show. That's when we became buddies. I just loved him. We were such kindred spirits. We made each other laugh so hard, and I just loved his singing.

When Kenny died, it was like losing a brother. That's the way we were with each other, like brother and sister.

You never know how much you love somebody until they're gone. I had so many wonderful years and wonderful times with Kenny, but above all the music and the success, I loved him as a wonderful man and a true friend.

When we got the chance to do "Islands in the Stream" together, the rest is history. We should have done a great duet album to follow it, but we just never did it.

When the idea came up to do a Christmas album, we thought, "We'd be perfect," because he looked just like Santa Claus. And that album does great every year. It's one of those classic albums. People say, "Oh I play you and Kenny every year at Christmastime." And I do, too. It brings back so many great memories.

I know Kenny is in a better place than we are today. I'm for-sure he's gonna be talkin' to God, and he's gonna be asking Him to spread some light on a bunch of this darkness going on here.

I loved Kenny with all my heart, and my heart was broken when he passed. A big ol' chunk of it went with him.

God bless you, Kenny. Fly high, straight to the arms of God.

I love everything about Christmas. After the holiday album with Kenny, I made a solo Christmas record in 1990, and that's when I wore this wintertime costume. To this day, the holiday season is a big deal at Dollywood.

Wait 'Til I Get You Home

With Mac Davis (Dolly Parton / Mac Davis) 1989

WHEN DOLLY DECIDED SHE WANTED to make Hollywood inroads, she turned to Mac Davis for advice. At the time, he was hot with his own NBC TV variety series (1974–1976) and hits such as "Baby Don't Get Hooked on Me," "I Believe in Music," and "Stop and Smell the Roses." He paved the way for her pop music acceptance by introducing her to his high-powered LA manager. Dolly had a 1969 hit with Mac's socially conscious song "In the Ghetto," and they became co-writers in the following decade. This duet appeared on Dolly's *White Limozeen* LP.

(Dolly)
You never cease to amaze me.
You can still make me crazy.
Baby you can turn me on with just your eyes.

(Mac)
You're just so darn appealin'.
Ooh, you stir up sexy feelin's.
Every man in the room would love to try you on for size.

DUET CHORUS
Baby, wait 'til I get you home,
Wait 'til I get you alone.
Wait 'til I get my hands on you,
Wait 'til I get you home, sweet baby,
Wait 'til I get you home.

(Dolly)
Oh baby you still make me
Feel feelin's that can take me
To places where I've never been before.

(Mac)
Well honey, I've got a feelin'
We'll make some shadows on the ceilin'
Tonight by candlelight behind closed doors.

REPEAT CHORUS

(Dolly)
Your lovin' gets better
Each time we're together
It's always exciting and new.

(Duet)
Each time we discover,
We're still like young lovers,
It's always been magic with you.

REPEAT CHORUS

I met Mac Davis when he was doing his big network television show out of LA [in 1976]. We automatically liked each other, and so we stayed in touch. Anytime he'd come to Nashville, he'd call and we'd get together for supper or something.

He was in Nashville working on a record when I was leaving Porter. I was kind of at a low point and in a mix-up of not knowing what all I wanted to do. So I called Mac. He said, "Well, come on down here," and we ordered room service at his hotel. We talked a lot, and I told him what my plans were. He said, "Well, let me put you in touch with Sandy [Gallin, Mac's manager]. I don't know if Sandy would want to manage a country artist, but at least he can kind of guide you."

I started working with Sandy, and that worked out wonderful. And Mac let us be his opening act on the road for a while. He was very, very helpful to me.

We started writing together, any time we could. When we write, it's such a fun time. The lines that we come up with are sometimes awful, sometimes vulgar, sometimes funny. But we always have a good time.

I think this song is very clever. It's based on how your mom or your daddy would say, "Young lady, you wait until I get you home." But it's like a love song instead.

Mac Davis is my buddy. We write songs together and sometimes sing together, too. I'll always be grateful to him for helping me to make it in Hollywood. Mac lives in LA, but we're both in the Nashville Songwriters Hall of Fame. I live in Nashville, but we both have stars in the Hollywood Walk of Fame, too.

Light of a Clear Blue Morning 1977

THIS SONG IS THE CENTERPIECE of *New Harvest . . . First Gathering*, an album Dolly produced with the assistance of her new musical director, Gregg Perry. It is her musical declaration of independence. It also had a prominent spot on the soundtrack of her 1992 comedy movie *Straight Talk*. Among those who have also recorded it are Glen Campbell, Allison Moorer, and Irish fiddler-singer Mags.

It's been a long dark night,
And I've been a waitin' for the morning.
It's been a long hard fight,
But I see a brand new day a-dawning.

I've been looking for the sunshine.
You know, I ain't seen it in so long.
But everything's gonna work out just fine,
And everything's gonna be all right
That's been all wrong.

CHORUS
'Cause I can see the light of a clear blue
morning.
I can see the light of a brand new day.
I can see the light of a clear blue morning.
Oh, and everything's gonna be all right.
It's gonna be okay.

It's been a long long time
Since I've known the taste of freedom.
And those clinging vines
That had me bound, well I don't need 'em.

Oh, I've been like a captured eagle.
You know, an eagle's born to fly.
Now that I have won my freedom,
Like an eagle, I am eager for the sky.

REPEAT CHORUS FOUR TIMES

"Light of a Clear Blue Morning" was my song of deliverance. I felt like I was trapped in a situation and needed to be free, because God was calling me, life was calling me, to something bigger. But I felt like my feet were nailed to the floor.

When I finally said, "I have to go," I remember walking out the door of Porter's office that day. It was raining. As I was driving back to my home with Carl in Brentwood, I was thinking, "It's been a long, dark night." I was almost to Brentwood, and all of a sudden the clouds started parting and the sun was coming out. I thought, "Well, if that ain't a sign, I don't know what is." I started saying the song's words. By the time I got home, I pretty much had the song done, in my head.

I felt like God had spoken to me. I had a good talk with myself, and I was free, thinking: "I've won my freedom like an eagle, and I'm eager for the sky. So let me go, and look out, world."

Applejack 1977

THIS BANJO TUNE IS DOLLY'S SALUTE to traditional country music on the *New Harvest . . . First Gathering* collection. Dolly is joined on the song's recording by a who's who of classic country stars, including Kitty Wells, Grandpa Jones, Carl & Pearl Butler, Wilma Lee & Stoney Cooper, Roy Acuff, Chet Atkins, and Minnie Pearl, as well as her parents.

He lived by the apple orchard in this little orchard shack.
His real name was Jackson Taylor, but I called him Applejack.
Now old Applejack was loved by everyone he ever knew.
Applejack picked apples, but he picked the banjo, too.

CHORUS
Play a song for me Applejack, Applejack.
Play a song for me, and I'll sing.
Play a song for me Applejack, Applejack.
Play a song, let your banjo ring.

Now I'd go down to Applejack's almost every day.
We'd sit and we'd drink applejack that old Applejack had made.
Then he'd take his banjo down. Then he'd ask me if I'd sing.
And he would play the banjo, and I'd play my tambourine.

REPEAT CHORUS

That's when I was just a kid, and now that I am grown
All I have are memories. Old Applejack is gone.
Oh, but he left me his banjo, and it always takes me back.
And every time I play it, I still hear Applejack.

REPEAT CHORUS THREE TIMES

"The rest of the stars loved the song and loved being part of what I was doing. I was a new, progressive person, but I loved the older folks, so I just had to get them on that song. That was a very fun day for all of us."

Uncle Phillip inspired "Applejack" because he was my banjo teacher as a girl. I still play the banjo in his old-time clawhammer style.

I kind of based Applejack on two people. My [great] uncle Philip, Grandpa Jake's brother, played the tar out of that old clawhammer banjo. He's the one who taught me how to play in that old clawhammer style.

And there was another man named Perry Lindsey, an old guy we called "Sawdust." He lived up in the woods, and he played the banjo. He had a bunch of old hunting dogs, and he stunk like crazy, but I would sneak off to his place. Mama said, "Don't go up there." But I was so intrigued, because I'd heard him playing the banjo and just loved how he played. I thought, "Well, I'll just hold my nose and go."

Neither one of them was named Applejack. I just created my own little person to tell that story.

The recording session for the song was such a fun thing. The guy that was doing Applejack's voice was Bob Ferguson, a wonderful man who was a producer at RCA who'd worked with Porter and me. The rest of the stars loved the song and loved being part of what I was doing.

I was a new, progressive person, but I loved the older folks, so I just had to get them on that song. That was a very fun day for all of us.

Where Beauty Lives in Memory 1977

IN THE SUMMER OF 1977, *New Harvest . . . First Gathering* became Dolly's first No. 1 country album. This saga of a madwoman is another of its standout compositions.

She stands before the mirror,
Smiles at her reflection,
Striking sexy poses in the glass.
She paints her lips a brilliant red,
Piles her hair high on her head,
Struggles to replace a false eyelash.

She powders up her face,
Paints her cheeks to match her lips.
She wears a dress cut low in front
Fittin' tight around her hips.
And there, inside her room,
She stands and gazes at herself.
Where beauty lives in memory,
She lives in fairy tales.

CHORUS
"Mirror, mirror on the wall,
Who's the fairest of them all?"
She sings as she goes waltzing 'cross the floor.
She keeps a candle burning
And she waits for his returning.
When beauty lives in memory,
It lives forevermore.

She was a fairy princess once
And was by all adored.
They say she was the fairest of them all.
They called her Cinderella
And they say that every fella
Would gladly answer to her beck and call.
So the story went.
They tell of how this handsome prince
Stole her heart and wandered far away.
He took her heart and took her mind.
Now she has lost all track of time.
Forty years have passed and still she waits,
singing,

REPEAT CHORUS

Meanwhile, back inside her room
The shades are pulled. It's half-past noon.
But in her mind, why, it's forty years ago.
She recalls the beauty of their love.
She remembers he was beautiful.
And of course, she always knew she was.
And so the past unfolds.

Then all at once, inside her mind
She sees him at the door.
And as he's leading her away
She feels the room begin to sway.
Where beauty lives in memory,
She falls dead upon the floor.

REPEAT CHORUS

This song is a movie I want to do, and I want to play the old lady. I'd love to play that part because it's like a Cinderella story. She fell in love with the handsome prince. Then he left and broke her mind. She's never turned him loose, and she's old now. She still thinks he's going to come waltzing through that door. She thinks she sees him in the mirror, and he's coming back for her. But, really, she's going right over the edge and falling dead. I call that dark, dark, dark.

When I'm writing, I throw myself into the characters in my songs. I might not be as nuts as the lady in "Where Beauty Lives in Memory," but I can certainly relate to her sadness and heartbreak.

Me and Little Andy 1977

DOLLY ACHIEVED HER POP MUSIC BREAKTHROUGH with the Grammy-winning "Here You Come Again." It was written by the famed team of Barry Mann and Cynthia Weil (who'd previously provided huge hits to the Righteous Brothers, the Animals, Elvis Presley, the Crystals, Paul Revere & the Raiders, and dozens more). This song was on the million-selling single's flip side and was the last title she recorded for her chart-topping *Here You Come Again* LP. Pop critics decried it as "maudlin" and "tasteless," but she sang it to much applause during her debut appearance on *The Tonight Show* on her thirty-first birthday, January 19, 1977.

Late one cold and stormy night I heard a dog a-barkin'.
Then I thought I heard somebody at my door a-knockin'.
I wondered who could be outside in such an awful storm.
Then I saw a little girl with a puppy in her arms.

Before I could say a word she said, "My name is Sandy
And this here is my puppy dog. It's name is Little Andy."
Standing in the bitter cold in just a ragged dress,
Then I asked her to come in and this is what she said,

Ain't ya got no gingerbread?
Ain't ya got no candy?
Ain't ya got an extra bed for me and little Andy?

Patty cake and baker's man,
My mommy ran away again
And we was all alone and didn't know what else to do.
I wonder if you'll let us stay with you.

Giddy up trotty horse, going to the mill
Can we stay all night?
If you don't love us, no one will.
I promise we won't cry.

London Bridge is fallin' down.
My daddy's drunk again in town.
And we was all alone, and didn't know what we could do.
I wonder if you'll let us stay with you.

She was just a little girl, not more than six or seven.
But that night as they slept, the angels took them both to Heaven.
God knew Little Andy would be lonesome with her gone.
Now Sandy and her puppy dog won't ever be alone.

Ain't ya got no gingerbread?
Ain't ya got no candy?
Ain't ya got an extra bed for me and Little Andy?

I performed dressed like a little girl with a stuffed-dog toy for one of my TV specials. It seems like I can always tap into my "inner child" when I am writing songs.

This was an odd song to be putting on a pop album. A lot of people said, "That is so out of place." I said, "Well, I was just trying to get some of my own songs on that record." And I love performing that little song.

It's a sad story, but I think people get a kick out of me doing my little-kid voice when I sing, "Ain't ya got no gingerbread? Ain't ya got no candy? Ain't ya got an extra bed for me and Little Andy?"

I used to do the song on the road a lot. I remember once we were in Las Vegas, and I had it in my act. This guy in the audience hollered out, "Don't sing that damn song in a nightclub! It's bad enough that the kid died! Did you have to kill the damn dog, too?"

I thought, "Well maybe he's right. Or maybe he's the daddy in the song who's drunk again." So I took it out of my club act, where people drink. I thought, "It's hard enough for regular people who ain't drunk to deal with some of the sorrow that I throw at 'em." Some people want to kick my ass for writing such sorrowful songs. That guy cussed me out, big time.

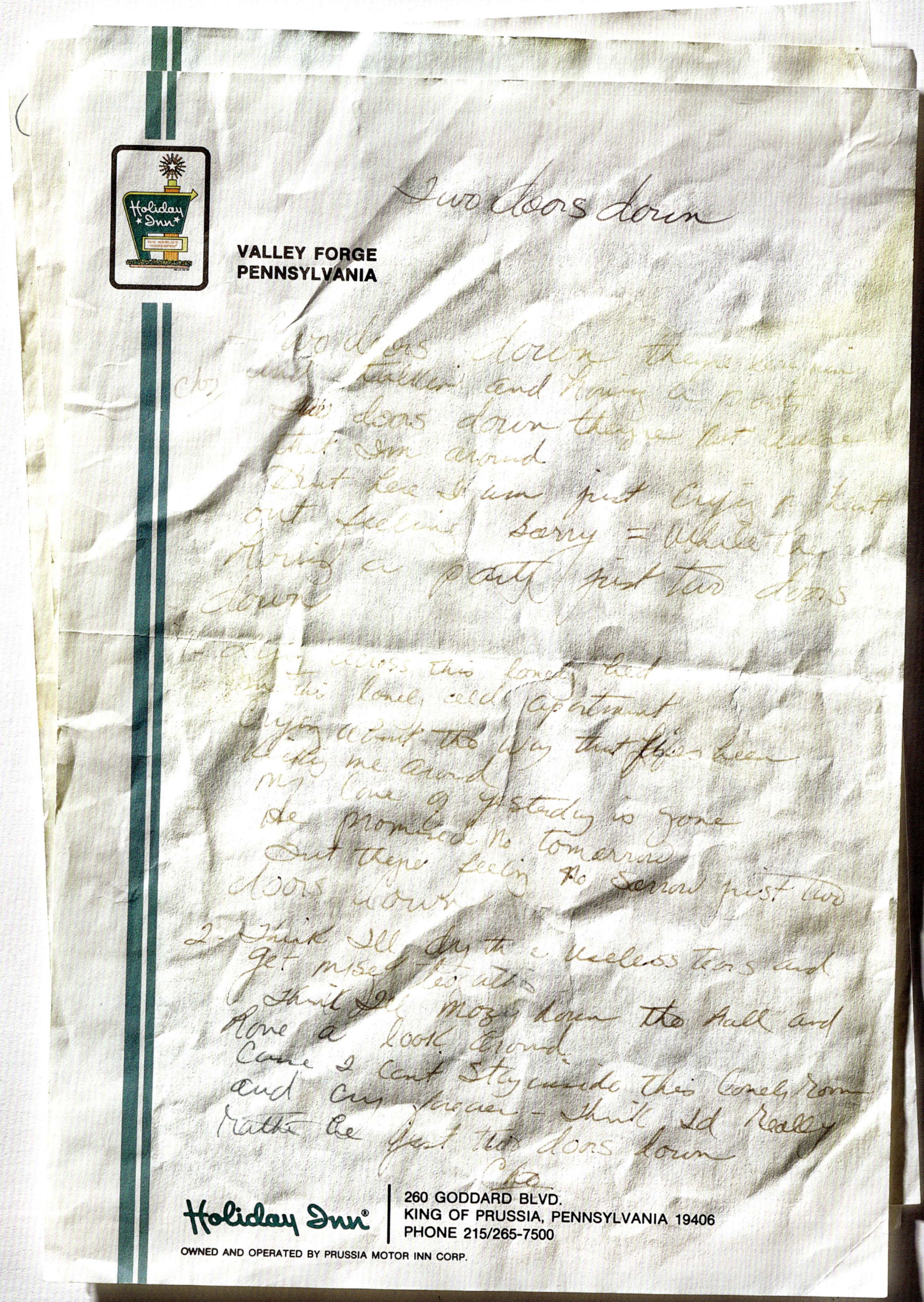

VALLEY FORGE
PENNSYLVANIA

Two doors down

Two doors down they're laughin' and having a party
Two doors down they're not aware that I'm around
But here I am just crying my heart out feeling sorry while they're having a party just two doors down

Lying across this lonely bed
In this lonely, cold apartment
Crying about the way that fate's been kicking me around
My love of yesterday is gone
He promised no tomorrow
But here feeling the sorrow just two doors down

2- Think I'll dry these useless tears and get myself fixed up
Think I'll mozy down the hall and have a look around
'Cause I can't stay inside this lonely room and cry forever
Think I'd really rather be just two doors down

Holiday Inn®
260 GODDARD BLVD.
KING OF PRUSSIA, PENNSYLVANIA 19406
PHONE 215/265-7500
OWNED AND OPERATED BY PRUSSIA MOTOR INN CORP.

Two Doors Down 1978

THIS SONG, THE SECOND SINGLE drawn from the *Here You Come Again* album, became a No. 12 adult contemporary hit and a No. 19 pop-music success. On the country charts, *Hee Haw* TV regular and former circus unicyclist Zella Lehr took it to No. 7. In 2019, the song inspired a Netflix movie in an anthology series based on Dolly songs.

Two doors down, they're laughing and drinking and having a party.
And two doors down, they're not aware that I'm around.
But here I am, crying my heart out, feeling sorry.
But they're having a party, just two doors down.

I think I'll dry these useless tears and get myself together.
I think I'll wander down the hall and have a look around.
'Cause I can't stay inside this lonely room and cry forever.
I think I'd really rather join 'em two doors down.

Two doors down, we're laughing and drinking and having a party
And two doors down, they're all aware that I'm around.
'Cause here I am no longer crying and feeling sorry.
We're having a party just two doors down.

I can't believe I'm standing here dry-eyed, all smiles and talkin',
Making conversation with the new love I have found.
I ask him if he'd like to be alone and we start walkin'
Down the hall to my place waiting two doors down, yeah.

FINALE CHORUS
Two doors down, they're laughing and drinking and having a party.
And two doors down, we're not aware that they're around.
'Cause here I am feeling everything but sorry.
We're having our own party two doors down.

Oh oh oh oh, two doors down
Oh oh oh oh, two doors down
Oh oh oh oh, two doors down
Oh oh oh oh, two doors down

REPEAT FINALE CHORUS TWICE

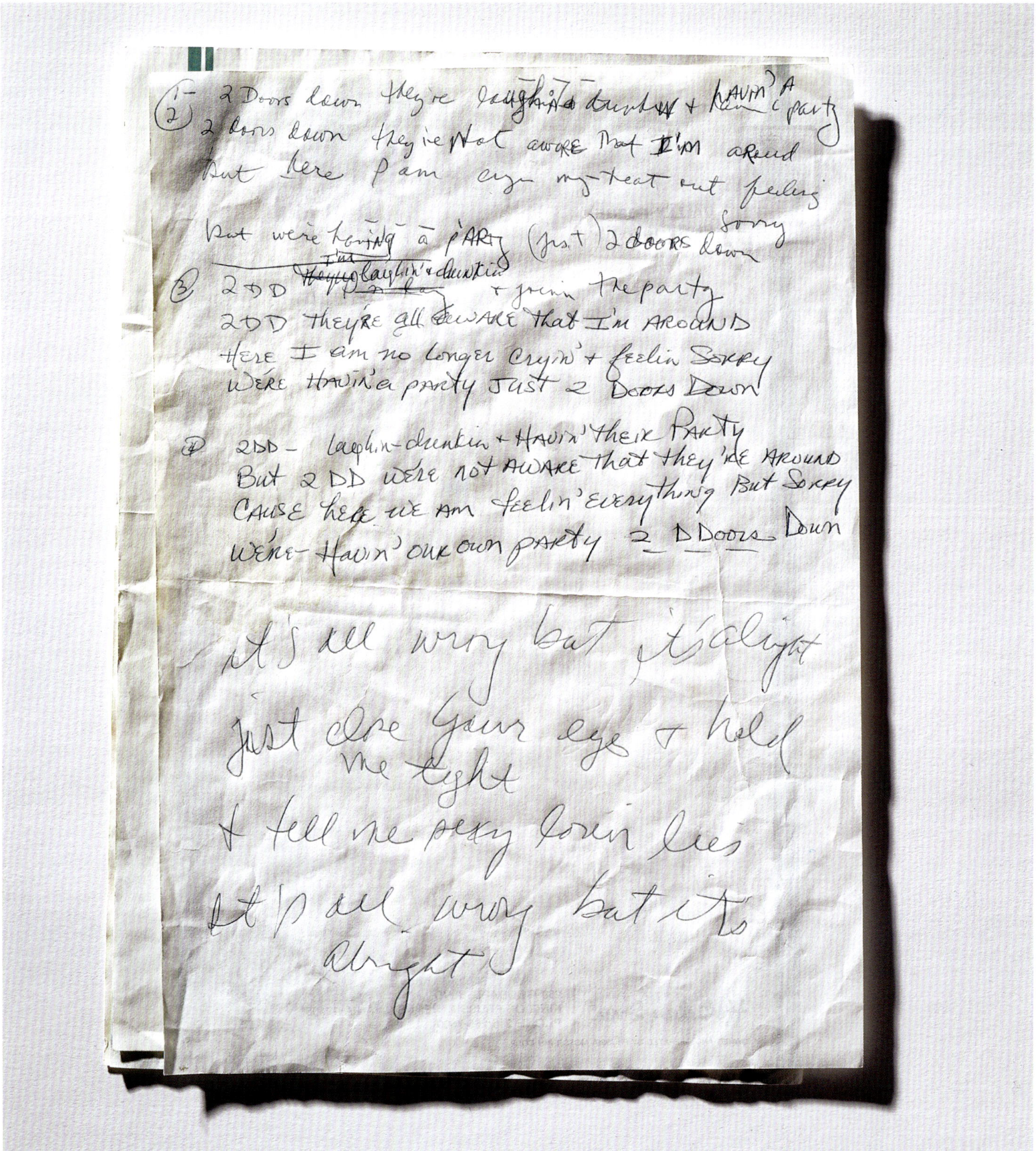

2 Doors down they're laughin' drinkin + havin' a party
2 doors down they're not aware that I'm around
But here I am cryin' my heart out feelin' sorry
but we're having a party (just) 2 doors down

2DD I'm laughin' & drinkin + joinin the party
2DD they're all aware that I'm around
Here I am no longer cryin' + feelin sorry
We're havin' a party just 2 Doors Down

2DD - laughin-drinkin + havin' their party
But 2DD we're not aware that they're around
Cause here we am feelin' everything but sorry
We're havin' our own party 2 D Doors Down

It's all wrong but it's alright
Just close your eyes & hold me tight
& tell me sexy lovin lies
It's all wrong but it's alright

Because I remember those fried clams so well, I am positive that I wrote "Two Doors Down" at a Howard Johnson's Motor Inn. I guess the stationary from a Pennsylvania Holiday Inn was the closest paper I had on hand to write it down. It looks like I started writing "It's All Wrong But It's All Right" on those same pages.

I had gained a lot of weight. I have a tendency to do that. At the time, I had tried everything to get the weight off, and there was this new diet out. It was like a liquid protein, and it was just the awfulest tasting stuff. You had to drink it three times a day, and you just gag when you are doing it.

We were staying at a Howard Johnson's hotel. It had these great fried clams, which I loved. The band was down there in the restaurant. I could hear them laughing and talking. I was in my room, because I couldn't go down there and eat. I remember just feeling so sorry for myself in this lonely-ass room while they were having a party.

I thought, "Well, I can't eat. I can't just sit here and feel sorry for myself. Why don't I just write a song?"

DOLLY PARTON
FRAGILE
BUTTERFLY EXPRESS
PO BOX 4499
N. HOLLYWOOD, CA.
91609
213-273-4210

It's All Wrong, But It's All Right 1978

THIS FLIP SIDE OF DOLLY'S "Two Doors Down" pop single reached No. 1 on the country charts. Both songs are on the *Here You Come Again* album, her first to earn a Platinum Record for sales in excess of one million. As recently as a decade before, it would have been unthinkable for a country-music woman to sing this lyric about having casual sex.

Hello, are you free tonight?
I like your looks, I love your smile.
Could I use you for a while?
It's all wrong, but it's all right.

The amber sunset glow has died.
My needs are very much alive.
Is it okay if I stop by?
It's all wrong, but it's all right.

CHORUS
It's all wrong, but it's all right.
Just close your eyes and hold me tight.
Tell me sexy, loving lines.
It's all wrong, but it's all right.

It may be wrong if we make love,
But I just need someone so much.
And who knows? It might last for life.
It's all wrong, but it's all right.

REPEAT CHORUS

ALTERNATE CHORUS
It's all wrong, but it's all right.
Just close your eyes and fantasize.
Tell me sexy, loving lines.
It's all wrong, but it's all right.

REPEAT CHORUS AND ALTERNATE
CHORUS

I thought this was a clever title and a clever idea for a song. I've always been drawn to sexy songs, and this happens to be one of my favorites. This character in this one just kinda throws caution to the wind, as most of us have done at one time or another.

I ask you, is this the face of a bad girl? I have always said my weakness is food, sex, and music . . . but not necessarily in that order.

Bally
1st Player
2nd Player
Dolly
PARTON
High Score To Date
Ball in Play
Credit
3rd Player
4th Player
1 to 4 Can Play
Game Over
SHOOT AGAIN
When Lit
DOLLY PARTON
INSTRUCTIONS
Bally
1 PLAY
QUARTER
DOLLAR
5
PLAYS
1 PLAY
QUARTER

Baby, I'm Burnin' 1979

THIS UP-TEMPO RAMPAGE from Dolly's *Heartbreaker* album reached No. 15 on the disco charts, No. 11 on the adult contemporary charts, No. 25 on the pop charts, and No. 48 on the country charts. It was her first song to score on the disco/dance charts, but not her last. Dance remixes of "9 to 5" (1981), "House of the Rising Sun" (1981), "Potential New Boyfriend" (1983), and her version of the Cat Stevens song "Peace Train" (1997) have also been club favorites. In early 2020, she was at No. 1 on the dance charts for five consecutive weeks with "Faith," her collaboration with the Swedish electronic duo Galantis.

You look at me that way, I know what your
eyes say.
Your eyes reflect love and desire.
I see that you need me. I need you to please me.
You touch me and set me on fire.

The way that you love me, the way that you
touch me,
The way that you whisper my name,
I cannot resist you each time I kiss you.
Then everything goes up in flames.

CHORUS
Baby I'm burnin', out of control.
Baby I'm burnin', body and soul.
Hot as a pistol of flamin' desire,
Baby I'm burnin'.
You've got me on fire.
I'm on fire.

This red-hot emotion puts fireworks in
motion.
It looks like the Fourth of July.
There's no use in fighting this fire you've
ignited.
Just stand back and watch the sparks fly.

REPEAT CHORUS

I like any kind of music, including disco. "Baby, I'm Burnin'" was the first time I wrote something made to be a disco song. Then they put dance beats to different songs of mine to play in nightclubs, including "Jolene."

I used to go to Studio 54 all the time and hang out with Andy Warhol and Calvin Klein and so many people. Steve Rubell, who owned Studio 54, I just loved him to death. He was the sweetest little guy.

Everybody was dancing. I didn't. I just liked watching, sitting there and being part of the whole scene. I'd just sit on the couch and talk to Andy Warhol. My friend Sandy Gallin, my gay manager, would get me out there every once in a while to dance a little with him. But I mostly just loved the commotion and the excitement and the thrill of that whole scene. It was the hottest thing going at the time.

I think that the [2020] Galantis song "Faith" is saying what we need to hear right now: Just have a little faith, show a little respect. I got to write a little piece of it: "Let me shine and radiate / With your love and light. And help me make / Any change I can in this world today / Help me, Lord and show me the way." I loved the song, loved being a part of it, and loved doing the video. And boy, it got so much attention, so much airplay and streaming and whatever. The next thing I know, it became this huge hit. So I was lucky to get to work with that group.

Nickels and Dimes

(Dolly Parton / Floyd Estel Parton) 1978

DOLLY'S CO-WRITER ON THIS SONG from the *Heartbreaker* LP is her younger brother Floyd Parton (1957–2018). She was eleven when twins Freida and Floyd were born. Both became recording artists, and Floyd also wrote Dolly's 1991 No. 1 hit duet with Ricky Van Shelton, "Rockin' Years."

I used to stand on the corner
When I was a child.
And I'd play my guitar
And sing as the people went by.
The sidewalks were crowded, but I'd just sing louder,
Because I didn't mind
Spending my time, spinning my rhymes
And singing for nickels and dimes.

CHORUS
Nickels and dimes, a song at a time
For nickels and dimes.
I'd brighten their day as they go on their way,
And they'd brighten mine.
A sidewalk rehearsal for dreams
That I held in my mind.
I knew that someday in my own special way
I'd repay all their nickels and dimes.

I recall the sidewalk each night
As I stand on the stage,
As I play my guitar and sing
For the people who paid.
Because I finally made it
To what they all call "the big time."
But I still remember,
I still owe some nickels and dimes.

ALTERNATE CHORUS
Nickels and dimes, a song at a time
For nickels and dimes.
A sidewalk rehearsal
For dreams that I held in my mind.
So if you remember
A child on the corner of time,
You'll know that I wrote this
To repay your nickels and dimes.

REPEAT CHORUS TWICE

My little brother Floyd gave me his song "Rockin' Years," which became a No. 1 hit duet with Ricky Van Shelton [in 1991]. Floyd was also one of my favorite songwriting partners in those days.

My brother Floyd was such a talent. He was the greatest singer, a great guitarist, and a great, great writer. He wrote "Rockin' Years" about our parents, and that was one of my favorite records, ever.

We used to love to get together and write. I don't like to sit and work with many people, but he was one of the few.

When I was a kid working at the Cas Walker show, I would sometimes ride the bus there from my aunt Estelle's house. While I would wait for the bus, I'd sometimes take my guitar out and just sing and play and leave my guitar case open. I really wasn't singing for money or begging, but people would drop some in the guitar case. So I'd go buy Jiffy burgers.

Floyd knew that story. One night, he just started playing his guitar and singing, "Nickels and dimes, a song at a time." We wrote some really special songs together, and this one is based on a true story.

My brother Floyd passed away in December 2018. He had lung cancer, and we did not know it. He was a smoker, but we didn't know he was that sick. Seven weeks after we found out, he was gone. It was shattering, because he did so many wonderful things. I put a display in my museum about him. He was a special boy.

CHAPTER 9

WORKING 9 TO 5

BEGINNING IN 1980, DOLLY GRADUATED FROM MUSIC FAME TO MOVIE stardom. From this point on, she made it a point to tie many songs to film projects created for television or the big screen.

Up to this time, much of her show-business experience had occurred in front of the cameras on Knoxville television, on early morning TV in Nashville, and during her seven years filming *The Porter Wagoner Show*. She had also hosted her own weekly variety series. But becoming a movie star was an entirely new adventure.

Dolly's debut film was an artistic and commercial success. Jane Fonda cast her in the 1980 workplace comedy *9 to 5*. Co-starring Fonda, Lily Tomlin, and Dabney Coleman, *9 to 5* became the third-highest-grossing film of 1981 (trailing the blockbusters *Raiders of the Lost Ark* and *Superman II*). Moreover, her mega-hit title song earned her two Grammy Awards and an Oscar nomination. ("Fame" beat both "9 to 5" and Willie Nelson's "On the Road Again" for the Academy Award.)

She followed that film by starring opposite superstar Burt Reynolds in *The Best Little Whorehouse in Texas*, which became her second straight box-office hit. She re-recorded "I Will Always Love You" for its soundtrack. This version became a No. 1 hit in 1982, making Dolly the only person in history to have two different chart-topping recordings of the same song.

Dolly composed fourteen new songs for her third film, *Rhinestone*, more than for any other film. Although the movie was panned by critics, the publicity surrounding *Rhinestone* resulted in her getting a star on the Hollywood Walk of Fame in 1984.

She followed her cinematic debuts with more than a dozen movies that provided outlets for her music. Her Hollywood experiences also inspired several compositions. These are highlights.

The character of "Doralee Rhodes" will always be special to me. In real life, I would probably have made a lousy secretary, but in *9 to 5*, "Doralee" made me a movie star instead.

Knowing you has made me
very happy, taught me
alot and it sure has been
fun — so let's keep
it up!
Love
Jane
SIGNED...

9 to 5 1980

"9 TO 5" BROUGHT DOLLY'S SONGWRITING to the top of the pop hit parade for the first time. It was also a No. 1 country and adult contemporary smash, won two Grammy Awards, and was nominated for an Oscar. The movie *9 to 5* subsequently became a TV sitcom (1982–1988) with Dolly's sister Rachel Dennison in the "Doralee Rhodes" role. Both Rachel and sister Freida Parton issued pop solo LPs in 1984. Freida wrote "Sing for the Common Man," the flip side of Dolly's million-selling "9 to 5" single.

Tumble outta bed and I stumble to the kitchen
Pour myself a cup of ambition
And yawn and stretch and try to come to life.
Jump in the shower and the blood starts pumpin'
Out on the street the traffic starts jumpin'
With folks like me on the job from 9 to 5.

CHORUS
Workin' 9 to 5, what a way to make a livin'.
Barely gettin' by, it's all takin' and no givin'.
They just use your mind, and they never give you credit.
It's enough to drive you crazy if you let it.

9 to 5, for service and devotion
You would think that I would deserve a fair promotion.
Want to move ahead, but the boss won't seem to let me.
I swear sometimes that man is out to get me!

They let you dream just to watch 'em shatter.
You're just a step on the boss-man's ladder.
But you got dreams he'll never take away.
You're in the same boat with a lotta your friends
Waitin' for the day your ship'll come in
And the tide's gonna turn, and it's all gonna roll your way.

REPEAT CHORUS

9 to 5, yeah, they got you where they want you.
There's a better life, and you dream about it, don't you?
It's a rich man's game, no matter what they call it
And you spend your life puttin' money in his wallet.

REPEAT CHORUS

9 to 5, yeah, they got you where they want you.
There's a better life, and you think about it, don't you?
It's a rich man's game, no matter what they call it
And you spend your life puttin' money in his wallet.
9 to 5, working 9 to 5.

Nine To Five

Tumble from the bed - Stumble to the kitchen
Pour myself a cup of ambition
And Wonder if I might be rich in another life
Jump in the shower and my blood starts pumpin - Out in the streets the traffic starts jumpin
With folks like me on the job from nine to five

Workin nine to five - what a way to make a livin -
Barely gettin by - its all takin and no givin
They will steal your mind and never give you credit
Its enough to drive you crazy if you let it -
Nine to five for service and devotion
You would think that I would deserve a fair promotion
Want to move ahead but the boss wont seem to let me -
I swear sometimes that man is out to get me ...

They let you dream just to watch em shatter
You're just a step

When Lily Tomlin and Jane Fonda arrived on the set of *9 to 5* they went straight into hair and makeup. I got there every morning ready to go as "Doralee," with my makeup on and my hair styled. I never leave the house unless I'm "camera-ready," no matter where I am.

I remember when I first started doing TV [in Knoxville], I was a little scared of the camera. One cameraman said, "Just follow those two red lights on the camera with your eyes and pretend that they are the eyes of somebody you know. Pretend you're singing to a friend." So I kind of became friends with the camera. Because of all my TV experience, I was more comfortable with cameras than most people.

But the movies are a whole different world. As far as lighting and standing on your marks are concerned, there's a whole lot of stuff to learn. And you're not allowed to look at the camera, so I had to unlearn some things.

Lily and Jane were very helpful. Jane is the one who got me in the movie. She was thinking, "Dolly will get us the South." I told her later as a joke, "Well, I might get you some North and East and West, too," because I had a lot of fans. I memorized the whole script. They thought that was the funniest thing they'd ever heard. But it helped them, because I was feeding them lines when they didn't remember theirs.

Jane said, "Don't worry about acting. Just be yourself. The director will tell you what to do, and you'll learn." Dabney Coleman [who played "Mr. Hart"] taught me a lot, too. He's a Texas guy, and we had a great connection. They all knew it was my first time in the movies, so they were all helpful. People are generous.

The thing I hate about the movies is all the waiting-around time. I realized early on that I had to do something besides just sitting there or going to the crafts [food] table. I did that and gained weight. Jane gave me good advice, so I said to myself, "Dolly, you've got to stop eating. They do scenes out of sequence, and you can't go in the door slim and come out fat. You've got to watch what you're doing."

So I spent my time watching everything, just soaking everything up like a sponge. I couldn't play my guitar; I didn't want to disrupt everything on the set by making music and attracting attention when other people were trying to work. So I would just take my nails and make them sound like a typewriter. Off by myself, I would click my nails and use that sound as my music.

I wrote "9 to 5" in my head that way. I'd go back to my hotel at night and put down what I had written that day, playing my guitar and getting it on tape. Over a long period of time, I wrote the song on my nails. I'm famous for that now. Every time I go on TV, I have to "play" my nails like a typewriter.

Working Girl 1980

DOLLY CREATED A CONCEPT ALBUM titled *9 to 5 and Odd Jobs* to frame her blockbuster hit. The album spent ten weeks at No. 1 on the country charts and became a Gold Record. This single from the collection made it to No. 14 on the country hit parade.

Some men find her sexy, some men disagree.
But if she's not, it's not because she doesn't
want to be.
She wears a push-up bra from Frederick's,
five-inch high-heel shoes,
Maybelline and Rubinstein, and Avon's
best perfume.
She's a working girl.

CHORUS
She's a working girl, she is single and free
She's a mother and wife and she's proud to be
A working girl

Some find her too aggressive. She don't know
how to stop
'Cause she's the kind that don't look down
until it's from the top.
She's elegant and stylish, French perfume
and a fur
Designer clothes by Halston and
Diane von Furstenberg
And she's a working girl.

REPEAT CHORUS

She has taken her place among the tallest
of trees.
But she weeps like a willow when she's
brought to her knees
'Cause she's a working girl.

You'll find her dressed according to standard
uniform
'Cause she must dress in comfort for the job
she must perform.
She has so many faces, she wears so many
names
She goes so many places and she does so
many things
'Cause she's a working girl.

REPEAT CHORUS TWICE

OPPOSITE PAGE: A stylist usually brushes out my wigs for me. Every now and then, I'll do my own touch-up. A girl's gotta do what a girl's gotta do to keep up her image.

When I wrote that song, I was thinking of all the working girls. They are all different. This one might have a push-up bra from Frederick's, or she might be wearing Halston. She might wear makeup by Maybelline or [Helena] Rubenstein. The lyrics are like a contrast between all different kinds of women who work.

I wrote it years before the [Melanie Griffith] movie *Working Girl* ever came out [in 1988]. But I thought the characters in that film were close to being like the ones in these lyrics.

I think it's a fun little song. We had a lot of fun recording it, too. [Producer] Mike Post worked on that with me. We had boards laying on the floor, and I remember smacking them to get that tramp-tramp-tramp sound.

Tennessee Homesick Blues 1984

RECORDED FOR THE SOUNDTRACK OF *RHINESTONE*, this No. 1 country hit became the film's best-known song.

New York City ain't no kinda place
For a country girl with a friendly face.
If you smile, people look at you funny, they
take you wrong.

The greenest state in the land of the free
And the home of the Grand Ole Opry
Is calling me back to my Smoky Mountain
home.

I wish I had my ol' fishin' pole,
And a-sittin' on the banks of the fishin' hole
Eatin' green apples and waitin' for the fish to
bite.

Life ain't as simple as it used to be,
Since the Big Apple took a bite outta me
And Lord I'm so Tennessee-homesick that I
could die.

CHORUS
But I ain't been home in I don't know when.
If I had it all to do over again,
Tonight I'd sleep in my old feather bed.

What I wouldn't give for a little bitty taste
Of Mama's homemade chocolate cake.
Tennessee homesick blues is runnin' through
my head.

Mama you can fluff my feather bed.
Just as soon as I can I'm a-gonna head
Back to the Tennessee hills, and it better be
soon.

Daddy, you can load the rifles up.
We're gonna load them dogs on the pickup
truck
And head out to Calhoun County and catch
us a 'coon.

REPEAT CHORUS

Eatin' grits and gravy and country ham.
Go to church on Sunday with dinner on the
ground.
Tennessee homesick blues is runnin' through
my head.

REPEAT CHORUS

Good Lord have mercy on a country girl
Tryin' to make a livin' in a rhinestone world.
It's hard to be a diamond in a rhinestone
world.

Tennessee homesick blues is runnin' through
my head.
I've got those Tennessee homesick blues
runnin' through my head.
Tennessee homesick blues.

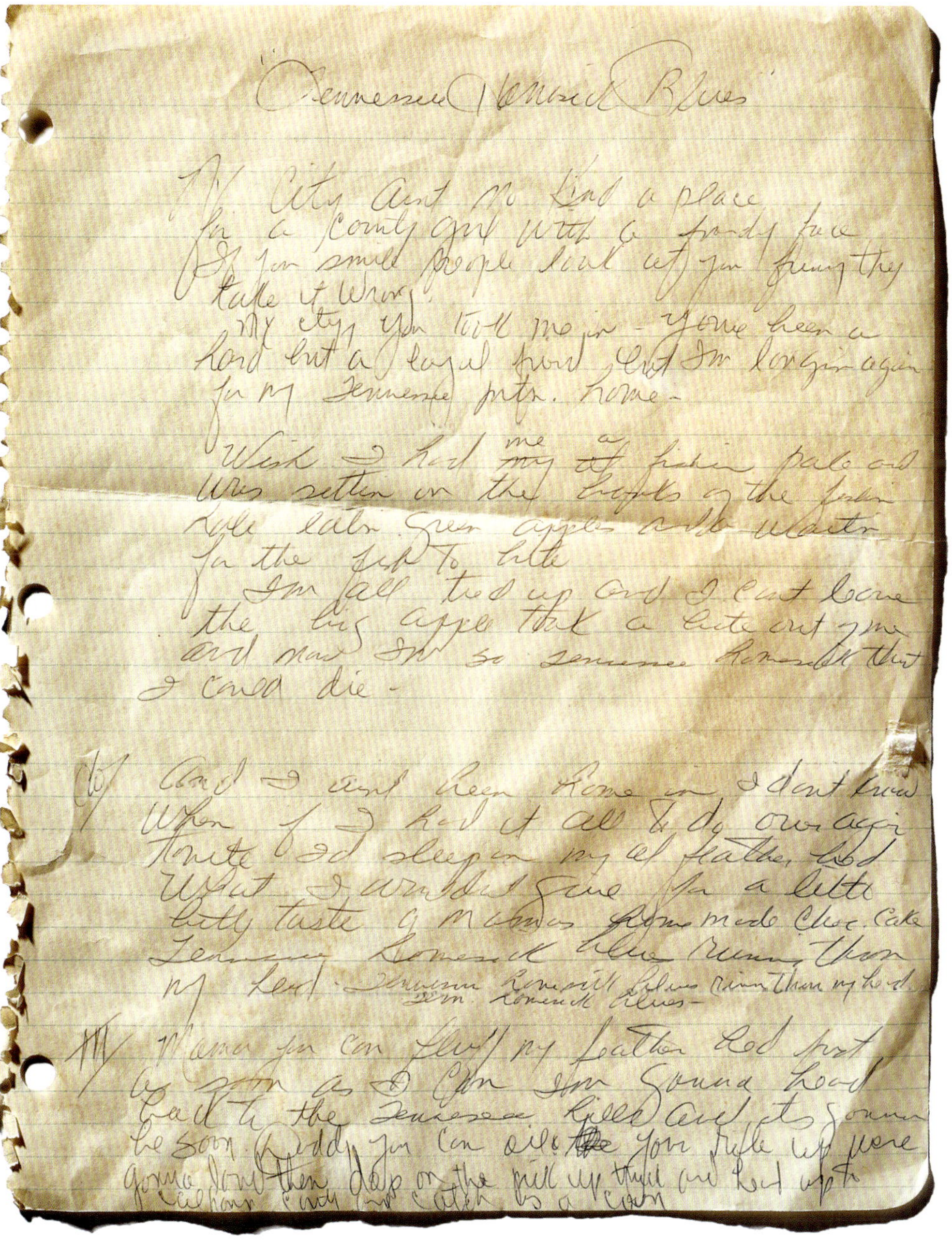

"Tennessee Homesick Blues"

V/ City ain't no kind a place
for a country girl with a friendly face
If you smile people look at you funny they
take it wrong.
My city you took me in - you've been a
hard but a loyal friend, but I'm longin again
for my Tennessee mtn. home -

Wish I had me a fishin pole and
was settin on the banks of the fishin
hole eatin green apples and waitin
for the fish to bite
I'm all tied up and I can't leave
the big apple that's a bite out of me
and now I'm so Tennessee homesick that
I could die -

Ch/ And I ain't been home in I don't know
when if I had it all to do over again
Tonite I'd sleep in my ol feather bed
What I wouldn't give for a little
bitty taste of Mama's homemade choc. cake
Tennessee Homesick Blues runnin through
my head. Tennessee Homesick Blues runnin through my head.
Tenn. homesick blues -

III/ Mama you can fluff my feather bed first
as soon as I can I'm gonna head
back to the Tennessee hills and it's gonna
be soon. Daddy you can oil ~~the~~ your rifle up we're
gonna load them deep on the pick up truck and head up to
[illegible]

As a songwriter, I think *Rhinestone* is one of my very best albums. I wrote all the songs for the movie based on the stories in it. Even though the movie did not do well and didn't get good reviews, if you listen to the songs I wrote for it, they hold up. I loved a lot of the songs in that soundtrack. I enjoyed writing that as much as anything I've ever done.

"Tennessee Homesick Blues" was the theme song for *Rhinestone*. It reminded me of when I first started writing songs about home. "Tonight I'll sleep in Mama's feather bed" and lines like that kind of took me back.

Stay Out of My Bedroom

With Sylvester Stallone 1984

THIS SONG FROM THE *RHINESTONE* SOUNDTRACK features one of Dolly's most overtly sexual lyrics. The film is about Dolly's character attempting to teach Sylvester Stallone's character to be a country singer.

(Sylvester)
Stay out of my bedroom.
Don't be messin' up my pillows and sheets
With your powder and perfume
If you don't have some understanding of me.

Don't be knockin' on my door
If you don't want to play in my fantasies.
Stay out of my bedroom,
Baby, if you can't take the heat.

If you want it, come and get it, baby,
Satisfaction guaranteed.
I'm a pleaser, free and eager.
I ain't never had as much as I need.

Easy lovin', that's down my alley.
I may be easy but at least I am cheap.
Stay out of my bedroom, baby,
Baby, if you can't take the heat.

Stay out of,
Stay out of
You're dealin' with some hot stuff.
Baby, can you deal with the heat?

We might burn on forever. We might
burn out tonight.
Where there's smoke, there is fire from
the flames I ignite.
The heat is intense when desire's blazin' high
Slavin' over all those red-hot lovers at night.

If you come to my bedroom to the heart
of the heat
I will pleasure your body into sheer ecstasy.
I will touch you in places no one else
ever reached
'Til you won't remember anybody but me.

(Duet)
If you want it, come and get it.
If it burns you don't come cryin' to me.
Don't come knockin' on my door
Baby, if you can't take the heat.

Don't be peepin' through my window
If you don't appreciate what you see.
Stay out of my bedroom,
Baby, if you can't take the heat.

Stay out of,
Stay out of
You're dealin' with some hot stuff.
Baby, can you deal with the heat?

Stay out of my bedroom . . .
Stay out of my bedroom . . .
If you can't take it, stay out of my bedroom
Stay out of my bedroom . . .
Stay out of my bedroom . . .

Well, it's true that Sylvester Stallone cannot sing country music. But I'll tell you what he can sing: old '50s rock 'n' roll songs. That's what he sang on the set, and it sounded good.

I had to write songs for him to sing, and a lot of people didn't like that, because he really didn't execute them very well. But I think that had to do with the fact that they were so out of his realm. It wasn't fair to him. I'll take responsibility for that.

But "Stay out of my bedroom if you can't take the heat" was a lot of fun. Stallone was fun to work with, and he was always singing.

I was coming out of a big gloom at the time, and I had some health problems and was not feeling so good. But he was so health-conscious, crazy, and funny. It was good for me. So the movie was a hit to me, personally.

That's Stallone, wearing his "country singer" outfit for the big finale music scene in *Rhinestone*. The gown I wore in that scene is now on display in the Chasing Rainbows Museum at Dollywood.

God Won't Get You 1984

THIS SONG FROM *RHINESTONE* went to No. 10 on the country charts. The lyric makes references to other notable songs, including "(If Loving You Is Wrong) I Don't Want to Be Right," "Your Cheatin' Heart," "Rock of Ages," "Amazing Grace," "Angel in Disguise," and "Torn between Two Lovers."

Sometimes in my sleep I hold you close against my skin.
Wakin' up, I wish that I could sleep and dream again.
'Cause only in my dreams can I know how it might have been.
But cheaters never win. Their heartaches never end.

But sometimes I get crazy, as lovers often do,
Trying to please him and wondering if she's pleasin' you.
Though they have every right to any part of us they choose,
I still live just for you and our secret rendezvous.

"Torn between Two Lovers" on the jukebox,
I'm thinkin' how I could have wrote that song.
Wonderin' if God loves us when we're cheatin',
Oh, but why he lets us feel things if it's wrong.

CHORUS
And I guess I should be singing "Rock of Ages,"
"Amazing Grace," and some of those good songs.
But my cheatin' heart will tell on me tomorrow.
If you think that God won't get you, well you're wrong.

Thou shalt not commit it, it's written in the Ten.
The spirit's always willin', but the flesh is weak again.
And you're as close to Heaven as I might ever fly,
An angel in disguise, a wrong that feels so right.

"Torn between Two Lovers" just keeps playing.
"I Don't Want to Be Right If Lovin' You Is Wrong."
I'm wonderin' if God loves us when we're cheatin',
Oh, but why do we have to feel things if it's so wrong.

REPEAT CHORUS

My cheatin' heart will tell on me tomorrow
If you think that God won't get you, well you're wrong.

Some songs come to me right away, but through the years I rewrote "God Won't Get You" two or three different ways. In my final version, I mention the song titles "Torn between Two Lovers," "Rock of Ages," "Your Cheatin' Heart," and a few more. I was making reference to them to illustrate the emotions in my song, and I love doing that. I do that pretty often in my songwriting.

Stallone and I are sharing a *Rhinestone* movie moment here. He is into physical fitness and was shocked at the junk food I ate. I think that's when I began to realize that I should change my ways and get healthier.

Smoky Mountain Christmas 1986

THIS WAS THE TITLE TUNE of a 1986 ABC TV movie that paired Dolly with Lee Majors, famed for starring in the series *The Six Million Dollar Man* (1973–1978), plus *The Big Valley* (1965–1969) and *The Fall Guy* (1981–1986). Directed by Henry Winkler, this was the first of her holiday TV movies. Others have included *Christmas of Many Colors* (2016), *Christmas at Dollywood* (2019), and *Christmas on the Square* (2020). To date, she has not included this song on any of her albums, but it can be experienced via a YouTube clip from a 1986 appearance on *The Tonight Show*.

CHORUS
I'm dreaming of a Smoky Mountain Christmas
With the kids around the fireplace
Stringing popcorn for the tree.
I'm dreaming of a Smoky Mountain Christmas
With nothing much that money buys
But everything worthwhile in life,
Dreamin' of a Smoky Mountain Christmas.

You can take the girl from the country
I have heard 'em say.
But you'll never take the country from the girl.

And me I've been a rambler
For the better part of life,
But no matter where I ramble in this world,

I keep dreamin' of a cabin in my Smoky Mountain home
Rememberin' my life there as a child,
Just as free as the butterflies, the hummingbirds, and bees,
As different as the snowflakes on the windows of my life.

And I'm dreamin' of a Smoky Mountain Christmas
With the kids around the fireplace
Makin' angels for the tree.
I'm dreamin' of a Smoky Mountain Christmas
With nothing much that money buys
But everything worthwhile in life,
Dreamin' of a Smoky Mountain Christmas.

REPEAT CHORUS

Yes, I'm dreaming of a Smoky Mountain Christmas

That movie seems to play every year. The film's title song says that Christmas is not all about money; it's not all about presents; it's what you share with one another and how the kids are entertained.

When you're mountain people, you don't have money to go out and buy big ornaments for the tree and all of that. You don't have money to go out and buy presents. You make stuff for each other. You do things for your neighbors. You cook stuff. You just make the most of it. To me, that's what Christmas is about. That's the true meaning of Christmas.

What I remember best about the *Smoky Mountain Christmas* movie are the kids who played the orphans in it. They were adorable. Notice that there were seven of them, just like in *Snow White and the Seven Dwarfs.*

White Limozeen

(Dolly Parton / Mac Davis) 1990

A NO. 20 HIT ON THE COUNTRY CHARTS, this Hollywood-themed song was co-written with Mac Davis. It was the title tune of her 1990 LP, which won a Gold Record award. This album was produced by country/bluegrass star Ricky Skaggs (who first topped the charts with 1982's "Crying My Heart Out Over You," co-written by Dolly's childhood mentor Carl Butler). Skaggs was inducted into the Country Music Hall of Fame in 2018.

Fresh scrubbed, hot off the bus,
Dressed up and feeling good,
Eyes full of stars, a heart full of dreams,
Daisy Mae in Hollywood

Struttin' down that boulevard,
The Walkway of the Stars,
With a vision of her name in lights
Reflecting off the cars.

And dreaming of a white limozeen.
She wants to have a white limozeen.

Well the days to come were long and dark,
And the nights were hard and cold.
She met the devil in the City of Angels,
But she never lost her soul.

She kept her dreams close to her heart
Like a family photograph.
She cried sometimes and died sometimes,
But still knew how to laugh.

Dreaming of a white limozeen
Dreaming of a white limozeen

Now she's a-living her dreams like a movie
queen,
Diamond rings and all things good.
From the breadlines to the headlines,
She's the toast of Hollywood.

White limozeen
White limozeen

Now she's really riding high.
She's a woman of the world.
But deep inside she never changed.
She's the same old down-home girl.

And when the airplane brings the kinfolk
To visit for a while,
There's a friendly guy in a red bow tie
To take 'em around in style.

He drives 'em in a white limozeen.
She finally got a white limozeen.

Now she's a-living her dreams like a movie
queen,
Diamond rings and all things good.
From the breadlines to the headlines,
She's the toast of Hollywood.

REPEAT FIRST TWO VERSES

Limozeen
A white limozeen
A big white limozeen
Limozeen
A white limozeen
A big white limozeen
Limozeen
A white limozeen
A big white limozeen

DOLLY PARTON
IN
WHITE LIMOZEEN

"I feel that Ricky is more like me musically than anybody else I know. He understood the 'old Dolly,' as far as the pure mountain music and what country music really is."

I felt very strongly about Ricky Skaggs producing this record, because I feel that Ricky is more like me musically than anybody else I know. He understood the "old Dolly," as far as the pure mountain music and what country music really is. What I wanted to do was an album that was really authentic sounding.

A lot of people thought I had lost my mind. People even at the record company and even within my own management company were saying, "Are you crazy? What are you choosin' Ricky Skaggs for?" I said, "Well, I happen to believe that Ricky Skaggs is one of the most talented people in the music business." And Ricky did a wonderful, wonderful job. I loved working with him. He's so even tempered, has a great sense of humor, is sweet, and has great ears. Ricky was fantastic, just as I thought he would be.

The song "White Limozeen" came from a very funny place. When I was doing the *Dolly* TV series, I called Mac [Davis] to see if he'd be interested in writing some songs. He was thrilled. I had a limousine that was paid for by the studio. I called Mac up and said, "I'm comin' up to your house. We're gonna write like we're hungry again." Mac lives in a mansion in Beverly Hills. As we headed up the hill, I realized what I had said. I thought, "Oh sure, we're gonna write like we're hungry again, and here I go in a white limousine up to Mac's mansion."

When I got out of the car, I said to Mac, "I feel like such an idiot telling you we were gonna write like we were hungry. We have got to write something about a white limousine!"

He said, "Well, let's just do it." He got out his guitar and started picking. It turned out that we were very complementary as songwriters. We were matching each other line for line. We were impressed with each other. That was the first song we ever wrote together. The other one we wrote that night was "Wait 'Til I Get You Home."

My "White Limozeen" dress, designed by the late, great Tony Chase, was dripping with faux pearls.

OPPOSITE PAGE: It's hard to tell who is more tickled about meeting Wolfman Jack, me or my producer buddy Ricky Skaggs.

Straight Talk 1992

THIS IS THE TITLE of Dolly's 1992 film and its soundtrack album. Reviews generally praised the performances of Dolly and co-star James Woods, but the script was panned. The single only made it to No. 64 on the country charts.

Gimme some straight talk, straight talk
And hold the sugar please
Straight talk, straight talk
Sounds plenty sweet to me

Don't talk to me in circles
In some mumbo-jumbo jive
Gimme just straight talk, straight talk
And we're gonna be alright

'Cause I like to know just where I stand
I don't like guessing games
And I hate a bunch of gibberish
So just spit it out real plain

Don't use big educated words
From your BS degree
Straight talk, straight talk
Don't try BS-ing me

Straight talk, straight talk
Turn loose and let it go
You can tell me anything
Just like on Oprah's show

Just tell me how you really feel
Be on the up-and-up
With questions I can understand
For answers you can trust

Pick up the 'phone, you're not alone
We've all got something to say
So listen in and listen up
We'll find a better way

With honesty and common sense
It's really hard to miss
Straight talk, straight talk
Just tellin' it like it is

Straight talk, straight talk
There's nothing like the truth
Just tell me all your troubles
Pretend I'm Donahue

So don't be shy, 'cause we can talk
You know you've got a friend
Call me, call me
For simple straight talkin'

What's cookin', America?
Straight talk, straight talk
Straight talk, straight talk

So come on let's talk turkey
Just straight and to the point
About passions, about problems
About noses out of joint

Now I want you all to know
I care and I do understand
And hey, thanks for lending me an ear
Out there in radio land

Give me some straight talk, straight talk
Don't sugarcoat it please
Straight talk, straight talk
Sounds sweet enough to me

But don't talk to me in circles
In your mumbo-jumbo jive
Straight talk, straight talk
And we're gonna be alright

Straight talk, straight talk
Makes plenty sense to me
Don't talk to me in circles
In your mumbo-jumbo jive

Gimme just straight talk, straight talk
And we're gonna be alright
Gimme just straight talk, straight talk
And we're gonna be alright

Radio talk-show advice lady "Shirlee Kenyon" was right up my alley in *Straight Talk*. She was a character with the gift of gab and a down-to-earth approach to life. I like to think that I have good "horse sense," just like her.

I loved doing *Straight Talk*, because the character was very much like me. She was like a psychologist who had a radio show and gave out good advice. I threw in a lot of "Dolly-isms," a lot of me, when we were filming it. I guess I'm better [in movies] when I can just be myself.

When I wrote the songs for it, I realized that it's easier for me to write songs than it is for me to play a part. That's how I can really ad-lib whatever my wisdom is.

Pat Resnick, who wrote *9 to 5*, wrote this film, too. I thought it was a good idea for a show and that it was an entertaining movie. I had the best time doing it. I don't judge things by how much money they make or how good the reviews are. I just base it on how much fun it was or how much I got out of it.

We were in Chicago for about four months filming, and I just loved that town. We were there the whole summer, when the weather's great. The day we finished, somebody said, "You better get out of here, because this place is no place to be in the winter." On our way home, my bus was heading down the highway and somebody said, "God, it's snowing in Chicago. They are going to have a blizzard." We just missed it.

Big T 1991

AN ANTHEM FOR AND ABOUT TEXAS, this song title also references the name of her TV-movie character "Theola Rayfield." It was originally intended to be the title tune of the film, but the audience tittered when she announced this on *The Tonight Show*. The movie was retitled *Wild Texas Wind*, and she portrayed a battered woman opposite actor Gary Busey. To date, the song has never appeared on an album.

Cut my teeth on a cactus stalk.
In cowboy boots, I learned to walk.
Said my first words with a Texas drawl,
In Texas, the big "T."

Born and raised on the Texas plain,
In a Texas church, I's born again.
I swell with pride when I speak the name
Of Texas, or big "T."

CHORUS
Yippi-ki-yi-yay, yippi-ki-yo, yippi-ki-yee,
big "T."
Yippi-ki-yi-yay, yippi-ki-yo, yippi-ki-yee,
big "T."

Got the best and got the most,
The best cowboys and rodeos,
Prettiest girls and livestock shows
In Texas, the big "T."

Bluest skies you've ever seen.
Home of Bob Wills' western swing,
The biggest fans and biggest teams
In Texas, big "T."

REPEAT CHORUS

Native of the Lone Star State,
Greatest place God ever made,
Love you more than I can say,
Sweet Texas, big "T."

Might boast too much and talk too loud.
Can't deny the fact I'm proud.
You've placed your brand on me,
Big "T," big "T."

REPEAT CHORUS TWICE

"Big T" stood for "Big Texas." So that's what I wanted to call the movie. Someone said, "You can't call it that." I said, "Why not?" They said, "Because everybody's going to think it stands for your big T's." I said, "That goes to show you how everybody's mind goes to that place." Any titty joke, they'll go for. So we wound up calling it *Wild Texas Wind*.

In the film, Gary Busey was being abusive. "Gary Abusey" is what I said as a joke. I thought he did a really good job, but people didn't like to see me getting beat up. I think my fans don't want to see me playing that kind of role.

Unlikely Angel 1996

ALTHOUGH ITS LYRIC does not exactly mirror the film's plot, this song became the title of Dolly's 1996 TV movie about an angel trying to win her wings. She later included it on her 2014 album *Blue Smoke*.

Like the Phoenix
From the ash and dirt
I rose up from the pain and hurt
When I was at my very worst
I found you

Thought I could never love again
When a spark of light came beaming in
A thread of hope
For me to spin around you

Unlikely angel
Standing there in front of me
As if you were my destiny
Like we were always meant to be together

Unlikely angel
It feels so right inside your love
Like God has sent you from above
To honor, cherish, and to love forever

The smile upon your angel face
The Heaven in your eyes replace
The Hell that I've been going through
Before you

How long have you been there for me
I once was blind but now I see
A future full of hope, how I adore you
Unlikely angel

Standing there in front of me
As if you were my destiny
Like we were always meant to be together
Unlikely angel

You never know where one might be
In sacred halls or crowded streets
But God sent one straight down to me from
Heaven
Unlikely angel
Unlikely angel
Ah ah, unlikely angel
Unlikely angel
Ah ah, unlikely angel

Blue Valley Songbird 1998

THIS WAS THE TITLE TUNE of Dolly's 1998 Lifetime TV movie, which was filmed in Nashville. The song also became a track on her *Hungry Again* CD the following year.

She was born in a place called Blue Valley
At the foot of the Tennessee hills
With the blue birds and blue bells
And blue mountain water
And the sound of the blue whippoorwill

But there was no peace in the valley
Her daddy, a cruel, ruthless man
Used and abused her mind and her body
So her mama said, "Run while you can"

So at fifteen she took to the highway
Belongings and guitar in hand
And she buried herself in her music
The one thing she did understand

And she sings like a bird and she writes
like a poet
Her voice has that high, lonesome sound
She hurts, and her songs are the best way
to show it
So the Blue Valley Songbird keeps
traveling around

She hopes someday she will make it
And everyone says that she will
When she comes to town, crowds
flock around
To see the girl from the Tennessee hills

She writes her letters back home to her mama
In care of the preacher in town
They're sacred to her so she reads them
at church
And so her daddy cannot track her down

And she sings like a bird and she cries
like a baby
Whenever she turns off the lights
She's a whole lot lonesome and a little
bit crazy
From mem'ries and miseries and dreams
gone awry

Blue dress, blue shoes, a blue Cadillac
A band dressed in blue by her side
Instruments tied to the top and the back
'Cause the Blue Valley Songbird is singing
tonight

One nighters, honky tonks, years flying by
She's never made it, but Lord knows she tries
Expressing the feelings she holds inside
And the Blue Valley Songbird is singing
tonight

Oh the Blue Valley Songbird is singing
tonight
And she sings like a bird and she writes
like a poet

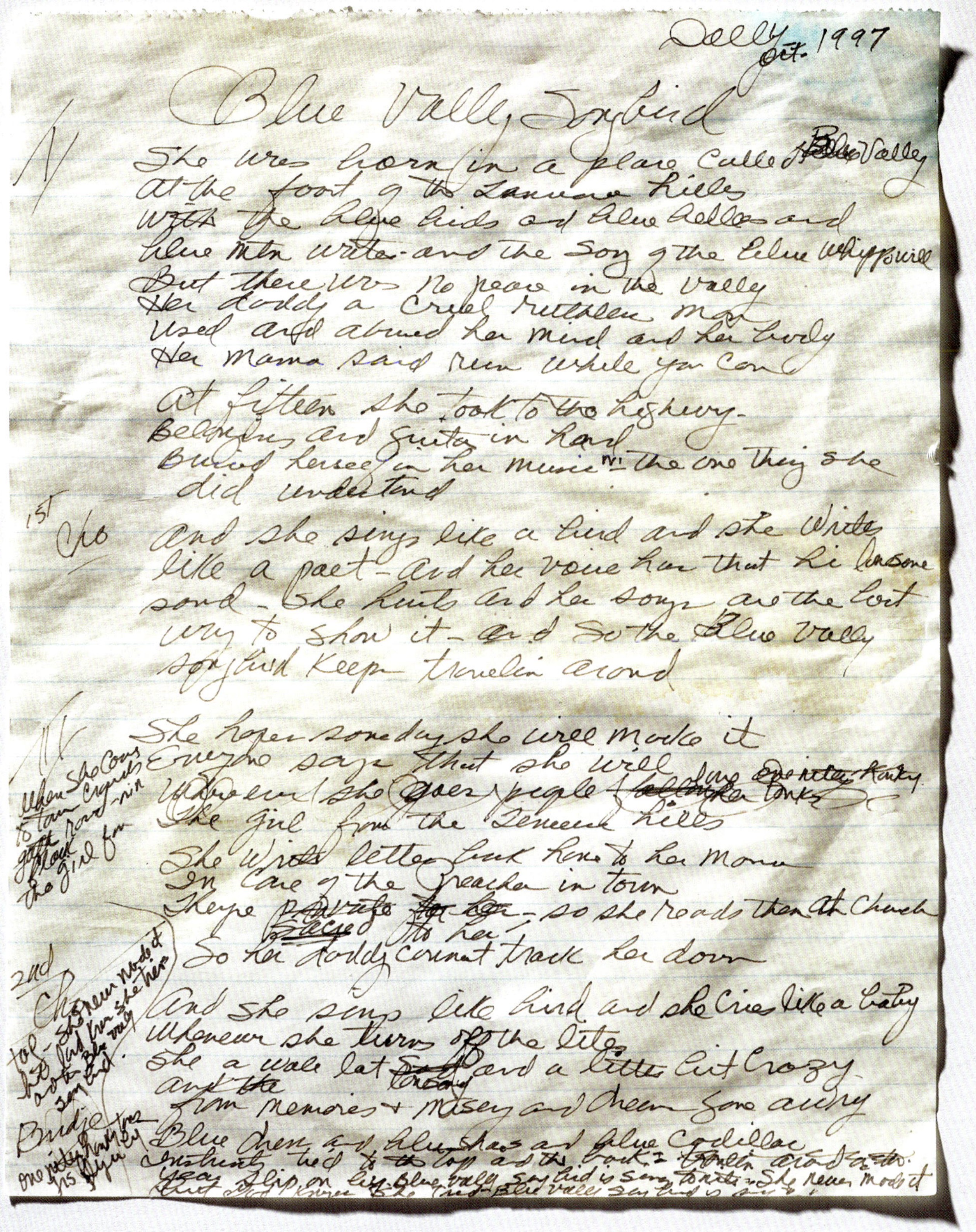
Dolly Oct. 1997

Blue Valley Songbird

I just love that title. There's a Blue Valley somewhere down around Chattanooga. I remember seeing that town's name and thinking, "The Blue Valley songbird is singing tonight." Then I thought I would create a girl singer for the lyric who is kind of "out there" in her personality. I think every woman in country music is "a little bit crazy," like the song says. I liked singing the song, because it has kind of an old-time country feeling about it.

I enjoyed doing the movie, too. I got the chance to really act.

Not Enough

With Queen Latifah 2012

THIS IS THE LEADOFF SONG on the soundtrack album of the movie *Joyful Noise*. It is one of three that Dolly wrote for the film.

(Choir)
Not enough, not enough, not enough love.
Not enough, not enough, not enough love.

(Queen Latifah)
There's no room for hate in a heart full of
kindness.
How long will it take then for that to ring
true?

(Dolly)
Our chances are fading, just stop all this
blindness.
A new world is waiting for us if we do.
But there's not enough love in our hearts.

(Dolly)
They write songs about it,
They put it in movies
How life would be better with just enough
love.

(Dolly and Queen Latifah)
Still we tend to doubt it
Though sometimes it moves us.
We settle for little when we could have much.
'Cause there's not enough love in our
hearts . . . no, no.

CHORUS
Not enough love, there's not enough love,
There's not enough love in our hearts.
There's not enough love, there's not enough
trust,
And it tends to keep us apart.
There's not enough carin'
There's not enough sharin'
Too much me, me, me and too much double
darin'.
Too much delayin' and not enough prayin',
I'm just sayin' it's not enough.
Just sayin' it's not enough.

(Dolly)
Hell and its road paved with real good
intentions.
We don't tend the garden; we just plant
the seed.
Promises broken, too many to mention
While people go hungry and naked in need.
'Cause there's not enough love in our hearts.

(Queen Latifah)
I often wonder what God must be thinkin'.
Lookin' down on us, He'd have to be sad.

(Dolly and Queen Latifah)
We'd better wise up now before we start
sinkin',
He gave us free choice, but we're messin'
up bad.
'Cause there's not enough love in our hearts,
No, not enough love in our hearts.

There's not enough love, there's not enough
love,
There's not enough love in our hearts.
There's not enough love and there's not
enough trust,
But it's never too late to start.
Why can't we try harder?
Why can't we see farther?
Why can't we do better?
Love's a good starter.
Too much nay-sayin',
And not enough prayin'.
I'm just sayin', it's not enough, it's not
enough.
Just sayin', it's not enough.

Not enough, not enough, not enough love
Not enough, not enough, not enough trust
Too much cryin', way too much lyin'
Too much hatin' and not enough tryin'
Not enough stayin', too much goodbye-in'
It's just not enough, not enough,
It's not, it's just not enough.

Not enough, not enough, there's not enough
love,
Not enough, not enough, between us
Let's build a foundation, change situation,
Strive for salvation, heed this revelation,
Fall on your knees and avoiding temptation.
I'm just sayin' it's just not enough, no-no-no.
I'm sayin' it's just not enough.
Oh, there's not enough, there's not enough,
There's not enough love.

(Choir)
Not enough, not enough, there's not enough
trust
Not enough, there's not enough
Just not enough
There's not enough love in our hearts
Not enough, there's not enough love, no, no
There's not enough love in our hearts
Not enough love in our hearts
Just not enough
Not enough, we're not doin' enough
Not enough

Joyful Noise is another one of those movies I did that didn't set the woods on fire. I wish it had done better, because of all the good people involved. But it was a hit with me; I had a great time with everyone.

We had wonderful dancers and singers. They were so giving and just so sweet. It was a little hard for me, because I really can't dance. But here I was, this little, white, sawed-off honky, up there with all these great rhythmic people. We had the best time.

Working with Queen Latifah was great, too. Her real name is Dana Owens, by the way. My mother's people are the Owens family. I said, "We must be kin. We must be kissing cousins or something." We had a good time together.

"Not Enough" is about treating each other with love. When I was honored by Musi-Cares [in 2019], Mavis Staples sang this song on the show. I was so excited by that, because I love Mavis.

Girl in the Movies

(Dolly Parton / Linda Perry) 2018

PART OF THE SOUNDTRACK of the Jennifer Aniston–Danielle Macdonald film *Dumplin'*, this song was nominated for a Grammy Award. This marked Dolly's forty-ninth Grammy nomination. The plot of the film centered on an overweight girl who is an obsessive Dolly Parton fan.

Popcorn, soda, box of Raisinets
Velvet-cushioned seats and soft armrests
Best seat in my favorite movie house
Start my dreaming as the lights go out
Up on the silver screen, I picture me
Living out my passions, hopes, and fantasies

I want to be the girl in the movies
The one with the glint in her eyes
The girl that seldom loses
Beautiful, with grace and style
Acting out her story
Standing in her glory
Happy ever after
I want to be the girl in the movies

Wish I had a nickel for each dime I've spent
Watching others live their lives with
confidence
Here's a preview of some things to come
It's not too late for me to be someone
I can't keep living in their make-believe
Coming attractions will be starring me

I want to be the girl in the movies
The one with the stars in her eyes (In her
eyes)
She gets the roles she chooses
She can laugh or she can cry
Acting in her story
Standing in her glory
Always happy endings
I want to be the girl in the movies

It's time I show the world just what I'm about
I'm steppin' up and I'm steppin' out
I'm feelin' bold and I'm feelin' proud
I want to be that girl

I want to be the girl in the movies
I want to be the girl in the movies

Gonna stand up
And I'm gonna matter
'Cause I've had enough of my dreams being
shattered
And I've had enough of my tears being
splattered
I've already been that girl

Oh, I want to be (I want to be)
I want to be (I want to be)
I want to be the girl in the movies
I want to be (I want to be)
Hey look at me (Hey look at me)
I want to be the girl in the movies
I want to shine (I want to shine)
I want to shine (I'm gonna shine)
It's my time
And I want to shine
I want to be happy, I want to be free
Just like the girl in the movies

Since this movie was about my music and about me, they contacted me to ask if they could license some of my songs that they wanted to use. I said, "Of course." Then they asked if I would write a theme song and if I would do it with Linda Perry. She had gotten involved with the film early on.

So Linda and I got together, and we clicked just like that. We started writing all kinds of stuff. All of a sudden, we said, "Maybe we could just do a whole [soundtrack] album."

"Girl in the Movies" was one of the first things that we wrote. It was about the little *Dumplin'* character. She lived in a kind of fantasy world through my music.

Linda Perry has worked with big pop stars like Pink, Alicia Keys, Christina Aguilera, Celine Dion, and Gwen Stefani, so I was pleased that she wanted to work with me on our country songs for *Dumplin'*.

Hollywood Potters 1982

DOLLY'S EXPOSURE TO HOLLYWOOD inspired several songs. This one appeared on her album *Heartbreak Express*.

Mothers hold on to your sons and your daughters
Should Hollywood claim them, you'll hold them no more
Cause they'll become clay to the Hollywood potters
And there's no escape once they walk through that door

CHORUS
Hollywood, Hollywood, Dungeon of Drama
Center of sorrow, city of schemes
Hollywood, Hollywood, Terrace of Trauma
Palace of promises, dealer in dreams

Some, they go hungry and some go insane
Some go to the bottle and some to the veins
Some become users and some become used
And some even make it, but most never do

REPEAT CHORUS

You spin them around like a merry-go-round
You mold them and shape them and then throw them down
All of your glitter and all of your gold
Is that what you give in exchange for a soul

'Cause they sell their souls for the likes of you
While you chew up and spit out what you cannot use

Mothers hold on to your sons and your daughters
Should Hollywood claim them, you'll hold them no more
Cause they'll become clay to the Hollywood potters
And there's no escape once they walk through that door

REPEAT CHORUS

I think being in Hollywood opened up a whole other world for me as a songwriter. I always thought that Hollywood was this great, glamorous place—a Disneyland with all the stars you see on TV. It was a real eye-opener the first time I went there. It was the most depressing place I'd ever seen. Down on Hollywood Boulevard there were all these people on the streets, homeless people and pitiful, crazy nuts running around. Oh my Lord, it was just a horrible setting.

When we first went there as musicians playing in places like the Roxy and staying at the Holiday Inn, I felt I was in a really strange town. There was weird craziness. It was not what I thought it was going to be.

Even when I had the chance to live in better quarters, I could see how depressing it still could be. All the rich people live in other areas. So I got to where I could see the good side of it.

Still, I would see these young people who'd come there and be willing to sell their souls to make it in show business. They'll do whatever they have to do, like the "casting couch." If their plans don't work out, they wind up selling themselves on the streets to get money for shooting up dope.

I wrote "Hollywood Potters" when I was doing [the movie] *9 to 5*. This one kid, an extra, killed himself. He was a struggling actor who believed himself to be a finer actor than to be working as "atmosphere," as they called it.

I think this song really nails what Hollywood's about. It's a "dungeon of drama." That's what it really is, a "dealer in dreams."

Sandy's Song 1979

THIS SONG WAS DEDICATED to Dolly's beloved manager, Sandy Gallin (1940–2017), the man who guided her to multimedia superstardom. Dolly and Sandy formed the movie-production company Sandollar Productions. It won an Academy Award in 1990 for the AIDS documentary *Common Threads: Stories from the Quilt* and went on to produce such popular fare as *Buffy the Vampire Slayer*, *Sabrina*, and *Father of the Bride* (with Steve Martin). "Sandy's Song" is set to the ancient English melody of "Greensleeves," whose authorship is often ascribed to King Henry VIII (1491–1547). It was not published until 1580. This is also the tune of the Christmas carol "What Child Is This?"

Sometimes I think of you, and tears fill my eyes
To think of the meaning you've given my life
You've touched me in places no one ever reached
You've given me reason and cause to believe

You are my rainbow; you've colored my life
And you are my sunshine; I'm warm in your light
You are my fountain that never runs dry
You're my inspiration, my reason to try

CHORUS
I'll love you 'til green grass turns lavender blue
And all the stars fall from Heaven and vanish
like dew
When horses and chariots chase down the wind
That's when I'll leave you, I'll love you 'til then

REPEAT CHORUS

That's when I'll leave you, I'll love you 'til then
That's when I'll leave you, yes
I'll leave you then
I'll need you 'til then
I'll love you 'til then

I'm drawn to weird, unusual, strange people, and Sandy fit all of that. Sandy Gallin was the character of the world. He was smart and funny and clever. He was quirky and nuts.

He knew the words to every song of every Broadway musical. And he would sing them, just for fun, right in the middle of a restaurant or something. I'd be going, "Sandy, hold it down." He would pull things like that just to embarrass me. Later, it's the kind of thing that makes a great memory.

There was no damper on his spirits. He wanted to be a star, at one time. Since he was a little boy, he'd gone to every movie and every Broadway show.

He was gay, and that's how we could get away with doing so many things together. Nobody was threatened by that. I was in no danger of him coming on to me. We could go anywhere and have fun doing it.

We were so close and our relationship was so loving. We were from two completely different worlds, but we just clicked, somehow. He was just one of those friends that you find who you just know are going to be your friend forever.

He knew how to put things together. He knew how to push people to get the deal he wanted. He was so smart. He added so much to my career and to my life. He was my buddy, and I miss him so bad. There are just some spirits you can't imagine being gone.

I wrote this song because I wanted to give him something. If it ever made any money, I was going to give him half of it. It's called "Sandy's Song," but it has nothing to do with Sandy, really. I just wanted him to have a song because I loved him. It's a pretty little song with a great melody, "Greensleeves."

Sandy was so dear to me. He was so crazy that he'd stop his car in the middle of the street and go buy donuts while I was still sitting in it, cringing from the honking horns from other drivers. After his years as my manager, he became a fabulous decorator who worked on big movie-star homes.

Travelin' Thru 2005

DOLLY WROTE THIS FOR THE FILM *Transamerica*, which centered on a transgender character. She earned her second Academy Award nomination for this composition and performed it on the 2006 Oscar telecast.

Well I can't tell you where I'm going, I'm not sure of where I've been
But I know I must keep travelin' 'til my road comes to an end
I'm out here on my journey, trying to make the most of it
I'm a puzzle, I must figure out where all my pieces fit

Like a poor wayfaring stranger that they speak about in song
I'm just a weary pilgrim trying to find what feels like home
Where that is no one can tell me, am I doomed to ever roam
I'm just travelin', travelin', travelin', I'm just travelin' on

Questions I have many, answers but a few
But we're here to learn, the spirit burns, to know the greater truth
We've all been crucified and they nailed Jesus to the tree
And when I'm born again, you're gonna see a change in me

God made me for a reason and nothing is in vain
Redemption comes in many shapes with many kinds of pain
Oh sweet Jesus if You're listening, keep me ever close to You
As I'm stumblin', tumblin', wonderin', as I'm travelin' thru

I'm just travelin', travelin', travelin', I'm just travelin' thru
I'm just travelin', travelin', travelin', I'm just travelin' thru

Oh sometimes the road is rugged, and it's hard to travel on
But holdin' to each other, we don't have to walk alone
When everything is broken, we can mend it if we try
We can make a world of difference, if we want to we can fly

Goodbye little children, goodnight you handsome men
Farewell to all you ladies and to all who knew me when
And I hope I'll see you down the road, you meant more than I knew
As I was travelin', travelin', travelin', travelin', travelin' thru

I'm just travelin', travelin', travelin', I'm just travelin'

Drifting like a floating boat and roaming like the wind
Oh give me some direction Lord, let me lean on You
As I'm travelin', travelin', travelin' thru
I'm just travelin', travelin', travelin', I'm just travelin' thru

I'm just travelin', travelin', travelin', I'm just travelin' thru

Like the poor wayfaring stranger that they speak about in song
I'm just a weary pilgrim trying to find my own way home
Oh sweet Jesus if You're out there, keep me ever close to You
As I'm travelin', travelin', travelin', as I'm travelin' thru

Going to the Academy Awards is so exciting. There are movie stars everywhere. I'm singing "Travelin' Thru" at a pre-Oscars party in this photo. I also got to sing it the next day on the Big Show.

I got involved with *Transamerica* because of the director, Duncan Tucker. He loved my music, so he called me to see if I was even interested in writing anything about that subject. I have a friend and a relative who are transgender. I said, "I'll be happy to make a stab at that." It came really easily, because I had personal stuff to draw from. I completely relate to anybody who's not allowed to be themselves and to be all that they feel they can be. I know gay people who are not accepted and have to live in the shadows.

The [movie] story is about transgender people. I tried to write "Travelin' Thru" from a broader scale, to make it about people who are trying to find out who they are or what their purpose is in life. It's about people and their life's journey: "I don't know where I'm going. I don't even know where I've been."

I think the song turned out really good. Duncan was in the studio helping me when we recorded it. He put in a lot of good ideas. It was really a labor of love.

I was honored to be nominated for an Oscar for "Travelin' Thru." I got to sing it on the Oscars, so that was good enough for me. The songwriters who did win [for "It's Hard Out Here for a Pimp" from *Hustle & Flow*] were Tennessee guys from Memphis, so that was fine. "It's Hard Out Here for a Pimp," and it's hard out here for a country singer, too.

CHAPTER

10

Eagle When She Flies

DESPITE DOLLY'S NEW MOVIE STARDOM AND ONGOING MUSIC SUCCESS, the early 1980s were the most troubled years in her life. She was beset by both physical and psychological difficulties.

She was financially stressed in the wake of the Porter Wagoner litigation. She suffered gynecological problems resulting in hospitalizations. She endured death threats. She spent years battling her weight. She felt betrayed by trusted associates and went into a deep depression.

One bright spot was a hugely successful 1983 tour of the British Isles. It resulted in a BBC TV special that aired in the United States on HBO as *Dolly Parton in London*.

In the late 1980s, Dolly Parton regained her footing. She was voted into the Nashville Songwriters Hall of Fame in 1986, the same year that her Dollywood theme park opened in East Tennessee.

Dolly turned forty while she was recording the landmark *Trio* album with Linda Ronstadt and Emmylou Harris. During 1987 and 1988, that collection earned her hits, awards, and critical acclaim. In addition, with more than three million in sales, *Trio* became her best-selling album to date.

In 1987, she starred in her own ABC TV variety series, was honored with a statue in front of the Sevier County Courthouse, and moved from her longtime label home RCA to sign with Columbia Records. This resulted in a flurry of new songwriting successes. In 1988, Dolly was chosen to be the first woman to host the CMA Awards.

In 1989, she co-starred in the hit film *Steel Magnolias* alongside Sally Field, Olympia Dukakis, Shirley MacLaine, Daryl Hannah, and Julia Roberts. Dolly capped the 1980s by hosting *Saturday Night Live*.

The music video era had begun with the launching of MTV (1981) and CMT (1983), and by 1990, Dolly already had eight music videos. During the next three years, she doubled that number. In the early 1990s, she also continued to place hits on the country charts. She was increasingly asked to participate on recordings with such superstars as Julio Iglesias, Smokey Robinson, George Jones, and Neil Diamond.

This was an era of huge changes in the music industry, but Dolly kept pace. These are the songs that carried her into the early 1990s.

I already had big pop hits and Hollywood success, but my top-selling music was still in front of me. My biggest-selling album was recorded with Emmylou Harris, left, and Linda Ronstadt. Linda was voted into the Rock & Roll Hall of Fame [in 2014], and Emmy is in the Country Music Hall of Fame [2008].

Heartbreak Express 1982

THIS SONG BECAME A NO. 7 COUNTRY HIT and the title tune of Dolly's 1982 album. In 1997, Bill Grant & Delia Bell transformed "Heartbreak Express" into a bluegrass tune.

Packin' my suitcase,
Writin' a tear-stained goodbye note.
Sayin' so long to a love gone wrong,
And that's all she wrote.
Leavin' behind what once was mine
With sad regrets.
But it's all gone now, and I'm leavin' town
On the Heartbreak Express.

Walkin' in the rain with a heart full of pain
To the train depot.
The only thing that's gonna keep
Me warm now is my overcoat .
Lost and lonely,
Waitin' in line at the ticket desk.
Hey mister, won't you give me a
one-way ticket
On the Heartbreak Express?

I'm gonna roll on down the line.
I'm gonna go so far I'm gonna get it off
my mind.
It hurts to know it ain't enough when you
give your best.
Got a ticket to ride, and I'm leavin' tonight
On the Heartbreak Express.

Oh, I couldn't hold a candle
To the flaming beauty that caught his eye.
It's killin' me now,
But I won't stay around and let him watch
me die.
Oh, it just goes to show you never do know
'Cause I never would'a guessed.
I'd be sittin' here now on a train,
sorrow-bound
Called the Heartbreak Express.

I'm gonna roll on down the line.
I'm gonna go so far I'm gonna get it off
my mind.
Maybe someday, somewhere, someway
I will forget.
But there's no goin' back, so roll down
the track
You ole Heartbreak Express.

Feelin' alone while a low whistle moans
On the Heartbreak Express.
Roll on, roll on down the line.
I'm gonna get it off my mind.

Roll on, roll on, roll on down the line.
Got a ticket to ride so I'm leavin' tonight
On the Heartbreak Express.
Roll on, roll on, roll on.

You know what they say, that which does not kill us makes us glad it didn't. Here I am, smiling after a ride on the "Heartbreak Express."

During the early '80s, I went through a lot of health problems and emotional things. I was overweight and having female problems that can affect your mind. I really went through a bad time.

When I look back, I really feel like everything in my life has been for a reason. I think God just smacked me down. That was a hard time, but it made me understand other people a lot better. I related to how alcoholics become alcoholics. I related to how drug addicts become drug addicts. Sometimes your pain is just so great you can't hardly bear it on your own. I completely had an insight into other people's sorrows.

I had to take a good look at myself. I had to tear everything down, reshape myself, and get some priorities in order, so that I could pick up, move on, and become bigger than I ever was before. And I think that's exactly what happened.

It was all meant to be, because I really became a better person. I became a better writer, too. Even during the time when I was really not in a good place, I was always able to write songs. Songwriting was my therapy, because I did not go to a therapist. My music has always been my best doctor. My guitar and my words always get me through whatever slump I'm in. That's what helped me get myself back together, get myself back in shape, and get myself out of that whole world of darkness.

"Heartbreak Express" was a song that I wrote during that lower time in my life. So was "What a Heartache You Turned Out to Be" [in the movie *Rhinestone*]. Both of them were "heart" songs. "Heartbreak Express" was saying, "I've just gotta get up, get on this train, and get out of here. I've got to move on down the line and get right on out of this heartache."

In addition to writing, traveling is great therapy. I'm sure my subconscious was making that feeling into a story and a song. But it was really about just moving on, in general.

A Gamble Either Way 1983

THIS SONG APPEARED ON DOLLY'S Top 10 hit album *Burlap & Satin*.

Being born was the worst and the first mistake
I ever made.
The doctor didn't spank me, he just slapped
me in the face.
And the cup of love was always quenching
someone else's thirst,
Leaving me to swallow the bitter taste of hurt.

'Cause I was raised an orphan, never wanted
as a kid
Until the year I turned thirteen.
Then everybody did.
Strangers passed me back and forth. Men just
took me as they pleased.
And others had a Cinderella slave to cook and
clean and weep.

Though the deck is stacked against you, win
or lose, you have to play
The hand that life has dealt you, and it's a
gamble either way.

On a dust road at fifteen in a yellow
cotton dress,
With the desert sun like an angry dragon
breathing down my neck,
And the dry cracked plains would make me
think of a prehistoric time.
Or should I fear what lay before me less than
what I'd left behind?

A fifteen-year-old girl don't have no trouble
hitching rides
But sometimes when you're riding free,
you'll pay the highest price.
On back roads and in back seats and in a
cheap highway motel
But what's a few more strangers in a life of
nothing else?

Sixteen caught me crying, underneath the
scarlet light
On the doorstep of a stranger on a cold and
rainy night.
When I walked into the parlor here, other
pieces seemed to fit.
I was good at pleasing strangers, so I made
the most of it.

Either way, it's all a gamble, so view the
stakes and know the odds.
And lay your cards upon the table. Do all the
dealing from the top.

Sometimes I start a song just because I love a title, and it was like that with "A Gamble Either Way." I was trying to write about all the chances we take, all the troubles we make, and all the gambles we take. Life is a gamble, and that idea just sounded good to me.

I was inspired by a distant cousin of mine. She was a beautiful, beautiful girl who could not be happy with the poor life we were living, and someone told her she could be a model. She thought she could be more than what she was ever going to be back home. So she met someone who took her to New York, and she became an escort. She worked in the prostitution business for years and years and years.

She eventually met someone, like the Julia Roberts character in *Pretty Woman*. She later married and had a wonderful life. She turned out to be a wonderful person. But that's where I started from to make up that song's story.

Could I Have Your Autograph 1987

THIS SONG APPEARED ON DOLLY'S *Rainbow* album.

Hello, I don't know you from Adam, you don't know me from Eve.
I just came here tonight 'cause I was lonely.
You're no Elvis Presley, I'm no Marilyn Monroe.
But I do think you're sexy, just thought I'd tell you so.

Hey could I have your autograph
Your name and your number on a small photograph?
I'd like to know you and what you're all about.
Hey could I have your autograph?

I've had my eyes on you and you're worth lookin' at.
Could I ask you out, or should a lady do that?
You may not be famous, but you look like a star.
You should be in movies as cute as you are.

Hey could I have your autograph
Your name and your number on a small photograph?
Could I interest you in a romance, perhaps?
Hey could I have your autograph?

Got my heart in my hands and my head in the clouds
And you're everything every girl dreams about.
And being with you would be Heaven, no doubt.
What I wouldn't do for your autograph.

Oh could I have your autograph?
Oh could I have your autograph?

Hey could I have your autograph?
I like your body, could I help you work it out
Maybe moving to the music playing on the phonograph?
Hey could I have your autograph?

Oh could I have your autograph?
You know you're just the kind to makes a woman real proud.
Would you take a chance on a girl from the South?
Could I have your autograph?

I know exactly how men are, so I used a pickup line that a man might use, like "What's your sign?" or "Whose pretty little girl are you?" In this case, it was "Could I have your autograph, your name, and your number on a small photograph?" The song does say, "Could I ask you out, or would a lady do that?" But I don't think that's the case with women anymore. Things are different for them these days.

The Pain of Loving You

With Linda Ronstadt and Emmylou Harris
(Dolly Parton / Porter Wagoner) 1987

1987'S *TRIO* LP teaming Dolly with Linda Ronstadt and Emmylou Harris was a landmark of women's music. Both Linda and Emmylou maintained that Dolly was that collection's artistic focus. This Dolly song was previously recorded in 1971 as a duet with Porter Wagoner. After the *Trio* version, it became evergreen, with versions by Ronnie Reno (2002), Patty Loveless (2008), and others.

You just can't stand to see me happy.
Seems you hurt me all you can.
Still I go on loving you.
But I never understand.

CHORUS
Oh, the pain of loving you,
Oh, the mis'ry I go through.
Never knowing what to do,
Oh, the pain of loving you.

To love and hate at the same time,
The line between the two is fine,
But two have bound me heart and soul,
So strong that I can't let you go.

REPEAT CHORUS

Oh, the pain of loving you . . .

The *Trio* album was something that each of the three of us was just as excited about as the other two were. Ever since we met in LA when we were all young, we'd always wanted to do something together. When we finally got to do it, we knew it was special. It's some of the best music that I have ever been a part of, and working with the two of them was just wonderful.

I was very honored to get some of my songs on that album. "The Pain of Loving You" is one that Porter and I had worked on together. Then the trio did a great version of it. The song is just such a singable, straight-ahead country melody, the kind of melody that lends itself to harmonies. It was the perfect song for three-part harmony. Just perfect.

The famous western-wear designer Manuel created our outfits for the cover of the *Trio* album. Mine is on display in my museum with a photo of the album jacket nearby.

Appalachian Memories 1983

THIS ANTHEM DESCRIBES THE EPIC, twentieth-century migration of Southerners to Northern factories and its emotional impact on those who lived it. Dolly featured it on 1983's *Burlap & Satin*. The following year, Jane Fonda won an Emmy Award for *The Dollmaker*, which dramatized the song's theme.

You oughta go north, somebody told us
'Cause the air is filled with gold dust
And fortune falls like snowflakes in your hands.
Now I don't recall you said it,
But we'd lived so long on credit,
And so we headed out to find our Promised Land.

Just poor Appalachian farm folk
With nothing more than high hopes,
We hitched our station wagon to a star
But our dreams all fell in on us
'Cause there was no land of promise
And it's a stuggle keepin' sight of who you are.

CHORUS
Oh and these Northern nights are dreary,
And my Southern heart is weary.
I wonder how the old folks are back home.
But I'll keep leanin' on sweet Jesus.
I know He'll love and guide and lead us.
Appalachian memories keep me strong.

Ya know I've been thinkin' a whole lot lately
About what's been and what awaits me.
It takes all I've got to give what life demands.
You go insane if you give in to it.
Life's a mill and I've been through it.
I'm just thankful I'm creative with my hands.

REPEAT CHORUS

I'll keep lookin' to the Father.
Keep our heads above the water.
Appalachian memories keep me strong.

I do so relate to "Appalachian Memories," because my own daddy went up there to try and work in Detroit. Some of his brothers and friends had gone up there and were doing pretty good. But Daddy didn't fit in anywhere but in the mountains, and he came home after a very short while.

I was really inspired to pull from that experience, because so many of my people did that. Relatives and neighbors and friends moved their families during that period of time. I've got relatives who still live in those areas, in Ohio and Detroit.

At the time, Jane Fonda was doing a movie called *The Dollmaker*. I told her I had a perfect song for it, "Appalachian Memories." She had adapted the film from a book about that subject. They never did use the song, but I still think it would have been ideal.

Yellow Roses 1989

BETWEEN 1985 AND 1989, DOLLY had seven Top 10 hits written by others. "Yellow Roses" brought her back to No. 1 with one of her own songs. It was included on her *White Limozeen* album.

"Hello," you said the day we met,
Handing me a yellow rose.
You asked me out and to your surprise,
And to mine, I said I'd go.

I thought it so romantic
And I found you sweet and bold.
Though we'd only met, I still said, "Yes"
To a single yellow rose.

And for years to come you were the one
To sleep with me at night,
To laugh and talk and share my thoughts
And hold me when I'd cry.

And on every occasion
And for no good reason to
A big bouquet or a single yellow rose
Was sent from you.

CHORUS
Yellow roses, the color of sunshine.
You loved me at one time
Why did you have to go
Yellow roses, are you sending your new love
My bright yellow rosebuds? I still love you so

I never see a yellow rose
That I didn't think of you
It's still my favorite flower,
Though the yellow's turned to blue

The day you left, my teardrops fell
Upon your farewell note,
You said goodbye like you said hello,
With a single yellow rose.

REPEAT CHORUS TWICE

Even when I was sick, I was always writing. I never had a dry spell. But during that time, I was recording with a lot of people who had pop-music ideas of what I should be doing. For the style of what we were doing at the time, I guess I just went along with what the new producers I was working with wanted me to do. I was probably writing stuff that was too "country."

When I wrote "Yellow Roses," I knew I wanted it to be something sad, and I knew I had a good theme. I've always loved "Yellow Roses," so I was really happy when it became one of my songs that finally did so well during that period of time.

Romeo

With Billy Ray Cyrus & Friends 1993

DOLLY WAS JOINED ON THIS LIGHTHEARTED SONG by fellow country stars Pam Tillis, Kathy Mattea, Tanya Tucker, and Mary Chapin Carpenter, with Billy Ray Cyrus portraying the title character. Despite the star power and a popular music video, it only reached No. 27 on the country charts and No. 50 on the pop charts. The song is on Dolly's LP *Slow Dancing with the Moon*.

A cross between a movie star and a hero in a book
Romeo comes struttin' in, and everybody looks
'Cause he's just got that special thang that everybody needs
And everybody wants him, but not as bad as me.

Hey, Romeo, where art thou? Get out here on the floor.
I want to dance you, darlin', 'til you forget wherefore.
Let's two-step to a new step. We'll keep it all in line
And we'll call this the Romeo, 'cause you're so mighty fine.

Romeo, Romeo, Romeo come dance with me.
And that sexy little body beats all I've ever seen.
I ain't never seen a cowboy look that good in jeans.
My temperature keeps risin' every time we meet.

I may not be in love, but let me tell you, I'm in heat.
Romeo, Romeo, I just know I'll get you yet.
Romeo, Romeo, I want to be your Juliet.

CHORUS *(Billy Ray)*
So step it high, step it low
Step it out and in
Step to the side and let it slide
Then steppin' up again

Step on toes, it all goes, steppin' as you please
But I'm one step away from love so don't step out on me.
Romeo, Romeo, Romeo with the magic feet

REPEAT CHORUS *(Dolly and Billy Ray)*

But I'm one step away from love so don't step out on me
Romeo, Romeo, I just know I'll get you yet
Romeo, Romeo.

(Billy Ray)
Won't you be my Juliet?

Romeo, Romeo
Romeo, Romeo

I wrote "Romeo" about my nephew Bryan. When he was a teenager, he was the cutest thing, and all the girls were absolutely crazy about him. He was breaking one heart after another. I called him "Romeo." I kept saying to him, "You Romeo, one of these days you're going to get your heart broke like that." After I wrote it, I sang the song to him and the whole family, and we all got a kick out of it.

Then when Billy Ray [Cyrus] came along with "Achy Breaky Heart," and he was the cutest thing, too, I said, "Well, I'm going to record that song, and I'm going to get Billy Ray to be Romeo."

I thought it was a commercial little song. I thought, "Well, why not get as many in here as we can?" We brought in Tanya and Kathy and all the other girls. And we had a whole lot of fun. It didn't matter to me whether it was a hit or not, it was fun, and it was a "hit" with us.

Bryan still loves saying to people, "No, she did not write that about Billy Ray. She wrote that about me!" And I did!

We filmed the video for "Romeo" at a club in Murfreesboro, south of Nashville.

ABOVE: Kathy Mattea cast eyes on Billy Ray Cyrus with me.

TOP: From left are Mary Chapin Carpenter, me, Kathy, and Tanya Tucker with Billy Ray at far right. Pam Tillis is just off camera. At the end of the video, I wound up with "Romeo."

More Where That Came From 1993

THIS SONG STALLED AT NO. 58 on the country charts, but the popularity of the videos for "More Where That Came From" and "Romeo" probably explain why her *Slow Dancing with the Moon* album earned a Platinum Record certificate.

I've been through Hell and half of Louisiana
Lookin' for a man like you
I know you could have any woman you want
And I know you've had a few
I know I've got some stiff competition
They ain't got nothin' on me
'Cause I've got something that you've
been missin'
I practice what I preach

CHORUS
'Cause I wanna be your lover. I wanna be
your friend.
And I wanna be your full-time woman,
closer than your kin
I wanna be your satisfaction, be your
number one.
And just when you think I can't love you
any better,
Well, I have just begun
'Cause there's more where that came from
There's more where that came from

And I want your clothes in my closet
My name on your mail
And I want my love to be your faucet
Drinkin' from an endless well
I want your kids to call me mama
I want you to call me hon
I wanna be the one you love and honor
When it's all been said and done

REPEAT CHORUS TWICE

Yes, I wanna be your full-time woman
I wanna be that, I wanna be that
Oh, I wanna be your lover, lover, lover
I wanna be that, I wanna be that
And I wanna be your satisfaction
I wanna be that, I wanna be that

You never know what's going to be a hit. You just write them and sing them and hope for the best. When this song didn't become a big radio hit, I don't remember thinking about whether they loved me anymore or not. I don't remember having any major thoughts about it.

It's just that they weren't playing artists over a certain age. I thought, "Well, it doesn't matter if you have something good or not. It has more to do with an age limit." I think they wanted "new country," and I represented "old country." They probably thought I was "over" at that time.

I'll Make Your Bed 1993

THIS SONG WAS ON THE FLIP SIDE of Dolly's "More Where That Came From" single. Both songs appeared on her *Slow Dancing with the Moon* collection.

I'm not the kind of girl that married
dear Dad.
I don't bake apple pies and cookies
from scratch.
I'm not even handy with a needle or thread.
But you'll never go hungry, and I'll make
your bed.

CHORUS
I'll make your bed a place you can't wait
to go,
Softer than feathers and as sweet as a rose.
Smooth satin pillows I will fluff for your head.
And you'll want for nothin', and I'll make
your bed.

I'll love you to sleep at night, wake you with
a kiss.
Things that I can't do, I swear you
won't miss.
I promised forever on the day that we wed.
That's I love you truly, and I'll make
your bed.

Do-do-do-do-do-do, de-de-de-oh-h
I'll love you truly, and I'll make your bed.

I'll clothe you in dreams, or I will feed you
with love,
Show you a magic life that few have
dreamed of.
I know this can be the love you'll never regret.
'Cause I'm your forever, and I'll make
your bed.

REPEAT CHORUS

I'll love you to sleep at night, wake you with
a kiss.
Things that I can't do, I swear you won't
miss.
Forever and always I will prove what I said.
And love you a lifetime, and I'll make
your bed.
And you'll want for nothing, and I'll make
your bed.

Do-do-do-do-do-do, dumb-de-de oh-h
I'll love you truly, and I'll make your bed.

Do-do-do-do-do-do, da-de-de-de-oh-h
I'll love you truly, and I'll make your bed.

I'm not much of a homemaker. When I wrote this song, I was going, "I may not be the best cook in the world. I may not be the best sweeper or mopper. I may not be the best to do laundry. But I'll make your bed. I'm pretty good at that."

Actually, I'm getting better at all those other things as I get older. And I have always been a pretty good cook. I just don't like to clean up. Most guys won't go for that. They want you to cook *and* clean up.

Country Road

(Dolly Parton / Gary Scruggs) 1991

DOLLY'S CO-WRITER ON THIS SONG, Gary Scruggs, is the son of Hall of Fame banjo wizard Earl Scruggs (1924–2012), who helped give birth to the bluegrass-music genre in 1945. The single made it to No. 46 and is on *Eagle When She Flies*.

Saw you turnin' down Main Street
In your big, black, fancy car.
You were dressed up fit to kill
With a pretty girl on your arm.
You spun around and you headed uptown
Where the neon lights all shine.
Left me choking in a cloud of dust.
You never pay me no mind.

CHORUS
You're livin' in the fast lane.
I guess I'm just too slow.
I never wore silk or fancy furs,
Just plain ole calico.
I'll never be a fast-lane lover,
And they're the only kind you take uptown.
I am just a country road
That you keep turnin' down.

If you ever hit a dead-end street,
If it's love that you're looking for,
You can always turn around
And beat a path right to my door.

Do I have to draw you a map?
You seem to know your way around.
So when you're tired of spinnin' your wheels,
Baby, we can go to town.

REPEAT CHORUS

I am just a country road
That you keep turnin' down.
You're livin' in the fast lane.
I guess I'm just too slow.
I never wore silk or fancy furs,
Just plain ole calico.

OPPOSITE PAGE: You know what I always say, "Leave no rhinestone unturned." Not even on my musical instruments.

I got to know Gary Scruggs in the studio. He's so quiet, so I was always trying to bring him out, me and my big, loud mouth. One day, he was playing guitar on one of my [recording] sessions. During a break, he was playing this tune. I said, "What is that?" He said, "It's a song I'm writing." And I said, "Well, let's do it together." That turned out to be "Country Road."

I found him to be very interesting, very tenderhearted, and very creative, but very shy. He was so sensitive. He reminded me a lot of my brother Floyd. Gary was a joy to be around.

Let Her Fly

With Loretta Lynn and Tammy Wynette 1993

AS EVIDENCED BY *TRIO, 9 TO 5, Steel Magnolias*, and *Joyful Noise*, Dolly has often succeeded with female co-stars. She teamed up with her fellow Music Row groundbreakers Tammy Wynette (1942–1998) and Loretta Lynn for *Honky Tonk Angels* in 1993. The album included this song about a mother's death. Dolly's mom actually lived for a decade beyond this recording.

There's a wreath on the door.
She don't live here no more.
As of today, she flew home.
And we all gathered here in sorrow and tears.
It won't be the same with her gone.

There's a place on the hill
That's peaceful and still
Where she'll sleep beside Daddy again.
The ol' family tree is shedding its leaves,
But we'll all meet in Heaven again.

CHORUS
Oh, she's an angel. Let her fly, let her fly.
She's gone home to glory to her home in the sky.
When God sees her comin', Heaven's choir will smile
And sing, "Oh she's an angel, let her fly, let her fly.
Ooh, she's an angel, let her fly."

She used to rock me when I was a child.
Sing "Rock of Ages" and "In the Sweet By and By."
Her life wasn't easy, oh but how hard she tried.
You know she's an angel, Lord, so let her fly.

REPEAT CHORUS

Ooh she's an angel, let her fly.

Tammy Wynette, Loretta Lynn, and I with our buddy Mark Collie backstage at a media event for *Honky Tonk Angels*.

I love men. But I love my girls, too. I love singing and working with them. And it's true that I have had some of my biggest successes by working with women. I've had a great relationship with every guy that I've ever worked with. They "get" me, and I "get" them, and we always have fun. It's just that I have been most productive with the women, and I always get along with the gals. None of us have ever fought.

I love Tammy [Wynette] and Loretta [Lynn]. We're all very similar and were good friends. We were competing on the charts with our records, but we never took it personal. We were just happy that we were all doing good. And in the beginning, they were doing better than me.

There are no catfights. You are professionals, so you're going to work that way. You know your space. You know your place. It was the same way with Linda [Ronstadt] and Emmylou [Harris]. We're like sisters. I felt the same way about Tammy and Loretta.

When I wrote "Let Her Fly," I knew that Mama was never going to be dead to me, and she never will be. So in my song, I gave her wings, just as I'm sure God did in the spirit world. So the song was, "Lord, she's an angel, so let her get on up there and be with You, sailing around, being happy and healthy and looking down on all of us." It was more than just saying goodbye to Mama, whenever that time was going to be.

I think that's how everybody wants to think about their parents. It's like they are angels, so give them wings and let them go. My mother was very, very dear to me, to all of us.

Family

(Dolly Parton / Carl Perkins) 1991

AFTER BECOMING A 1950S ROCKABILLY STAR with "Blue Suede Shoes" and "Honey Don't," Carl Perkins (1932–1998) thrived as a member of the Johnny Cash road show and as the author of Cash's hit "Daddy Sang Bass." Still later, he became one of Dolly's favorite songwriting partners. This collaboration is possibly the first country song to mention the word "gay." It appeared on *Eagle When She Flies*.

When it's family, you forgive them
For they know not what they do
When it's family, you accept them
'Cause you have no choice but to
When it's family, they're a mirror
Of the worst and best in you

And they always put you to the test
And you always try to do your best
And just pray for God to do the rest

When it's family
Some are preachers, some are gay
Some are addicts, drunks, and strays
But not a one is turned away

When it's family
Some are lucky, others ain't
Some are fighters, others faint
Winners, losers, sinners, saints
It's all family

And when it's family, you trust them
And your heart's an open door
When it's family, you tolerate
What you'd kill others for
When it's family, you love and hate
And take then give some more

Somehow you justify mistakes
Try to find some better way
To solve the problems day to day
In the family
You take the trouble as it comes
And love 'em more than anyone
Good or bad or indifferent
It's still family

You choose your lovers
You pick your friends
Not the family that you're in
They'll be with you 'til the end
'Cause it's family

When it's family, you forgive them
For they know not what they do
When it's family, they're a mirror
Of the worst and best in you
When it's family, when it's family
Let me be all that I should be
To the family

Carl Perkins and I have always loved each other. Back in the day, we worked "package shows" together. He was a very special guy. We had him up at Dollywood to perform, doing his '50s stuff. That's when I got to know him more personally.

He lived down in Jackson [Tennessee]. He said, "Come on down here to Jackson. I've got a little studio, and we'll just write some stuff together." I said, "You know, I just might do that, because I've always just loved you to death, and I love your writing."

So I went down there and got me a little motel room as close as I could get to his house. The first time, I stayed down there for two or three days. We got in his studio and wrote our brains out. We had so much fun talking about our early days. Because he was as poor as Job's turkey, just like me. So we'd laugh about that.

We both came from big families. I said, "Let's write a song called 'Family.'" It fits everybody's family. We have some preachers. Some are gay. We've got crazy ones. We've got smart ones. Some are saints and some are druggies. I just put in everything that all families have, or at least certain families, like his and mine.

Even though it was a serious subject, you can imagine how much we laughed while we were writing it. He would relate certain stories, and so would I. It was so much fun working with him that after this first visit, I would go down there at different times to write more with him.

I'm "all ears" during one of my songwriting sessions with Rock & Roll Hall of Fame member Carl Perkins. He and his sons wrote my 1991 hit "Silver and Gold," and I always loved the times I spent writing with him in those days.

Eagle when She Flies

June 23, 1989

I

Shes been there God knows
shes been there
She has ~~been~~ and ~~seen~~ done
it all
Shes a woman ~~she can take~~ She knows how to
~~it~~ dish it out – or take it all
Tho her hearts as soft as feathers ~~she~~ still
~~still~~ she weathers stormy skies
~~Heaven knows how hard she tries~~
Shes a sparrow when shes broken
But shes an eagle when she flies

Chs

Gentle as the sweet magnolia
Strong as steele her faith + pride
An everlasting shoulder
The leaning post of life
She hurts deep and when she weeps
Shes fragile as a child
~~She~~ "a sparrow when – shes broken
an eagle when she flies

II

A Kaleidoscope of Colors
You can toss her round and round
You can keep her in your vision
But you'll never keep her down
She a mother shes a lover – shes a friend + shes a wife

Eagle When She Flies 1991

THIS SONG'S MUSIC VIDEO FEATURED images of women from all walks of life in a visual tapestry. Conservative radio programmers branded the single as "too feminist," hampering its airplay. It reached No. 33, was nominated for a Grammy Award, and is the title song of Dolly's Platinum-selling 1991 album.

She's been there, God knows, she's been there
She has seen and done it all
She's a woman, she knows how to
Dish it out or take it all

Her heart's as soft as feathers
Still she weathers stormy skies
And she's a sparrow when she's broken
But she's an eagle when she flies

A kaleidoscope of colors
You can toss her around and round
You can keep her in your vision
But you'll never keep her down

She's a lover, she's a mother
She's a friend and she's a wife
And she's a sparrow when she's broken
But she's an eagle when she flies

Gentle as the sweet magnolia
Strong as steel, her faith and pride
She's an everlasting shoulder
She's the leaning post of life

She hurts deep and when she weeps
She's just as fragile as a child
And she's a sparrow when she's broken
But she's an eagle when she flies

She's a sparrow when she's broken
But she's an eagle when she flies
Oh, bless her, Lord
She's an eagle when she flies

When we [Julia Roberts, Sally Field, Shirley MacLaine, Daryl Hannah, Olympia Dukakis, and Dolly] got together to film *Steel Magnolias*, we all knew who we were. We all had names and were important in our own ways. We all knew what our roles were. We never argued about anything. We just enjoyed being together and learning about each other. We enjoyed the things we could find out about each other's lives. When I worked with those women, they were like my sisters or my aunts or my cousins. I take to everybody as if they are family.

I wrote "Eagle When She Flies" to be the theme song for *Steel Magnolias*. That's why I used the lines "Gentle as the sweet magnolia, strong as steel, her faith and pride."

They wound up not using a theme song [of any kind] in the movie. I still think "Eagle When She Flies" is one of my best songs. I think it covers all kinds of women, "a kaleidoscope of colors."

I relate to eagles, somehow. Eagles are the strong ones, flying the hardest, the fastest, the highest. I didn't realize how much I write about eagles until somebody brought it to my attention. I must just relate to the idea of soaring. I like things with wings. If I ain't writing about angels, I'm writing about eagles or butterflies. I just love things that can move and get on out of here.

We have an eagle sanctuary at Dollywood, where we take injured eagles, nurture them, and release them back into the wild. Back when we started it, bald eagles were beginning to be extinct. We've helped to get it back to where they aren't so scarce anymore.

CHAPTER 11

HUNGRY AGAIN

DOLLY'S SONGWRITING ENTERED A NEW PHASE OF EXPERIMENTATION and creativity as she rounded out the 1990s and entered the new millennium. Her albums *Hungry Again* (1998) and *Halos & Horns* (2002) were widely praised as containing some of her finest songwriting yet.

Her established song catalog continued to pay dividends. In the wake of Whitney Houston's blockbuster, worldwide pop hit "I Will Always Love You" in 1992, dozens of artists recorded the song. As a result, Dolly reaped millions in royalties. Dolly herself revisited her iconic composition via a 1995 duet with Vince Gill. This No. 15 country hit won a CMA Award and was nominated for a Grammy.

Between 2000 and 2010, more than a dozen artists performed versions of "Jolene." Her classics "Coat of Many Colors" and "Down from Dover" also received fresh interpretations during those years.

After years of offers, a reluctant Dolly was at last persuaded to write a memoir in 1994. She pointedly titled it *My Life and Other Unfinished Business* to indicate that she was far from through. The book spent more than two months on the *New York Times* bestseller list.

In 1995, she launched her Imagination Library free books initiative. This led to her new nickname, "The Book Lady." To help her raise funds for the program, the state of Tennessee soon began offering a Dolly Parton license plate.

Dolly Parton was inducted into the Country Music Hall of Fame in 1999. Without the slightest nostalgic glance at the accomplishments that had brought her there, she continued to forge forward. During the next ten years, her new recordings were nominated for thirteen more Grammy Awards.

I like to think that I'm peeking around the corner at the new century in this photo. I felt musically renewed and was working harder than ever on my songwriting at the time.

Hungry Again 1998

THIS IS THE TITLE SONG of an album co-produced by Dolly's cousin, musician Richie Owens. He is the son of her sometime song collaborator and business associate, Uncle Louis Owens.

The thrill, the desire, the excitement is gone.
We seem to have found a safe comfort zone.
We worked so hard to get where we are.
That romance got lost on the way.

It used to be never enough.
We'd melt with each look and each burning touch.
We laughed and we loved and we just ate it up,
Back when we were hungry that way.

CHORUS
Let's love like we're hungry again,
Bring back the passion we had back then.
The time has gone by, we forgot what it meant.
Let's love like we're hungry again.

Don't you miss those feelings we had at the start,
And that fire that got started from each little spark?
Oh it's good where we are, but I miss where we've been.
Let's love like we're hungry again, now and then.

ALTERNATE CHORUS
Let's love like we're hungry again,
Bring back the passion we had back then.
The time has gone by, now we've grown too content.
Let's love like we're hungry again, now and then.

Let's love like we're hungry again.

This is the garden outside the little meditation chapel I had built next to my home. I do some of my most creative work there, including writing new songs.

When I was getting ready to do the *Hungry Again* album, I decided to fast and pray. I'd bought and fixed up the old Tennessee Mountain Home [on Locust Ridge, about ten miles from Dollywood], so it was like a personal retreat. I thought I would go up there in the mountains for a couple of weeks. Fasting is something that comes out of the church. If you fast, it cleanses your body as well as your mind, so you can leave yourself more open to God. I wanted to get more spiritual. I'd been working too hard and not taking care of myself.

Fasting is awful. You've gotta pray hard, and you gotta have a lot of faith. It takes me about two or three days to get into it. You do a water fast for a day or so, and you get these god-awful headaches. Then you do a juice fast to get your mind open, and you get light-headed. That's when I feel like I am getting into that "God space," where I really feel like I'm communicating on a spiritual level. And then the songs start coming, and I go with it. I wrote a lot of songs during that period. Any time I can allow myself the time to do that, my songs are usually better.

"Hungry Again" is one of the songs I wrote during that time. It was kind of saying two things. One of them was "Let's love like we're hungry again." But it was also about being hungry for something new and getting out of the doldrums. It was "Let's live like we're hungry again." At the time, I felt like I wasn't losing ground, but I wasn't gaining any. And I don't like being in neutral.

PMS Blues 1994

THIS SINGLE WENT TO NO. 70 on the country charts. The song was introduced on Dolly's *Heartsongs* album.

Eve you wicked woman, you done put your
curse on me.
Why didn't you just leave that apple hangin'
in the tree?
You make us hate our husbands, our lovers,
and our boss.
Why I can't even count the good friends I've
already lost
'Cause of PMS blues, PMS blues.

I don't even like myself, but it's something I
can't help.
I got those god-almighty, slap-somebody
PMS blues.
Most times I'm easygoing, some say I'm good
as gold.
But when I'm PMS, I tell ya, I turn mean and
cold.

Those not afflicted with it are affected just the
same.
You poor old men didn't have to grin and say
"I feel your pain."
PMS blues, PMS blues

You know you must forgive us for we care not
what we do
I got those can't-stop-crying, dishes-flying
PMS blues
But you know we can't help it. We don't even
know the cause
But as soon as this part's over, then comes the
menopause
Oh, lord, oh, lord

We're going to always be a heap of fun,
Like the devil taking over my body,
Suffering, suffering, suffering, everybody's
suffering, huh?

But a woman had to write this song, a man
would be scared to,
Lest he be called a chauvinist or just fall
victim to
Those PMS blues

You know we'd kill for less than that
PMS blues

You don't want to cross my path,
'Cause a pitbull ain't no match
For these teeth-a-clenchin', fluid-retention,
Head-a-swellin', can't-stop-yellin',
Got-no-patience, I'm-so-hateful

PMS blues, premenstrual syndrome
Got those moods-a-swingin', tears-a-slingin'
Nothin' fits me when it hits me
Rantin', ravin', misbehavin'
PMS blues

It's the only time in my life I ever think about
wishing I'd been a man,
But you know that only means one thing,
If I'd have been a man, I'd be somewhere
right this very minute
With some old cranky, naggin', raggin',
hateful woman
With those old PMS blues, PMS blues

I don't want to talk about it. We both could
do without it.
Got those treat-your-kids-bad, don't-you-
talk-back
Gone-ballistic, unrealistic,
Awful lowdown, bitch-to-be-around
PMS blues

Well, *somebody* had to write a song called "PMS Blues"! When I did, I thought, "I'll just cover every emotion that women go through." Then, when that PMS part's over, comes the menopause! How we make these poor old men and our kids suffer. You guys are never going to get any rest.

I sing the song on my shows. It always gets a belly laugh when I do. The guys love it, because I point the finger right at us women. I pretend that I am "PMSing" on some guy in the front row. And that gets a big laugh, too.

Speakin' of the Devil 1995

THIS SONG WAS ORIGINALLY INTRODUCED in Dolly's 1991 TV movie *Wild Texas Wind*, but it achieved wider exposure as a number on her 1995 album *Something Special*.

He's got a way of walkin',
He's got a way of talkin',
A way to fascinate me all the time.
Ah, and he's got a way with women
A way to keep my head a-spinnin',
But he's got away too many times.

Ah, he's got his spell upon me,
Got to be his one and only
Burning with passion and desire.
Caught up in all his magic
It surely would be tragic
To never share the heat from all this fire.

CHORUS
Ooh, speakin' of the devil, well here
he comes now;
Lookin' like an angel, got my defenses down.
He's got me dreamin', got me schemin'.
Oh, and speakin' of the devil, he is driving
me wild
With that wicked little grin and that fire
in his eyes.
He's got me dreamin', got me dreamin'.
Oh, and speakin' of the devil, I feel mighty
close to Heaven
And I'd go through Hell to make him mine.

REPEAT CHORUS

REPEAT FIRST VERSE

REPEAT CHORUS

Speakin' of the devil, speakin' of the devil,
Speakin' of the devil, here he comes now.

I love Asleep at the Wheel, Ray Benson's band. When I got ready to do *Wild Texas Wind*, I thought, "Who better to do this movie with me than Ray Benson? He's from Texas. He's the best western-swing bandleader." The filmmakers didn't particularly want to use him, but I had a little power then. I said, "You don't have him, you ain't getting me." Because I thought he was the perfect one for the part. We struck up a really good relationship and wrote a few songs together.

But I wrote "Speakin' of the Devil" on my own. I had recorded it in that western-swing style. I took it to the band, and they did a really good job playing it. Ray really liked it, because it had that little swing to it.

Honky Tonk Songs 1998

THIS SINGLE REACHED NO. 74 on the charts. It is a selection from Dolly's *Hungry Again* album.

Just keep it coming 'til I don't have to think
And point out some cowboy that might want to dance
And make sure I get home if you see that I can't

You see I loved him, he left me for a girl half my age
I relate to each sad song that ole jukebox has played
I listen to Haggard, ole Hank, and George Jones
But why don't more women sing honky tonk songs?

Why don't more women sing honky tonk songs?
About the heartaches and the tough breaks
And the men that's done 'em wrong
There are others just like me that are hurtin' to the bone
So why don't more women sing honky tonk songs?

Why don't more women sing honky tonk songs?
Honky tonk angels are just queens without thrones
Judge not lest you be judged, who can cast the first stone?
Why don't more women sing honky tonk songs?

Bartender won't you pour me a very strong drink?
Just keep it coming 'til I don't have to think
And point out some cowboy that might want to dance
And make sure I get home if you see that I can't

Why don't more women sing honky tonk songs?
About the heartaches and the tough breaks
And all the men that's done us wrong
There's a whole lotta women I know would sing along
So why don't more women sing honky tonk songs?

Why don't more women sing honky tonk songs?

Well, why *don't* more women sing honky tonk songs? I wrote a song asking that and got a whole bunch of women in honky tonks singing along with it. But I don't know the answer to the question. I guess it's because there are just more honky tonk men than there are honky tonk women.

Halos and Horns 2002

THIS IS THE TITLE TUNE of one of Dolly's most acclaimed collections of the early 2000s.

CHORUS
Halos and horns, sinners and saints,
Hearts that are torn between what's wrong and ain't.
Just because it feels right does not make it so.
So we struggle through life in horns and halos.

Tempted and tried with each step we take.
We stumble and slide and make our mistakes,
Ask God to forgive us for all of our sins,
Then we take off our horns and wear halos again.

REPEAT CHORUS

Most people are both the angel and the devil. We all have both sides in us. I've never tried to deny it about myself. I'm as good as I know how to be. I'm not a sinner, and I'm not a saint. I just allow myself to feel whatever I feel and do whatever I think is the right thing to be doing.

"Halos and Horns" talks about that. That's why I think it's a song that a lot of people can relate to. You need to have a conscience about what you do. You might not know why you do something, and you hope the Lord will forgive you if it's wrong. I know I push Him to the limit, sometimes.

Sugar Hill 2002

IN 2019, THIS LYRIC INSPIRED a Netflix movie in an anthology series based on Dolly's songs. It was introduced on the *Halos & Horns* album.

Up on Sugar Hill we'd go walkin'
Hand in hand while the south wind blowed
Bobwhites callin', black crows cawkin',
Countin' the warts on a toad in the road

Down in the mill pond swimmin' naked
Showin' more than we should have showed
We were just kids explorin' nature
Learnin' more than we should have knowed

CHORUS
Sug, Sug, Sug, Sugar Hill memories
Stealing sugar on the mountainside
Sug, Sug, Sug, Sugar Hill sugar
Sweeter than candy and cake and pie

A yellow dress drapin' off of my shoulder
Seein' myself in the lookin' glass
Older now and a little bit bolder
Thinkin' about our summers past

Up on Sugar Hill we'd go walkin'
Hand in hand up the mountainside
Teenage lovers plannin' and talkin'
Dreamin' of a future for you and I

REPEAT CHORUS

Years have passed, we're married with
children
Our days are happy and our memories fond
We still find it quite appealin'
To go to Sugar Hill and swim naked in
the pond

REPEAT CHORUS

Up on Sugar Hill there's a wealth of treasure
Down its memory lane I go walking still
What it means to me is more than I can
measure
Golden moments up on Sugar Hill

Up on Sugar Hill with the fireflies glowin'
Sound of katydids and the whip-poor-will
Honeysuckle bloomin' and a mountain
stream flowin'
A little spot of Heaven up on Sugar Hill

Up on Sugar Hill with the bobwhite's callin'
Black crows cawkin', and the soft wind blows
Up on Sugar Hill there are lovebirds talkin'
Up on Sugar Hill where the good times roll

REPEAT CHORUS

A little spot of Heaven up on Sugar Hill

Even when you've been together your whole life and you're older, you will always love each other in the same way. "Sugar Hill" kind of takes you through a whole life. It shows you that you can be romantic all the days of your life, if you choose to be. Love is a frame of mind. Passion is the same. If you've always had a connection with that person, you're never going to lose that.

You may not be as crazy as you used to be. You may not "be there" as often. But you might be, sometimes. What is that old saying that [Opry star] Bill Carlisle used to say? "I can jump as high as I used to, but I can't stay up as long." It's kind of that way.

Shattered Image 2002

DOLLY'S VERSION OF THIS SONG on her *Halos & Horns* collection is a revival of a song she originally introduced on her 1976 LP *All I Can Do*.

I used to sit for hours as a kid
Dangle my feet from an old flat bridge,
Seein' myself in the water below
Shatter my image with the stones I'd throw.

I recall a vacant old shack
Down by the edge of the tobaccer patch.
A child's reflection in a dirty window
Shatter my image with the stones I'd throw.

CHORUS
A long time gone and a long time ago
When I shattered my image with the stones I'd throw.
The world is cruel and people are cold
They shatter my image with the stones they throw.
Shatter my image with the stones they throw.

I'm far from perfect, but I ain't all bad;
It hurts me more than it makes me mad.
You gather your stones by stoopin' so low
Then shatter my image with the stones you throw.

If you live in a glass house, don't throw stones.
Don't shatter my image 'til you look at your own.
Look at your reflection in your house of glass.
Don't open my closet if your own's full of trash.
Stay out of my closet if your own's full of trash.

REPEAT CHORUS TWICE

Shatter my image with the stones you throw,
Don't shatter my image with the stones you throw.
Shatter my image with the stones you throw,

Shatter my image with the stones you throw,
You shatter my image with the stones you throw.
Shatter my image with the stones you throw.

Shatter my image with the stones you throw,
You shatter my image with the stones you throw.
Shatter my image with the stones you throw.

Back in my early days when I wrote that song, I was really not used to people saying bad things about me. Especially if they weren't true. And you don't have to be in show business for somebody to shatter your image or ruin your reputation.

The line I love the best in this song is, "If you live in a glass house, don't throw stones / Don't shatter my image 'til you look at your own / Look at your reflection in your house of glass," and don't do whatever you do until you look at your own ass. Ha! Or whatever my rhyme word was there.

There are a *lot* of stories about me in the tabloids. I always say that they are based on some thread of truth, but usually it's so frayed by the time they get done with it, you don't hardly even recognize it. I don't mind what they say about me, as much as I do when it hurts other people I know. I hate that. I can handle it, myself. But I hate it when they drag other people into it.

I love the tabloids. I read them all. They're fun to read. I believe everything they write about everybody. Except me!

This is an Owens Resonator Guitar. It was designed and manufactured by my uncle Louis Owens and my cousin Richie Owens; pictured below are me and Uncle Louis.

These Old Bones 2002

DOLLY'S SISTER STELLA PARTON maintained that when Dolly sang in the old woman's voice on this record, she sounded just like their mother. This *Halos & Horns* song was the basis for a Netflix movie starring Kathleen Turner.

CHORUS
These old bones will tell your story.
These old bones will never lie.
These old bones will tell you surely
What you can't see with your eye.
These old bones, I shake and rattle.
These old bones, I toss and roll.
And it's all in where they scatter
Tells you what the future holds.

Oh, she lived up on the mountain
Eleven miles or so from town
With a one-eyed cat named Wink,
A billy goat, and a blue tick hound.
Her graying hair was braided
And wrapped around her head;
And her dress was long and faded;
And her home a rusty shed.

In a little pouch of burlap
Tied with a piece of twine
There were bones all shapes and sizes
Gathered through the course of time.
She'd throw them out before you
She swore that she could see
The present, past, and future
She could read your destiny.

Everybody knew about her
Came to get their fortune read
Concerning health and wealth and power
Who to love and when to wed.
Well, I just like helpin' people
I'm just glad that I could help.
Why, I know everybody's secrets
But I keep it to myself.

REPEAT CHORUS

Some called her witchy woman;
Some said she was insane;
Some said she was a prophet;
Still everybody came.

Just because a body's different
Well, that don't make 'em mad.
Well, they've crucified a-many
For the special gifts they've had.

I had often heard about her,
Dreamed about her now and then.
For I, too, was clairvoyant,
Came about when I was ten.

I was fascinated with her
And the things I'd heard about.
And I knew some day I'd meet her,
And one day it came about.

Well, I know'd that you 'uz a-comin'
I could feel it in my bones.
These old bones have also told me
That I won't be here for long.

Did you know that you 'uz adopted?
Did you know you once't was mine?
But the county took you from me,
Said I wasn't right in mind.

But I just know'd I had to see you
'Fore these bones was laid to rest.
So I conjured up a message
It must'a worked, I guess.

This gift runs in the family
I know you also know
And I passed this gift on to you.
These old bones, they're just for show.

REPEAT CHORUS

I held her hand while she was dyin';
And with the funeral through
I headed on back up the mountain
For Billy, Wink, and Blue.

And that little pouch of burlap
With those bones so worn and old
She give me somethin' special
Now every time I throw.

REPEAT CHORUS

Now I can't tell you what you want to hear,
I just tell you what I see.
It's these old bones a-talkin'.
Blame it on them; don't pack it on me.

It's just like that time that there boy died up
at the sawmill.
Well, I know'd who done it, but I never said.
And I know'd when somebody is a cheatin'
Or when somebody's baby was gonna be
born dead.

But unless somebody just plain out and
asked me
Well, I just figured there ain't no point
goin' around
Actin' like you know everything, just 'cause
you might.
Ah, you know, girl, I want you to take these
bones

'Cause I don't want no young'un of mine
A-goin' around unprepared.
You just remember that the magic is
inside you.
There ain't no crystal ball.

There were always those old people in the mountains who were clairvoyant or could prophesize. That kind of gift runs in our family. My mother would get visions of things. She once told my Dad, "Lee, get up! We gotta go over to Cove Bridge! Denver's had a wreck!" Daddy said, "Avie Lee, go back to bed." She said, "I'm telling you, get up!" He pacified her because she wouldn't shut up. So they went over to Cove Bridge, and my brother had wrecked there. The wheels were still spinning, that's how fresh it was. He laid in the hospital for a year with every bone in his body broke. But my mother had a premonition.

The character in "These Old Bones" was based loosely on a relative of ours who prophesized that I was going to do something special. She laid her hands on me and said, "This child is anointed." I was little, so I said, "Mama, what does 'anointed' mean?" She said, "That probably means that you're going to do great things for the Lord and do good things in life."

For "These Old Bones" I created this old woman who lived up in the woods that everybody was afraid of. They thought she was witchy. I sang the old lady's part in the song, the way my Mom and my aunts would sing. So that song is real special to me.

What a Heartache 2002

THE SONG WAS ORIGINALLY WRITTEN for the soundtrack of the 1984 movie *Rhinestone*. Dolly chose to revisit it first as a track on 1991's *Eagle When She Flies*, then again as one of her *Halos & Horns* selections.

I thought I saw the promise of forever in your eyes.
I thought that I was sure of what I saw.
You led me to believe that I was special in your life,
So I left my heart wide open for the fall.
I thought I'd found a safe and loving place inside your heart;
And I was warm and willing any time.
The same soft lips that kissed me sweet were lying from the start.
But I swear I thought your love was genuine.
What a heartache you turned out to be.

What a heartache, what a heartache,
Like a switchblade that cuts so quick and deep.
Oh, what a heartache, what a heartbreak,
Love ain't always what it appears to be.
Oh, what a heartache you turned out to be.

It just goes to show that you never can tell.
'Cause I really thought that I knew you well.
I still can't believe I could be deceived so easily.
Are all these wishes I'm wishin' to myself
Just rusty coins in a wishin' well?
Wishes come true, they come false as well.
It's too late for you and me.
Oh, what a heartache you turned out to be.

What a heartache, what a heartache,
Love is two-faced and easy to deceive.
Oh, what a heartache, what a heartache,
What a mistake to think I could believe.

What a heartache, what a heartache,
Like a switchblade that so cuts quick and deep.
Ooh, what a heartache you turned out to be.
What a heartache, what a heartache,
What a heartache, what a heartache,
What a heartache.
Ooh, what a heartache you turned out to be.
Ooh, what a heartache.
Oh, what a heartache,
What a heartbreak you turned out to be.

A heartache is as sharp as a knife. If you're going to hurt me like that, this is what it feels like. That's the way it is in this song. It's the way it is in "Dagger through the Heart," which is on that same album. In the old days, people would kill themselves over a broken heart.

I have a tendency to re-record a song if I really believe in it. That's why this is on three of my albums. I'm drawn to those songs that I think are some of my best work. So I try to bring them around and think, "Maybe this time people will get it." I believe this could be a hit, if not for me, then for somebody, somewhere, someday.

I can write songs anywhere and at anytime of the day or night. This shot was taken during the photo sessions for my *Little Sparrow* album.

Color Me America 2003

THIS PATRIOTIC DREAM OF PEACE and social justice can be found on Dolly's album *For God and Country*.

CHORUS
I am red and white and blue;
These are colors that ring true
To all I am and feel and love and do.
I stand proud and brave and tall;
I want justice for us all.
Color me America, red, white, and blue.

But I see red when evil speaks
Spilling red blood on our streets.
And I feel blue from grief and sorrow that it brings.
But the white, the light of love,
God's own Spirit like a dove
Lifts us up and hands to us an olive branch.

Oh, sweet freedom, may you stay
In our land and lives always;
And may peace and beauty fill our hearts anew.
And may we all stand up for you;
May our thoughts and deeds be true
And be worthy of your stripes . . . red, white, and blue.

REPEAT CHORUS

Oh, sweet America.
God, won't You shed, won't You shed Your grace on Thee.
And crown Thy good with brotherhood
From sea to shining sea.
Oh, color me, color me America
Red, white, and blue, color me America.

When I did the *For God and Country* album, I thought I needed to write something like this. I am a girl of many colors. I am an all-American girl. Peace is a color. It's the pure white color of everything. So I thought this was a really good Americana song. One of those good songs about and for America.

You can't go wrong with the stars and stripes, so I wrapped myself in the colors of the flag for the costume pictured on the jacket of my 2003 album *For God and Country*.

Hello God 2002

THIS SONG WAS INSPIRED by the terrible events of 9/11 in 2001. Dolly introduced it on the album *Halos & Horns*, and its single climbed to No. 60 on the charts.

Hello God, are You out there?
Can You hear me, are You listenin' anymore?
Hello God, if we're still on speakin' terms
Can You help me like before?
I have questioned Your existence,
My resistance leaves me cold.
Can You help me go the distance?
Hello God, hello, hello.

This old world has gone to pieces.
Can we fix it, is there time?
Hate and violence just increases,
We're so selfish, cruel, and blind.
We fight and kill each other
In Your name, defending You.
Do You love some more than others?
We're so lost and confused.

Hello God, are You out there?
Can You hear us, are You listenin' anymore?
Hello God, if we're still on speakin' terms
Can You help us like before?
Oh, the free will You have given
We have made a mockery of
This is no way to be livin',
We're in great need of Your love.
Hello God

Hello God, can You grant us
Love enough to make amends?
(Hello God) Is there still a chance
That we could start again?
Hello God, we've learned our lesson.
Dear God, don't let us go.
More than ever . . .
Hello God, hello, hello.

Hello God, we really need You.
We can't make it without You.
(Hello God) We beseech You
In the name of all that's true.
Hello God, please forgive us
For we know not what we do.

Hello God, give us one more chance
To prove ourselves to You.
Hello, God; hello, God.

Everybody remembers where they were on 9/11. I was out on a farm near Pigeon Forge, Tennessee, doing a video for a new ride that was going to be opening at Dollywood. We had rented this whole farm, and we had a film crew, mostly from New York. Because we were out on that farm so far out in the country, the cell phones wouldn't work. This woman in the farmhouse that we were using was watching TV. She came out screaming, "Oh, the Twin Towers!" Everybody went running into the house to see what was going on. Then they all went crazy, because their families were in New York—their children, their wives. They went running down the road, trying to get somewhere where their phones would work and they could call someone to find out what was going on.

We were all going crazy, going, "Oh my God, it's the end of the world." And then as we all got to see all that it really was, it was like the bottom had fell out of the world. It was like the world had stopped. It was like the end of time, somehow. It was just a horrifying thing. It was awful. People were freaking out and crying.

And that's when I started writing that song, "Hello God." I was thinking, "Are You out there? Are You listening anymore? Can You hear me? Have we gone against You so much that these things are happening to us, now? I've questioned Your existence." The song was very inspired. That was my 9/11 song.

CHAPTER

12

THE GRASS IS BLUE

IN THE 1990S, DOLLY BEGAN TO TURN AWAY FROM MAKING POP-influenced music and returned to her country roots with her albums *Honky Tonk Angels* (1993), *Heartsongs* (1994), and *Hungry Again* (1998).

The trend reached its fullest expression with the 1999 releases of *The Grass Is Blue* and her reunion with Emmylou Harris and Linda Ronstadt, *Trio II.* Both projects garnered critical acclaim and reaped awards. *Little Sparrow* (2001), *Halos & Horns* (2002), and *Live and Well* (2004) continued in this vein.

During these years, the press became interested in her as a savvy businesswoman. The success of Dollywood, her Velvet Apple Publishing income, her lucrative movie and television paychecks, and her investments in everything from real estate to agriculture led to her being dubbed an "Iron Butterfly."

Dolly already owned the copyrights to her songs. Now she wanted to own her recordings of them. Because she wanted to own her records, the major labels were no longer interested in her, nor she in them. In 1994 she formed her Blue Eye Records label. Producer Steve Buckingham was also fed up with entertainment corporations, so she asked him to run the label. He encouraged her to pursue bluegrass, a genre in which the major labels had no interest.

When Dolly was a girl, bluegrass songs were played on the radio alongside country hits. By the 1970s, bluegrass had been exiled from mainstream country music, and it developed its own festivals, radio programs, trade associations, publications, and promoters.

Bluegrass music had long been a favorite of hers, and now the style returned her affection. In 2000, she won her first award from the International Bluegrass Music Association (IBMA). She sang on *Smoky Mountain Sweethearts* and *Livin' Lovin' Losin'*, which won IBMA Collaborative Recording of the Year awards in 2002 and 2004.

She also recorded with such bluegrass luminaries as Ricky Skaggs, Rhonda Vincent, the Grascals, Alison Krauss, and Dailey & Vincent. Her songs became favorites with many others in the genre.

Dolly Parton has always been a champion of roots music. As the songs in this chapter indicate, Dolly's interest in bluegrass sounds both predates and postdates her "official" bluegrass recordings.

Mountain Music

Recorded by Porter Wagoner 1978

THE EARLIEST RECORDED DOLLY COMPOSITION with a bluegrass theme was this single released by Porter Wagoner in 1978. The recording never made the charts and did not appear on any of his RCA albums. Dolly has never recorded the song.

If you like mountain music and I know that
you do,
I know a place and I'll show it to you,
Where the old-timers gather on a
Saturday night,
And the sound of their music echoes through
the night.

If you like mountain music, you'll be glad
that you came,
And after you've been there, you won't be
the same.
If you like mountain music where the
old-timers touch,
There'll never be nothin' you'll enjoy
as much.

The bass is a string on a tub.
Some play the spoons and some blow in a jug.
Some take a paper and blow in a comb
There's ephin' and iphin' and the old
hambone

Some play the cowbells to join in the fun,
A bucket-led beat with a stick is the drum.
And there's the old rub-board and the old
hand saw,
And the fiddles and guitars just give it
their all.

Jews harps and french harps and
autoharps too,
Dobros and banjos and mandolins, too,
Hand-clappin', toe-tappin',
knee-slappin', too,
Lip-smackin' moonshine, just made
home brew.

So, if you like mountain music, I know
where to go,
Where the mountaineers gather and put
on a show,
And all through the night, they keep
playin' away
And I know you won't be forgettin' this day.

Even though bluegrass music is credited to Bill Monroe coming out of Kentucky, the mountain people in Tennessee made music that was basically the same. A lot of people played mandolins and fiddles and banjos. Through the years, I've written a lot of songs about that style of music, with its homemade instruments, even if it was just the spoons. I've always been writing bluegrass songs and recording bluegrass songs in different albums here and there.

Daddy's Old Fiddle

With Charlie Daniels 2007

WHEN CHARLIE DANIELS CRAFTED his *Deuces* album of celebrity duets, Dolly provided this lively toe-tapper. Her lyric mentions several titles of traditional fiddle tunes.

CHORUS
Daddy's old fiddle is a family treasure
Handed down from hand to hand.
I used to go with him when I was just little,
I was my daddy's biggest fan.

Hey diddle, diddle, my daddy's old fiddle.
Boy, he could play to beat the band.
He played it better than just a little,
Known and loved throughout the land.

Oh, back when I was just a young'n
I used to travel around with Dad.
He made a little money and we had a lot of
fun'n
And it was the best times I ever had.

Daddy played at every social function,
Even coulda played with Bill Monroe.
He offered him the job, but Daddy wouldn't
take it,
Said he'd miss me too much to go.

My daddy loved me.
Play one, Daddy!

Now every square dance and every pie
supper,
Even on the big Election Day
People would come from miles around
They didn't come to vote, but to hear him
play.

I'm votin' for you, Daddy.

"Cotton-Eyed Joe" and "Sally Goodin,"
"Soldier's Joy" and "Hasty Puddin',"
"Little Boy Blue" and the horn he had
Didn't have nothin' on my dad.

Said, "Chicken in the bread pan, pickin' out
dough.
Daddy does your dog bite? No child, no."
Hey diddle, diddle, my daddy's old fiddle
It rosin-ates throughout my soul.
Show 'em Daddy.

REPEAT CHORUS

And when they laid my daddy down
And I stood beside his grave
Held his fiddle in my hand
And I played "Amazing Grace
How sweet the sound."

REPEAT CHORUS

All day singing, dinner on the ground,
Weddings, funerals, parties in town,
In the Court House yard they'd spit and
they'd whittle
While Daddy entertained them with his old
fiddle.

REPEAT CHORUS

Daddy's old fiddle,
My daddy's old fiddle
I miss you, Daddy.

LEFT: The Grand Ole Opry stage is the perfect place for me to sing my mountain music.

ABOVE: Charlie Daniels shares my love of bluegrass music. He joined me as a member of the Opry cast [in 2008] and as a member of the Country Music Hall of Fame [in 2016].

Charlie Daniels was doing an album. He said, "I need a Dolly Parton song." I love Charlie, so I said, "Well, I'll write you one." So I tailor-made this song just for him. I know it sounds like an old song, but I wrote it.

My grandpa played the fiddle, and so did several of my other relatives, so I knew all the fiddle tunes from the old days. I incorporated as many of their titles as I could in the lyrics, because I knew Charlie would enjoy that.

Do I Ever Cross Your Mind

With Linda Ronstadt and Emmylou Harris 1999

THIS SONG HAS BEEN in Dolly's concert set list for decades. As the flip side of her 1982 version of "I Will Always Love You," it was a No. 1 hit in 1982. But it arguably achieved greatest prominence as a track on the Gold-selling *Trio II* collection of 1999, recorded with Emmylou Harris and Linda Ronstadt. Stars such as Randy Travis, Tom Jones, and Joan Osborne have recorded it, and Dolly has included the song on five different albums.

Oh, sometimes I go walking through fields
where we walked

Long ago in the sweet used to be.
And the flowers still grow, but they don't
smell as sweet
As they did when you picked them for me.

And when I think of you and the love we
once knew
How I wish we could go back in time.
Do you ever think back on old memories
like that
Or do I ever cross your mind?

Do you ever wake up lonely in the middle of
the night
'Cause you miss me, do you darling?
Oh, and do your memories ever take you back
Into another place in time?

And do you ever miss the feelings and the
love that we shared
When you were with me, tell me darling,
Or do I ever cross your mind?

Oh, how often I wish that again I could kiss
Your sweet lips like I did long ago.
And how often I long for those two
loving arms
That once held me so gentle and close.

And when I think of you and the love we
once knew
How I wish we could go back in time.
Do you ever recall those old memories at all
Or do I ever cross your mind?

Do I ever cross your mind, tell me darlin'?
Do I ever cross your mind?

"Do I Ever Cross Your Mind" has always been one of those fun songs for me to sing. We do it *a cappella* in my concerts, using our voices like instruments. When I first recorded it, it did not have that little bridge that goes, "Do you ever wake up lonely in the middle of the night 'cause you miss me?" I added that later, and that's the version that is on *Trio II*.

Linda and Emmy loved the song, and it seemed to fit so well on our trio vocal album. So we did our version of it. I keep recording it, anytime I can, because I think it is just one of those songs that someday somebody is going to have a perfect record of.

The cover of *Trio II* pictured the three of us as little girls. From left are Emmylou, Linda, and me.

The Grass Is Blue 1999

THIS IS THE TITLE TUNE of Dolly's first bluegrass collection. The album won both a Grammy and an IBMA award as the Bluegrass Recording of the Year.

I've had to think up a way to survive
Since you said it's over, told me goodbye.
I just can't make it one day without you
Unless I pretend that the opposite's true.

Rivers flow backwards, valleys are high.
Mountains are level, truth is a lie.
I'm perfectly fine and I don't miss you.
The sky is green and the grass is blue.

How much can a heart and a troubled mind take?
Where is that fine line before it all breaks?
Can one in their sorrow just cross over it,
And into that realm of insanity's bliss?

There's snow in the tropics, there's ice on the sun.
It's hot in the arctic and crying is fun.
And I'm happy now and I'm glad we're through
And the sky is green and the grass is blue.

And the rivers flow backwards, and my tears are dry.
Swans hate the water and eagles can't fly.
But I'm alright now, now that I'm over you.
And the sky is green and the grass is blue.

And I don't love you and the grass is blue.

First of all, Steve Buckingham is a wonderful man, and he knows his music. He knows everything about country music, about every artist, and about everything concerning it. He's also a great organizer. He knows how to put great musicians together. He knows how to make great records, and he's so easy to work with. I loved working with him on everything we did together. He was always there to help me, whether it was performing on shows or organizing a band for TV. He was just an all-in kind of guy. He was really a magic person for me, starting with [1991's] *Eagle When She Flies*.

Steve Buckingham and I used to go to dinner all the time, because we knew so many of the same people. We'd get caught up on the latest gossip and talk about whatever was going on in the [music] business. We just enjoyed each others' company.

I have always loved bluegrass music, and I grew up singing a lot of it. This one night we were at the table, and Steve said, "I saw a survey in one of the magazines that asked, 'Who would you most like to see do a bluegrass album who's never done one?' And your name was right at the top of the list." I said, "Well, let's do one."

In no time flat, he put together the best bluegrass pickers. He did such a great job pulling it all together with those great musicians, and we had such a fun time recording that.

We picked some of the best, great, classic bluegrass songs, and I wrote "The Grass Is Blue" as the theme song. The album got some of the greatest reviews I've ever had for my music. I'm really, really proud of that record.

Mountain Angel 2001

THIS SHORT STORY within the confines of a song was included on Dolly's *Little Sparrow* album.

Pretty as an angel from the day that she was born;
Skin as fair as lilies, hair as golden as the corn.
They knew that she was special from the moment she first cried.
She was a mountain angel, certified.

She was her mama's baby; she was her daddy's pride.
Good at home, at church and school, at everything she tried.
Everybody's darling, led a charmed and peaceful life;
The perfect mountain angel 'til he arrived.

And oh, oh, oh, she fell so deeply,
Oh, oh, oh, she couldn't stop.
She gave herself to him, yielded completely;
He lifted her so high, then let her drop.

She gave up everything for him that mattered in her life;
Oh, the others that had loved her, and she vowed to be his wife.
She dreamed of bearing children in an ivy-covered house.
The Mountain Angel's sunshine turned to clouds.

The wicked, handsome stranger left the way he came.
Broke her heart and broke her mind, she never was the same.
They say he was the devil, that had come to steal her soul.
She never loved another it was told.

They say she had a baby, some say that it had died.
They say it's just as well as it had been the devil's child.
They say good conquers evil, but here evil won the prize.
So the Mountain Angel took to the wild.

And oh, oh, oh, she couldn't take it.
Years passed and she had long since lost her mind.
She waited for him as her beauty faded.
Her parents died from grief before their time.

She tried to gather pieces of her life, they wouldn't fit.
Beside the tiny grave deep in the woods is where she'd sit.
Talking to the child, herself, to him, who knew for sure;
Possessed they say by Satan's insane lure.

High atop the mountain for years they say she's seen,
Looking down upon the town where she had once been queen.
She'd sneak around the playground, watch the little children play.
They'd see the crazy lady; they'd run away.

They say she roamed these hills for years wearing not a stitch.
The lovely Mountain Angel, now thought to be a witch.
She made those wailing, mournful sounds that you could hear for miles
Long after she'd laid down upon her baby's grave and died.

And oh, oh, oh, her ghost is calling
She's wailing for the ones that she adored.
Through spring and summer, fall, when snow
is falling
Her spirit roams these hills forevermore.

The Mountain Angel's voice is evermore.
Oh, Oh, Oh, Whoa, Whoa
Woo-hoo-hoo, Woo, Woo, Woo,
Oh, Oh, Oh, Oh, Oh,
Woo-hoo-hooo, Ooh, Ooh

When I was writing "Mountain Angel," it was like a movie. It's so picturesque. It's as well written as anything I've ever done, because I tried to create all of these things where you never lose interest and you never know what's going to happen next.

You can see it all. She falls in love with this guy who is almost like the devil, the way he puts a curse on her. He's just so evil and mean. He leaves her with a child. The child dies. She buries it up in the mountains. Her mind snaps. She's a mountain girl who runs wild in the mountains, living like a witch. She's naked, and her hair's all crazy. Since her baby's gone, she goes down to the schoolyard looking at all the little kids.

It's got that mournful old sound, like Mama used to do. I incorporated that, "Ooh, ooo, hoo," where she's crying. I got to create it, I got to write it, and I got to act in it.

Then she falls dead at the end on the baby's grave. I have to make it worse, right? If I ain't killing dogs and kids, I'm killing myself!

It's almost like I go into a daydream when I write my story songs. Sometimes I can't even predict how those stories are going to end. Except it's usually in tragedy, if I know me.

House of Blues
Dolly Parton

My Blue Tears 2001

THIS DOLLY SONG HAS BEEN a perennial favorite. A year after Dolly introduced it on 1971's *Coat of Many Colors* LP, Goldie Hawn came to Nashville to record it. Country/pop star Dickey Lee was next. The Incredible String Band cast it as a folk song in 1973. Dolly's brother Randy Parton did a version in 1981, and then Linda Ronstadt gave it a new wave of popularity the following year. After Dolly reintroduced it as a bluegrass tune on 2001's *Little Sparrow*, Rhonda Vincent, the genre's queen, drove the point home by recording her version in 2002.

Fly ye away from my window, little bluebird.
Fly ye as far as you can away from here,
And let not your song fall upon my ear.
Go spread your blue wings and I'll shed my blue tears.
For the one that I have loved, he has left me and gone;
And I am in no mood for to hear your sad songs.

And bring not your light into my dark gloom, yellow sunshine.
Waste not your warmth on the coldness in here.
Oh, trouble me not, go ye elsewhere
Go light your blue sky and I'll shed my blue tears.
For the only one that I have ever loved has gone away;
And I am in no mood for the sunshine today.

'Cause I don't know when or if ever again
I will see his sweet face; but I fear
It's forever goodbye though I can't say why
But I sit here and cry my lonely blue tears.
Go spread your blue wings, light your blue sky
I'll shed my blue tears.

Go spread your blue wings and I'll shed my blue tears,
My blue tears, my blue tears.

One day in the early 1970s, I got a call from somebody wanting to get a copy of "My Blue Tears" and my okay for it to be recorded. I was so excited. It was Goldie Hawn. That's when she was on *Laugh-In*. She was the cutest, sweetest thing, and who even knew that she could sing? She did a really good job. Look it up.

Sometimes I will go back and choose to record one of my old songs again. Because it might fit the album that I'm doing at the time. This one just seemed to lend itself to the whole concept I was trying to get across on *Little Sparrow*.

This Washburn guitar was a gift from the House of Blues. It dates from when I did my House of Blues Tour in 2002.

With Bells On 1984

THIS IS ONE OF THE SONGWRITER'S most recorded songs by bluegrass performers. It first appeared on *Once upon a Christmas*, Dolly's 1984 holiday LP with Kenny Rogers. After Jeff & Sheri Easter turned it into a bluegrass romp in 2001, it has been sung by Karen Peck & New River, the Sanders Family, and gospel's Gaither Vocal Band, not to mention superstar drag queen RuPaul.

CHORUS
I'll be home with bells on
I'll be home with bells on
Trim the tree and wrap the presents, turn the Christmas music on
This Christmas I'll be home with bells on

I've traveled around this country, crossed the waters deep and wide
Made lots of friends and memories, brought joy to other's lives
It's Christmas time again, another year has come and gone
And I can't keep from wonderin', how the old folks are at home

REPEAT CHORUS

When the snow is on the meadow and the sleigh bells jingle bright
And the kids are singing "Jingle Bells" around the Christmas lights
As Daddy stokes the fire and Mama puts the turkey on
There ain't nothing going to slow me down, this Christmas I'll be home

REPEAT CHORUS TWICE

You've heard that expression, "I'll be home with bells on." That's what I was thinking of when I wrote this. I thought it made a perfect little Christmas number, and now it seems to be becoming like a country classic Christmas song. Every Christmas, I find myself going around the house, singing, "I'll be home with bells on, ring, ring, ring." It's such a singable little tune. Bluegrass acts seem to love that one.

The Highlight of My Life

Recorded by Bill Emerson 2012

INDUCTED INTO THE BLUEGRASS HALL OF FAME in 2019, Bill Emerson is one of the most influential five-string banjo players of all time. Following stints with the Country Gentlemen, Jimmy Martin, Red Allen, Emerson & Waldron, and Country Current, he formed his Sweet Dixie Band in 2007. The group turned this Dolly tune from the *Jolene* album into a bluegrass event.

CHORUS
Darling, you're the highlight of my life.
You're the one that makes it all worthwhile.
You're the one that taught me how to smile.
Darling, you're the highlight of my life.

You're a part of ev'ry dream I dream,
You're my love, my life, my ev'rything.
I'll never love another, how could I,
When, darling, you're the highlight of my life.

REPEAT CHORUS

You're the one I always think about,
And you're the one I couldn't live without,
And you have always been my guiding light,
Darling, you're the highlight of my life.

REPEAT CHORUS

Darling, you're the highlight of my life.

I'm glad whenever I hear that someone records any of my songs. This is one of my older ones, so it was a surprise to me when it was recorded again, especially in bluegrass. It does have a melody that anybody can sing. Of course, it's about Carl. He has always been the highlight of my life.

Little Sparrow 2001

DOLLY ADAPTED THE TRADITIONAL TEXT of "Come All Ye Fair and Tender Ladies" in her album's title song. Both the lyric and the modal melody echo one of the most ancient and beautiful of Appalachian folk songs. Elements of the song were first collected in Scotland and published in 1727, when it was already considered to be antique. American versions were collected by folklorists between 1900 and 1920 as "Little Swallow," "Come All Ye Pretty Maidens," "Warning," "I Wish I Was a Little Black Bird," "Say Oh! Beware," "Young Ladies," and "Come All You Fair and Pretty Ladies."

CHORUS
Little sparrow, little sparrow,
Precious, fragile little thing.
Little sparrow, little sparrow,
Flies so high and feels no pain.

All ye maidens heed my warning,
Never trust the hearts of men.
They will crush you like a sparrow
Leaving you to never mend.

They will vow to always love you,
Swear no love but yours will do.
Then they'll leave you for another,
Break your little heart in two.

REPEAT CHORUS

I would flutter all around him
On my little sparrow wings.
I would ask him, I would ask him,
Why he let me love him in vain.

I am not a little sparrow,
I am just a broken dream
Of a cold, false-hearted lover
And his evil, cunning scheme.

REPEAT CHORUS

All ye maidens heed my warning,
Never trust the hearts of men.
They will crush you like a sparrow
Leaving you to never mend.

Little sparrow, little sparrow
Oh the sorrow never mends.

"Little Sparrow" is a favorite among the fans. In my shows, on stage, I sing it *a cappella*. I perform it like, "Come hear my voice and listen. Don't trust the hearts of men."

Mama used to sing a song I think is called "Fair and Tender Maidens." I used that whole idea and that whole old-timey sound and feeling for "Little Sparrow."

Marry Me 2001

A MOUNTAIN GIRL GETS GIDDY in love in this song from the 2001 CD *Little Sparrow*.

Well, I met a boy from Grassy Branch
Fine as he can be;
I met him at the big barn dance,
And he took a shine to me.

Sky blue eyes, a big wide smile,
Tall as a sycamore tree,
He's real smart with a real big heart,
And he's gonna marry me.

He's gonna marry me;
And we're gonna go to town.
We're gonna buy us a real good car;
And we're gonna drive around.

We'll hold hands, touch, and hug;
He talks so sweet to me,
He knows a lot about love and stuff;
And he's gonna marry me.

His mama don't like me one little bit,
But you know I don't care.
Let her pitch her hissy fit
'Cause I ain't a-marryin' her.

He's always been a mama's boy;
It's just plain jealousy.
She's as mad as an ol' wet hen
'Cause he's gonna marry me.

Oh, he's gonna marry me,
And he's gonna buy me a ring.
We're gonna be so free,
Cut mama's apron strings.

He's gonna build me a pretty little house,
Have a pretty little babe or three.
'Cause he's done kissed me on the mouth;
And he's gonna marry me.

Yeah, he's gonna marry me.
He's gonna buy me a ring.
We're gonna be so free.
Cut mama's apron strings.

He's gonna build me a pretty little house,
Have a pretty little babe or three.
'Cause he's done kissed me on the mouth;
So he's gotta marry me.

Yeah, he's done kissed me on the mouth,
And he's gonna marry me.
Yodel-ay-dee-dee, marry me

When I wrote "Marry Me," I made it to sound like an old fiddle tune. I gave it that little rompin' sound of banjo and fiddle. I like writing those kinds of songs. It just takes me back home.

I sang it like a girl from the country. "We're gonna go to town. We're gonna buy us a real good car, and we're gonna ride around. He done kissed me on the mouth, so he's gonna marry me." It's kind of like a "girl" thing.

Heartsong 1994

DOLLY TOUCHED HOME WITH ROOTS SOUNDS on several occasions prior to her full-scale bluegrass albums, as is the case in this title tune of her 1994 album *Heartsongs: Live from Home*. The album included her versions of such folk songs as "Barbara Allen," "Mary of the Wild Moor," "In the Pines," and "Wayfaring Stranger."

CHORUS
A heartsong melody plays like a symphony
The sweetest music I have ever known
A song of joy and pain
The mountain angels sing
A bittersweet refrain of my Smoky Mountain
home,
Heartsong

Farmer's daughter if you will
And I often wonder still
In memories where I rambled as a child
Makes me cry and makes me laugh
My reflections on the past
And the family, friends, and faith that shaped
my life

Ragged clothes and hand-me-downs
Just enough to go around
But the sweetest things in life are always free
Like the songs the birds would sing
And the sweet new grass of spring
And the sacred blossoms on the dogwood tree

REPEAT CHORUS

And I recall the thrill and joy
Of a Smoky Mountain boy
I remember my first kiss and my first love
And the songs I'd sing and write
And the dreams I'd clutch so tight
And the loved ones that gave me that extra
shove

And in that little house 'a prayer
Where I spent many hours
Praisin' God and liftin' up His name
And asking Him to lead and to keep watch
over me
As I headed up that rocky road to fame
And now this Smoky Mountain girl has been
all around the world

But it makes no difference
Just how far I roam
I still cling to that part
That is so dear to my heart
My faith in God
And memories of home

REPEAT CHORUS

I was planning to do an album of all those old mountain songs that Mama always used to sing. Songs like "Barbara Allen" and "Fair and Tender Maidens." I remember thinking, "What am I going to call this album, because these are songs of my past, songs of my heart, songs of my soul, my Smoky Mountain roots?" We had a theater at Dollywood called Heartsong Theater, so I thought, "I'll write a song called 'Heartsong,' and I'll call the whole album that, because that's what these songs are.

I was working with Steve Buckingham. We decided to record the whole album live [at Dollywood's larger Celebrity Theater], using all these great musicians. We had Alison Krauss, Randy Scruggs, Pig Robbins, Rhonda Vincent, Jerry Douglas, Carl Jackson, Suzanne Cox, Darrin Vincent, the Irish band Altan, and other people, too. We had all the sound equipment and stuff out back. It was a magic night of me getting to sing all those great old songs. We didn't have to touch up anything. We just did it, and it turned out like it was supposed to.

CHAPTER 13

ME, AN "ICON"?

ALTHOUGH THE TERM MIGHT MAKE HER UNCOMFORTABLE, BY THE year 2000, Dolly Parton was an internationally recognized icon. During the first decade of the new millennium, she was showered with career accolades, even while she was finding new musical challenges and new worlds to conquer.

She was voted into the national Songwriters Hall of Fame in New York in 2001, placing her alongside the likes of Irving Berlin, Lennon & McCartney, Bob Dylan, and Cole Porter. In 2003, BMI presented her with its Icon Award, an honor she shares with Carole King, Chuck Berry, Willie Nelson, Paul Simon, Merle Haggard, and James Brown.

Dolly was saluted by the Library of Congress in 2004, was chosen for a National Medal of Arts accolade in 2005, and was honored by the Kennedy Center in 2006. She was presented with a Grammy Lifetime Achievement Award in 2011.

Meanwhile, a musical who's who continued to seek her out to sing on their records. Among them were Rod Stewart, Don Henley, Chicago, Ronnie Milsap, and Elton John. In 2005, she returned to No. 1 on the country hit parade by singing with Brad Paisley on his gospel song "When I Get Where I'm Going." It won a CMA Award, her eighth.

Between 2001 and 2018, she acquired the Splash Country Water Adventure Park, Smoky Mountain Cabins, Pirate's Voyage Dinner & Show, and the luxurious DreamMore Resort. She also was affiliated with a line of gambling slot machines that played her music, and the Cracker Barrel restaurant chain began marketing her CDs in its gift shops.On April 30, 2009, *9 to 5: The Musical* opened on Broadway. Dolly's first stage musical earned four Tony nominations, fifteen Drama Desk nominations, a Grammy nomination, and two LA Drama Critics Circle awards. It later ran in London (2019) and Sydney (2020).

Her country music output continued unabated. During the decade, she issued seven new albums. Her new "icon" status threw a spotlight on some of her most self-referential lyrics.

Others might praise me for what I've already done, but I am always looking onward and upward to find my next inspiration, my next big dream.

Livin' a Lie 1992

THIS SONG ORIGINALLY APPEARED on the soundtrack of 1992's *Straight Talk*.

Spotlight's on and shining bright and I like
standin' in it.
It's only superficial light, but I don't want to
end it.
Its warmth and glow has taken hold
And I'm caught up in the shine;
A Cinderella fairy tale, I want to claim as
mine.

Fancy clothes, a magic coach, and happy ever
after;
Like something from a story book, the
Cinderella chapter.
But when the clock strikes midnight and I lie
awake in bed
Reality, not fantasy, keeps runnin' through
my head.

You gotta walk the straight and narrow
And to thine own self be true
You gotta aim straight as an arrow,
All eyes are upon you.
But sometimes it feels so good that I can
almost justify
Livin' a lie . . . livin' a lie.
But I don't feel right . . . livin' a lie.

Is it wrong for me to want
The sweeter grass that's greener?
To chase the all-American dream,
I've always been a dreamer.
At the top and still I've got a heavy heart
inside.
I keep rememberin' my daddy told me as a
child.

You gotta walk the straight and narrow
And to thine own self be true
You gotta hold fast to the right.
Gotta aim straight as an arrow,
Walk onward toward the light.
Oh, and when I'm out there in it, I think I
might get by
Livin' this lie . . . livin' a lie.

All the fame and fortune, glory and prestige
Can't make you happy if it goes against what
you believe.
And I've sacrificed my honor, my values, and
my pride
Livin' a lie . . . livin' a lie.
Livin' a lie . . . I'm livin' a lie.
Livin' a lie . . . mmm.
Lie, lie, lie, l-l-l-lie.
I'm livin' a lie, lie, lie . . . l-l-lie.

Oh, you gotta walk the straight and narrow
And to thine ownself be true.
You gotta aim straight as an arrow,
God's eyes are upon you.
And you'll never find contentment, no matter
how you try
Livin' a lie . . . livin' a lie.
You won't get by . . . livin' a lie.

Livin' a lie . . . livin' a lie.
Livin' a lie . . . I gotta make it right.

This song seemed to write itself. I started working on it for the movie *Straight Talk*, and it just seemed to take off on its own. And it turned out to be really good.

In my own life, I don't know that I am living a lie. I guess I might look like I am. I know I look phony. But I'm totally real. I'm comfortable with who I am and the way I feel. Sometimes if my spiritual self gets after me, I wonder if I am overdoing it a little bit. But there's no way to tame me down.

Fish out of Water 1992

THIS LYRIC FROM THE *STRAIGHT TALK* movie describes how out of place Dolly's character feels as a country girl mingling with the elite.

I feel so out of place here
With this high society
These highfalutin people
Don't know what to make of me

I feel like a minnow
In a sea of Moby Dicks
A small fry in a big pan
They're caviar—I'm fish sticks

Fish out of water
I know I don't belong
Fish out of water
Everything I do is wrong

My style of hair, the clothes I wear
The way I speak, the things I eat
The way I act, my lack of tact
Nothin' seems to fit

Fish out of water
Flounderin' round
Out of my element
But I'm just as good as they are

Why do I feel second rate
It's like, "Sorry Charlie,
We want only tuna
With good taste"

I guess you could say Wal-Mart
Is quite a way from Gucci's
I'm Timex, they're Rolex
I'm Captain D's, they're sushi

Fish out of water
I've had it to the gills
Fish out of water
With these yuppie-guppy frills

Yeah, I'm a square in a round hole
A catfish in a goldfish bowl
A little fish with lots of soul
Out of my element

Fish out of water
Flounderin' round just for the halibut
Save me, save me
S.O.S. somebody
Save me, save me
Somebody rescue me
Fish out of water
Somebody throw me in
Fish out of water

On a scale of one to ten
I'm a two, perhaps a three
Compared to the big fish in the sea
I'm washed ashore so save me please

I'm in an awful fix
Fish out of water
Rescue me
And you better do it quick

Fish out of water
It's such a culture shock
Fish out of water
My stomach's tied in knots

Fish out of water
Fish out of water

Feeling like a fish out of water applied to my character in *Straight Talk*, "Shirlee Kenyon." She was totally a fish out of water with all those highfalutin people. That was just not her world. So I thought this song was appropriate for that situation.

We went to the aquarium to shoot that scene in the movie. That's where the song worked out really good, being there in the aquarium and looking through the fish.

Backwoods Barbie 2008

THIS SONG IS IN *9 TO 5: THE MUSICAL* and also served as the title tune of Dolly's 2008 album. *Backwoods Barbie* was the first album issued on her own Dolly label, which succeeded Blue Eye Records.

I grew up poor and ragged, just a simple country girl.
I wanted to be pretty more than anything in the world.
Like Barbie or the models in the Frederick's catalog
From rags to wishes in my dreams I could have it all.

I'm just a backwoods Barbie, too much makeup, too much hair.
Don't be fooled by thinkin' that the goods are not all there.
Don't let these false eyelashes lead you to believe
That I'm as shallow as I look 'cause I run true and deep.

I've always been misunderstood because of how I look.
Don't judge me by the cover 'cause I'm a real good book.
So read into it what you will, but see me as I am.
The way I look is just a country girl's idea of glam.

I'm just a backwoods Barbie in a push-up bra and heels.
I might look artificial; but where it counts I'm real.
And I'm all dolled up and hopin' for a chance to prove my worth,
And even backwoods Barbies get their feelings hurt.

I'm just a backwoods Barbie, too much makeup, too much hair.
Don't be fooled by thinkin' that the goods are not all there.
Yes, I can see where I could be misjudged upon first glance;
But even backwoods Barbie's deserve a second chance.

I'm just a backwoods Barbie just asking for a chance,
Just a backwoods Barbie.

I wrote this for *9 to 5: The Musical.* Writing for Broadway was one of the biggest challenges I've ever had, but also one of my most fun experiences. After the show ran in New York, it went to England and Australia. And now it travels around everywhere. It has been a pretty big success out there on the road.

"Backwoods Barbie" is me saying, "Okay, here's who I am, just a backwoods country girl who wants to be pretty more than anything in the world." And I did. I loved anything fancy. I wanted to be pretty, like the pictures in the magazines.

When I wrote the song, I talked about all that I am and all that I wanted to be. But it was also saying, "Don't judge a book by the cover, because there's a lot underneath here." I might look artificial and corny to you. You might think I have no taste. But underneath the look is a person. There's a brain and a heart underneath the hair and the boobs. The song is really about that.

I actually had a Dolly doll back in the 1970s. Anne Warden, who was the wife of my manager Don Warden, created the Dolly. She did a beautiful job. They still sell some of them at Dollywood. I'm thinking about doing another one in the future.

The "Dolly" doll was curvy, just like a Barbie doll. Why not? So am I.

ABOVE: I posed with her in the 1970s, but some people save "Dolly" as a keepsake in her original packaging. As for being "backwoods," I have been known to go fishing, especially if Carl takes me and baits my hooks.

The Lonesomes 2008

THIS *BACKWOODS BARBIE* ALBUM SONG dives into Dolly's psyche as it describes a dark night of the soul.

My heart's as heavy as an anvil.
My tears are puddled in my eyes
And time seems to be at a standstill.
I've really got the lonesomes tonight.

Feels like I'm never gonna make it.
I'd like to lie right down and die.
It's so very hard to fake it.
I've really got the lonesomes tonight.

Just like that old song by Hank Williams;
I am so lonesome I could cry.
Can't seem to shake these sad old feelin's,
I've really got the lonesomes tonight.
'Cause I've really got the lonesomes tonight.
Oooh, I'm pretty sad, mm-mm-mm-mm

Oh, I hope tomorrow will ring truer.
And I'll awake and I will be all right.
But right now I couldn't feel much bluer,
Can't shake these lonely memories inside.

Oh, but my heart's as heavy as an anvil.
My tears are all puddled in my eyes.
And my mind has really got its hands full,
I've really got the lonesomes tonight.

You got that right, I've really got the lonesomes tonight.
But I'll be all right, I've really got the lonesomes tonight.
Got lonesomes, mm-mm-mm

I think we all get "The Lonesomes." The song reminded me of the ones that Hank Williams used to write. It reminded me of some old-timey songs like "In the Pines," those mournful, painful songs of feeling really, really, really alone and desperate and forlorn. I can write them as pitiful as ol' Hank sometimes. I ain't as good a writer, but I think I can feel as lonesome as he did. I do get "The Lonesomes."

That's when the songwriting becomes therapy. I never went to a therapist, because songwriting heals me. With my little guitar, my little head for writing songs, and my gift for rhyming, I can lift myself up.

Kiss It (and Make It All Better) 2016

THIS PLEA TO HEAL a wounded heart is on the *Pure & Simple* album.

When I was a child whenever I'd fall
Skinning my elbows and knees,
Mommie or Daddy would kiss away tears,
Kiss all the places in need.
Scraped, scratched, or broken,
A kiss was a token
That mended and cured every part.
Then I grew up and I fell in love,
Fell so hard that it broke my heart;
And now there you are.

CHORUS
So kiss it and make it all better.
Kiss me and heal all this hurt.
Kiss me all over and over, all over,
'Cause that's where it hurts the worst.

Damsel in distress in a red satin dress
And a knight with his armor askew.
Two broken hearts and all other parts
Left in lost-love residue.
Came in for a drink so I wouldn't think,
To erase every thought from my head.
But on second thought, I think we ought
To see each other safely to bed.

REPEAT CHORUS

I need a shoulder to cry on, to lean on,
Two loving arms to hold me,
Tender words said to make me forget
And two lips to kiss me to sleep.

REPEAT CHORUS

Kiss me tonight and make it all right.
Just kiss it and make it all better.
Oh, oh, oh, oh kiss it, make it better.
Kiss me and heal all this hurt.

And kiss me all over, all over and over,
'Cause that's where it hurts the worst.
Kiss it, kiss it (and make it better).
(Kiss it) Kiss it, make it better.

This was a fairly new song that I did for the *Pure & Simple* album. You know how, as a kid, you would say this when you fell and had an accident? This was playing off of that. Your heart's been broken and you've been hurt, so when you meet somebody you want them to kiss you and make it all better. It sort of has the same theme as "The Bargain Store": "Please put the pieces back together, and I'll be good as new."

Cologne 2008

THIS IS A RARE DOLLY SONG where she portrays the mistress. It was issued on *Backwoods Barbie*.

You ask me not to wear cologne,
She'll know you've been with me alone.
And you can't take our secret home
So you ask me not to wear cologne.
You can wipe the makeup off,
The lipstick or a little gloss;
But fragrance lingers on and on
So you ask me not to wear cologne.

You leave my bed and go to hers
Leaving me alone and hurt.
I love you whether right or wrong
And you ask me not to wear cologne.

I'm not out to hurt someone,
Not you, not her, not anyone.
But I've got heartaches of my own,
Why, I can't even wear cologne.
Oh, but I never meant for this to be,
It wasn't in my heart to cheat.
Love has a nature all its own
So I willingly gave up cologne.

Oh, and every time you come to me
I realize I'm in too deep.
I know you love us both and I keep holdin' on
You ask me not to wear cologne;
You say don't wear cologne.

Oh, whatever am I gonna do
'Cause I am so in love with you.
I know you love us both, but where
do I belong?
You ask me not to wear cologne?

You ask me not to wear cologne,
She'll know you've been with me alone.
And you can't take our secret home
So you ask me not to wear cologne.

Oh, how do I walk away
From the greatest love I've known?
You ask me not to wear cologne.
Oh, you ask me not to wear cologne.

You ask me not to wear cologne.
She'll know you've been with me alone
And I'm a scent you can't take home.
But will I ever get to wear cologne?

I like the melody in this one. I liked the way I could do my vocal a little bit differently. Sometimes, I write a song just so I can sing different than what people might expect.

I also like to act in my songs, and in this one I got to be the colorful "other woman." I usually complain about another woman taking my man, but this was the other way around. "You ask me not to wear perfume when you're coming in my bed, because you're going to take that home and your wife will know."

At one point, I had my own perfume, and I'm starting a new fragrance now. Yes, I do love perfumes.

My “Backwoods Barbie” guitar has a pink carrying case, of course. It’s a baby Martin, the kind of guitar I learned to play and first wrote songs on when I was a young girl.

From Here to the Moon and Back 2012

IN THE MOVIE *JOYFUL NOISE*, Dolly memorably slow-danced to this with Kris Kristofferson, who played the spirit of her deceased husband. On her 2014 album *Blue Smoke*, she sang it as a duet with Willie Nelson.

I could hold out my arms
Say "I love you this much."
I could tell you how long
I will long for your touch.

How much and how far
Would I go to prove
The depth and the breadth
Of my love for you?

From here to the moon and back,
Who else in this world will love you like that?
Love everlasting I promise you that,
From here to the moon and back,
From here to the moon and back.

I want you to know you can always depend
On promises made and love without end.
No need to wonder how faithful I'll be
Now and on into eternity.

From here to the moon and back
Who else in this world will love you like that?
Forever and always I'll be where you're at,
From here to the moon and back,
From here to the moon and back.

I blow you a kiss as I wish on a star
Counting my blessings for all that you are.
Thank Heaven for you and to God tip my hat
From here to the moon and back.

And I'll spend forever just proving that fact
From here to the moon and back . . .
From here to the moon and back.

This song is very much based on my husband, Carl. I'm using it in a musical for Broadway that I'm writing. It's my life story as a musical. This is going to be sung as a duet between the "Carl" character and the "Dolly" character in that.

I originally wrote it for the *Joyful Noise* movie soundtrack. That's where I got to dance with Kris Kristofferson, which was great. And it is such a pretty song, if I do say so myself.

Then Willie was doing an album of duets with girls. He said, "I like that song of yours. Why don't we do 'From Here to the Moon and Back'?" I said, "Okay. I think I can pick that on my guitar." And so we did it.

One of the most romantic scenes in any of my movies is when my "G. G. Sparrow" character in *Joyful Noise* slow dances with the ghost of her late husband, "Bernard," who was played by the dreamy Kris Kristofferson. Kris and I have known each other for years: This shot of the two of us is from the 1980s.

Lover du Jour 2014

FRENCH PHRASES PEPPER THE LYRICS of this song on Dolly's *Blue Smoke* album.

(Spoken)
What are you looking at, lover boy?
It won't do you any good
'Cause I know your kind.
If you want to be mine
We gotta get this understood . . .

Oh, I'm not gonna be your, be your lover
du jour,
Your special of the day, no way, adieu,
farewell, bonjour.
Pardon my French, but there's no chance in
Hell for you for sure.
If you think I will be your, be your lover
du jour.
Pas moi, not me.

I am well aware of your good looks and
sexy ways,
Serving up yourself to girls to satisfy
your taste.
The fresh catch of the day on your
Romeo buffet,
Served up hot and ready, just having it
your way.

Well, if I'm on the menu you'd better get
this straight.
Me 'n' you had better come to terms before
you grab your plate.
Don't even place your order if you believe
that I
Am just some cheesy little dish, just another
chick-ey pie.

No I'm not gonna be your, be your lover
du jour,
The flavor of the day, no way, adieu, farewell,
bonjour.
Pardon my French, but there's no chance
in Hell that I'll endure
The fact that I would only be your lover
du jour.
Oublie moi, forget me.

(Spoken)
Still lookin', lover boy?
Have you changed your view?
I told you once, I'll say it again
I'll take no merde from you . . . that's crap.

If you want somethin' appetizin', somethin'
real and satisfyin'
I'll be worth a second look, but that's the
only way.

'Cause I'm not gonna be your, be your amour
du jour,
Your playmate of the day, no way, adieu,
farewell, bonjour.
'Cause I won't be caught up in all your charm
and your allure.
No, I'm not gonna be your, be your lover
du jour.

No, I'm not gonna be your, be your lover
du jour,
The special of the day, no way, adieu,
farewell, bonjour.
Pardon my French, but there's no chance
in Hell that I'll endure
The fact that I would only be your lover
du jour.

No, I'm not gonna be your, be your lover
du jour, your lover du jour.
Mm-mm-mm, c'est dommage, too bad.

Now I am not for your amusement. I'm not
a toy.
You're nothin' but trouble. Oooh, you're
a bad, bad boy.

Well, I'm a tasty starter or I'm a full-course
meal,
Dessert or after-dinner drink and you can
have your fill.

Pardon my French . . .
Tu ne causes que des ennuis.

Tu es un mauvais garcon
Any questions?

Aw, my French is awful, but my love is
awesome.
Oooh, they're gonna laugh at me in
France . . . sorry.

I had my nieces with me out in LA. One of them, Rebecca, was about fifteen or sixteen at the time, and she was as big a flirt as I am. She came by that naturally. She always has a boyfriend somewhere. We were riding up and down the coast and stopped at this little fish restaurant. The menu said, "soup du jour," and my nieces said to me, "What is that word?" I said, "I think that means, 'soup of the day.'" Rebecca was flirting with this cute waiter. I said, "Oh Lord, Rebecca. Is that your lover du jour?"

So I went home and wrote it. I don't speak a word of French. I can barely speak English, much less French. I had a couple of people give me some French words to put in the lyrics. People who speak French say, "I don't hear a word of French in that song. It's either your accent, or you're using the wrong words." Anyway, I was trying to get that in there. Maybe somebody who speaks French should record it.

I know this photo looks like it takes a village to get me ready for the cameras. I'm really not that "high maintenance." I can put on my makeup, costume, and wig and be ready for anything in fifteen minutes or less.

Say Forever You'll Be Mine 2016

THIS WAS A BIG HIT for Porter Wagoner and Dolly Parton, reaching No. 5 on the charts in 1976 and becoming the title tune of an album. Exactly forty years later, Dolly turned it into a solo plea for lasting romance. Appropriately, she re-recorded it for the album celebrating her golden anniversary, *Pure & Simple*.

Forever is the love that is filled with understanding.
Forever is the love that is true and undemanding.
Forever is the love that can stand the test of time.
Forever I am yours, say forever you'll be mine.

Trouble clouds may fill our skies.
It might even rain awhile;
But the rain will go away.
There's always a brighter day.

Darlin' I won't promise you
That we'll be happy all the time,
But forever I am yours;
Say forever you'll be mine.

Say forever you'll be mine,
'Cause forever I am yours.
I'll do anything for you,
Anything you ask me to.

Darlin' I won't promise you
That we'll be happy all the time.
But forever I am yours,
Say forever you'll be mine.

So many of the songs on *Pure & Simple* I wrote because of Carl and me and our fifty-year marriage. When we had our fiftieth anniversary, we got remarried. We got all dressed up in fancy clothes, me in a fancy gown with a veil and him in his dressed-up duds. So several songs on that album were based on our love. And some were songs I had written years before.

"Say Forever You'll Be Mine" is one of the earliest songs I ever wrote for Carl and me; I wrote that way back in our first years together.

I think, for us, the secret [of a lasting marriage] has been that we have a lot of respect for each other. And we have trust. We have a great sense of humor. We're as funny as can be. You would absolutely roll on the floor if you saw us together. We just do these routines all the time, without even realizing that we're doing them. We're both very witty and very quick. He's really funny, and I've been known to be. So sometimes we just laugh so hard. I think that laughter has been one of the best parts of our relationship. I never know what he's going to do or say, and he never knows what I'm going to do or say.

I don't choke him to death, saying do this or don't do that. We love our freedom. We have a lot of things in common. We both like to travel around. We have our little camper, and we like to get out and just sightsee. We'll stop at a grocery store, get a few little things, and go picnicking. We'll go to drive-through restaurants. We just like to do simple things. We don't complicate our lives, and we don't overthink things. We live a pretty peaceful life, actually.

I think if you can be friends, that's a big, big part of it. There's nothing you can't do together. Being great friends is the secret of happiness.

LEFT: Carl and I have never called each other by our first names. Never have, never will. It just seems so impersonal to us to do that. We call each other all kinds of pet names. He calls me "Kid," and I call him "Dad."

ABOVE: Carl's done kissed me on the mouth, and how. He's made me one happy country girl for more than fifty years. We were dating when he enlisted in the National Guard. Of course, I figured out a way to visit him in Georgia at the army base where he did his basic training, pictured here. He squeezed, hugged, and kissed me so hard that he knocked my wig off.

The Sacrifice 2011

IN THIS RARE INTROSPECTIVE LYRIC, Dolly thinks back on her life and career with some questioning, contemplation, and self-doubt. She included this song on her album *Better Day*.

Well, I've sacrificed time with family and friends
Gave up vacations for work without end
Twenty-four seven, three hundred and sixty-five
But I was willing to make the sacrifice

But empty or full, I've carried my pail
You don't drink the water if you don't dig the well
Through blood, sweat, and tears I have built a good life
But it didn't come without sacrifice

But I was gonna be rich no matter how much it cost
And I was gonna win no matter how much I lost
All through the years I kept my eye on the prize
You ask if it's worth the sacrifice, the sacrifice

I think about Jesus and all that He gave
And the ultimate sacrifice that He made
He is my strength and my guiding light
And He's taught me that nothing's without sacrifice

I was gonna be rich no matter how much it cost
And I was gonna win no matter how much I lost
I wanted success and, brother, I've paid the price
And, yes, it's been worth the sacrifice, the sacrifice

I was gonna be rich no matter how much it cost
And I was gonna win no matter how much I lost
Grindstones and rhinestones have made up my life
But I've shined like a diamond through sacrifice

I was gonna be rich no matter how much it cost
And I was gonna win no matter how much I lost
But I hope God will tell me, 'Well done, my child
You've won your reward through your sacrifice,
The sacrifice

But sometimes I wonder in the still of the night
Is it really worth the sacrifice?
I've often laughed and I've often cried
I've often failed but I've always tried

I made the sacrifice
The sacrifice

I can't even guess how many miles I've traveled following my dreams. From riding in packed cars to cruising the highways in my custom tour bus, from Hollywood limousines to international jets, I've rambled and roamed all my life.

This is a song that I wrote that just came out of my heart and soul, my gut. Sometimes you wonder if you've made all the wise choices. Would you do things differently if you could?

People say, "How come all of this success happened to you?" I say, "Because I sacrificed whatever I had to in order to get it." You can't veer off into this and that. You can't lose your momentum if you've got a dream and a focus. I always felt like God was directing me. So I'm not going to let up until He says, "Stop." I just keep going, like a horse with blinders on.

I wrote "The Sacrifice" because somebody asked me that question. Well, the answer is, I gave up time with family and friends. I gave up vacations for work. I "carried my pail." Like the song says, "You don't drink the water, if you don't drill the well." One of my favorite lines I ever wrote is, "I was gonna be rich, no matter how much it cost / And I was going to win, no matter how much I lost."

It's only in the wee hours, when you're fading off to sleep, that you ask, "Is it worth the sacrifice?" I think I probably wouldn't have done anything different, because I believe that this is what I was supposed to do. Who am I not to sacrifice to make things better for the people here that I am responsible for?

Yes, I would do it all again. No doubt about it.

CHAPTER 14

BETTER DAYS

DOLLY PARTON IS BELOVED BY MILLIONS FOR HER POSITIVE ATTITUDE and chin-up optimism. These traits increasingly infused her music in the second decade of the twenty-first century.

There were certainly reasons to feel upbeat. New manager Danny Nozell helped stage a triumphant tour of Europe, North America, Australia, and New Zealand in 2014, capped by an appearance at England's Glastonbury Festival before 180,000 fans. Their enthusiasm was echoed by the equally wild crowds that greeted her concert tour in Australia.

Also in 2014, the Recording Industry Association of America (RIAA) certified her worldwide record sales at 100 million. In 2016, the CMA presented her with a Lifetime Achievement Award.

After wildfires decimated her East Tennessee homeland in 2016, Dolly organized and hosted an Emmy Award–winning telethon that raised $8.9 million for victims. By 2018, her Imagination Library had distributed more than 100 million free books to children. It expanded from a statewide Tennessee initiative to an international one, celebrated in the 2020 documentary *The Library That Dolly Built*.

Coat of Many Colors, based on her classic song, became one of the highest rated TV movies in history when it aired on NBC in 2015. She followed it with an Emmy-nominated, holiday-themed sequel in 2016. She issued her debut children's album in 2017, which followed her first effort as a children's book author, 2009's *I Am a Rainbow*.

Her iconic "I Will Always Love You" took one more trip to the top of the charts in 2016. It was the cornerstone song in the medley "Forever Country" saluting the fiftieth anniversary of the CMA. "Forever Country" was 2017's CMA Video of the Year, with Dolly "closing the show" in the star-studded production.

She ended the decade with a blizzard of activities. In 2019, eight of her songs inspired movies on Netflix in a series titled *Dolly Parton's Heartstrings*. Also in that year, she was honored as the Grammy MusiCares Person of the Year, starred in the NPR podcast *Dolly Parton's America*, co-hosted the CMA Awards on ABC, introduced her Hallmark Channel movie *Christmas at Dollywood*, wowed the crowd with a surprise appearance at the Newport Folk Festival, and celebrated her fiftieth anniversary as a Grand Ole Opry member on an NBC special.

She topped the gospel charts and won a Grammy in 2019 via "God Only Knows," a collaboration with the band For King & Country. She entered the new decade at the top of the dance charts performing with Galantis on its international hit "Faith."

These are the songs that illustrate indomitable Dolly's philosophy of life.

There's so much darkness in the world. I just hope that I can be a force for good and a light for others.

There'll Always Be Music

With Porter Wagoner 1973

THIS WAS A PORTER AND DOLLY DUET on their LP *Love and Music*. She sang it to Porter when she visited him for the last time in 2007.

(Dolly)
A mother sings as she rocks her babies
Children sing the noted nursery rhymes
(Porter)
The old church bell is ringing
For the Sunday morning singing
Music is as old as the time

(Porter)
As the farmer works the fields, he sings a song
The songbirds in the trees sing along
(Dolly)
And the wind makes melodies
As it whistles through the trees
Man's burdens are made lighter with a song

DUET CHORUS
There'll always be music as long as there's a story to be told
There'll always be music 'cause music is the voice of the soul
There'll always be music

(Dolly)
Rain makes rhythmic sounds when it's falling
There's music in a newborn baby's cry
(Porter)
There's music all around
And there is no sweeter sound
For that's the way a man expresses life

(Duet)
In Heaven there's a choir of angels singing
We often heard about God's angel band
Music will live on
When men on earth are gone
There'll still be music in that promised land

REPEAT DUET CHORUS

I sang once more for Porter during the celebration of his 50th anniversary as a member of the Grand Ole Opry in 2007. He passed away just five months later at age 80.

I wrote "There'll Always Be Music" many, many years ago, but I remember it well. It says that there will always be music, as long as there's a story to be told and because music is the voice of the soul. Music is so important in so many ways. I know that whenever I feel down or I am sick, music can bring me up. When I hear music or when I write music, it can weave all those good feelings around.

Music focuses your attention and allows the body to heal itself. Even when music is sad on your heart, you're caught up in it. I think from the beginning of man, it has been physically healing as well as mentally healing. I really do.

I believe that music is a healing profession. They use it for dementia and Alzheimer's patients, because when they play music, people connect. Music makes such a deep impression on your psyche that it can bring your mind back to a place where you're safe. You recognize it, because it is so deeply embedded in you.

If I Had Wings 2014

THIS SONG ON DOLLY'S 2014 *Blue Smoke* album became the basis of a Netflix movie in 2019.

If I had wings, I'd fly away from
All-a my troubles, all-a my pain.
And I would fly to a place of comfort,
Heaven knows I need a change.
If I had wings, Lord give me wings.

Oh, I've had my share of sorrow,
Walked a long and lonesome road.
I could use a new tomorrow;
If I had wings, I'd make it so.
One cannot predict the future.
One cannot undo the past.
But we can make the present useful,
Build a future that will last.

If I had wings, I'd fly away from
All-a my troubles, all-a my woes.
And I would fly 'til I found freedom.
If I had wings, I'd up and go.
If I had wings, Lord give me wings.

If I had wings, I'd fly away from
All-a my troubles, all-a my woes.
And I would fly 'til I found freedom.
If I had wings, I'd up and go.
If I had wings, Lord give me wings.

(If I had wings) Oh, if I had wings.
(If I had wings) Oh, Lord just give me wings.
(If I had wings) If I had wings, I'd make a
change.
If I had wings, if I had wings.

Oh-oh-oh, oh-oh,
If I had wings, if I had wings.

And here's me with wings. I'm a little happier in this photo than the song "If I Had Wings" implies, but I do have wings.

I like writing songs like this, both for myself and for other people. "If I Had Wings" is for people who are having troubles or heartaches. Think of people in prisons. They're thinking, "If I had wings, I'd fly until I found freedom." If you're bedridden or in a wheelchair, you're thinking, "If I had wings, I'd just get up and go." Maybe you want to fly out of a bad relationship. You're going, "If I could just get up far enough to move on out of here and get out of this." People want to fly away from their pain. If only we all had wings.

Red Shoes

(Dolly Parton / Linda Perry) 2018

THIS IS ONE OF THE SONGS Dolly created for the soundtrack of the film *Dumplin'*.

I remember as a child
I was absolutely wild
'Bout some red shoes that my
Aunt Lucy wore
She would let me stomp around
In those high heels up and down
'Round the house and 'round the
wrap-around porch

And from that moment on
I've had a pair of my own.
They make me feel at home
And brand new.
They build my confidence
As if they've been Heaven sent
I feel alone, I'm puttin' on my red shoes

I begged Mama pretty please
From the Wish Book order me
A pair of red shoes for my feet;
So Mama did.
Through the years I've thought about
Aunt Lucy's love and think of how
Such little things in life can make or
break a kid

I believe that every child
Needs to feel a sense of pride
And someone to love and guide
And see them through.
So many miles I've traveled,
Many times they've come unraveled
On the road both smooth or graveled.
But I've made it through . . .

Hell and half of Georgia,
A walkin' thru New Orleans,
Walked the streets of Memphis boldly
Strolled around a block or two.
And if God sees fit to own me
Anyone that's ever known me
Knows I'd walk the gold streets only
In a pair of red shoes.

And if I ever get to Heaven,
If I ever get to Heaven,
If I ever get to Heaven,
And Lord I hope I do.
I will walk the streets of Glory,
I will walk the streets of Glory,
I will carry my Lucy's story
And walk with her in red shoes

They're red, they have five-inch heels, they're decorated with my initials in gold, and they're over-the-top fabulous. Any questions?

There was a book called *Dumplin'* that came out a few years ago. Someone sent it to me and said, "This might be something you'd like to produce or adapt." I said, "No, that would be too self-serving. Because the story is about me." This little girl in the story liked me. I was an inspiration to her, and she loved my songs. So I said, "No, I would never do that." Then I forgot about it.

A few years later, Jennifer Aniston adapted it. At that point, they approached me to see if they could use my music [in the movie]. I said they could. Then they asked if I would write some additional music for it, and I said I would. So I started working with [producer/songwriter] Linda Perry.

One of the songs I love the most in that whole soundtrack album is "Red Shoes." It's kind of like my modern-day "Coat of Many Colors." In the movie, there was a pair of red shoes that represented dreams and plans and things.

In my real life, there was a pair of red, high-heeled shoes. The welfare people used to send boxes of clothes up to the mountains where we lived. When I was a kid, I found this pair of red shoes that were kind of like the shoes I wear now. I thought I could wear those shoes, but they were grown-people's shoes. I cried over those shoes, because they wouldn't let me have them. Those red shoes have always stayed in my mind.

We used a little bit of that story in the *Coat of Many Colors* movie, which was made before *Dumplin'* came out. In our movie, the town tramp gave me the red shoes.

In *Dumplin'*, the "Aunt Lucy" character just loved Dolly. So I used her name in the song. I loved writing that song, and I love singing it, too. Because it talks about "if I ever get to Heaven, I hope to tromp around on those golden streets in a pair of red shoes. Just like the ones that 'Aunt Lucy' let me wear to tromp around on her porch."

Better Get to Livin'

(Dolly Parton / Kent Wells) 2007

THIS SONG REACHED NO. 47 on the country charts and was included on the *Backwoods Barbie* album. Her co-writer on it is Kent Wells, who has been producing Dolly's records, off and on, since 2003.

People always comin' up to me and askin'
"Dolly, what's your secret?
With all you do, your attitude just seems to be so good,
How do you keep it?"
Well, I'm not the Dalai Lama, but I'll try
To offer up a few words of advice.

You better get to livin', givin'.
Don't forget to throw in a little forgivin'
And love along the way.
You better get to knowin', showin'
A little bit more concern about where you're goin'.
Here's a word unto the wise, you better get to livin'.

A girlfriend came to my house,
Started cryin' on my shoulder Sunday evening.
She was spinnin' such a sad tale,
I could not believe the yarn that she was weaving.
So negative the words she had to say.
I said if I had a violin I'd play.

I said you'd better get to livin', givin'
Be willin' and forgivin' 'cause all healin'
Has to start with you.
You better stop whinin', pinin'
Get your dreams in line
And then just shine, design,
Refine 'til they come true.
And you better get to livin'.

Your life's a wreck, your house is a mess,
And your wardrobe way outdated.
All your plans just keep on fallin' thru.
Overweight and underpaid, under appreciated,
I'm no guru but I'll tell you this I know is true.

You better get to livin', givin',
A little more thought about bein' a little more willin'
To make a better way.
Don't sweat the small stuff, keep your chin up,
Just hang tough and if it gets too rough,
Fall on your knees and pray,
And do that every day.
Then you'll get to livin'.

The day we're born we start to die,
Don't waste one minute of this life,
Get to livin'.
Share your dreams and share your laughter,
Make some points for the great hereafter,
Better start carin', better start sharin',
Better start tryin', better start smilin'
And you better get to livin'.

This is a good song for anybody to lift their spirits up. People are always coming up to me and asking me for advice. I'm not the Dolly Mama, not the Dalai Lama. But the song just tries to give you a little bit of advice. It tells you things you'd better do if you want to have a happy life.

Kent Wells and I have worked together for many years. He's been my bandleader, my musical director. He's also produced my records. We work so well together because we're so much alike. He's a country boy from Arkansas.

He knows music really well, and we've worked together on a few songs. One was "Home," which we had a lot of fun doing. He usually has the melody, and I write most of the words. But we work together on both. He'll add a few lines, and I'll add some music here and there. All in all, we've done well with the songs. "Better Get to Livin'" is one of our best.

Out of the Silence (Came a Song)

Recorded by Porter Wagoner 1971

THIS DOLLY PARTON MEDITATION was sung on the 1971 LP *Porter Wagoner Country*.

Silence was around me as I walked along.
My mind was so troubled. I felt so alone.
I had no desire to live.
I had not a will to go home.
Then out of the silence came a song.

The words were sharp
And they cut deep into my troubled mind.
The melody was piercing
As it tore into this heart of mine.

You have the legs to walk along
While others are born lame.
You have a mind to think with
While others are insane.
You live while others die
And yet no thanks are shown.
Out of the silence came this song.

(Spoken)
Then I saw a vision of myself.
My legs were bent and lame.
Not only was I crippled,
But I couldn't speak my name.
And then I saw a graveyard
With my own funeral going on.
Then out of the silence came a song.

You have the legs to walk along
While others are born lame.
You have a mind to think with
So why should you complain?
You live while others die
And yet no thanks are shown.
Out of the silence came this song.

Out of the silence came a song.

I wrote this song when I was still back home. I remember sitting up on Graveyard Hill with my guitar. I was thinking about all those people in their graves, wondering about their lives, of all the things that might have happened to them. I was thinking about what was going on in my life and about the other people around me.

Then, all of a sudden, a song came to me. It was really an inspired kind of song. It's unusual, a little different. But I really liked it. When I was writing it, I knew it was special. When you write as many as I do, there are some that you can take or leave. They're like your kids. Some of them are more well behaved. Some of them have better qualities. But they are all yours.

I remember that when I wrote this one, I thought, "That's a little deeper than what I've been writing." I took a lot of pride in it. I felt kind of "grown up," somehow, when I wrote it. I felt like somebody needed to hear something that I was so inspired to write.

Country Is as Country Does

(Dolly Parton / Mac Davis) 2011

THIS SONG WAS CO-WRITTEN with Mac Davis and appeared on the album *Better Day*.

I can live in a mansion or a double wide,
Eat sushi raw or my catfish fried.
Wherever I am, then that's where I belong.
'Cause I'm quite content with who I am.
And if you ain't, well kiss my ham.
Country is as country does and I'm country
to the bone.

Country is as country does,
It's the way I am and it's the way I wuz.
It's the way I always will be, that's for sure.
Country born and country bred,
Country-fied and country fed,
A country heart and a country head,
'Cause I'm country to the core.

Yeah, I can drive a tractor or a Cadillac,
I can fly first class or plum in the back;
But I'll be the same ol' gal when I arrive.
Oh, I can wear denim or I can wear silk,
Drink champagne or chocolate milk.
Take the best or live with less, 'cause a
country girl survives.

Country is as country does,
It's the way I am and it's the way I wuz.
And the way I'll be until they lay me low.
Country born and country bred,
I'm country-fied and I'm country fed.
And I'll be that way 'til I'm country dead.
'Cause I'm country head to toe.

And what you see is what you get.
Nothing's ever changed me yet
Nothin' will, it's a pretty safe bet
'Cause I'm country thru and thru. Yee-hoo!

Country is as country does.
It's the way I am and it's the way I wuz.
It's the way I'll be until my dyin' day.
I'm country born and country bred
Country-fied and country fed,
And nothin' done or nothin' said
Can change my country ways.
Nothin' done or nothin' said
Nothin's gonna change my country ways.

Uh-huh, I don't think so . . .
I wouldn't change if I could.
Country is as country does.
It's the way I iz and it's the way I wuz.
Country born and country bred,
I'm countrified and I'm country fed.

(Spoken)
Hey, yeah, you know that.
I'm country, but now that don't mean I can't
go to town.

I'm proud to be country. I love real country music, mountain music, bluegrass, and gospel, the stuff I grew up on. If I had my druthers, I'd pull back everything else and do just that, my first love. But you can't make a living doing it.

I could never be like some of the boys and girls who make it today and then don't want to be identified as being just country [performers]. I couldn't be anything but country, and I know that about myself. So why not be who you are?

"Country Is as Country Does" is a song I wrote with Mac Davis that puts it all out there where it belongs. It's a really fun song, and it sums me up.

Change It 2009

THIS WAS A STANDOUT TUNE in Dolly's score for *9 to 5: The Musical*. The Broadway cast included Allison Janney in the role originated by Lily Tomlin and Megan Hilty as Dolly's "Doralee Rhodes" character.

(Spoken)
Hello . . . I know you've got a world of
problems.
And you think you can't do anything to
solve 'em;
But I am here to tell you you can.

Somethin' got you down, got you chained
and bound
Well break it. (Face it)
If you've built a wall and know it needs
to fall,
Then shake it. (Replace it)
Somethin' that you know is dammin' up
the flow,
Tear the damn dam down.
Let me explain it.
If you don't take the reigns, it's going to stay
the same
Nothin's gonna change if you don't change it.

(Spoken)
Let's do this!
Don't let fear and doubt leave you empty
and without.

You got somethin' on your mind that's
naggin' all the time,
Well nix it. (Resist it)
Somethin' in your life that just ain't
sittin' right,
Well fix it. (Just kick it)
If you've lost your place somethin' in
your face
If there's an empty space and you can't
name it.
That feelin' in your gut that's got you in a rut,
You're made of better stuff and you can
change it.

Change it,
You don't want your little light to
never shine.
Change it,
Turn it up on bright and get your goals
in line.
There's a great new world out there
For those who dare to claim it.
A better day is on the way and only you
can change it.

Cha-cha-change, cha-cha-change, change it!
No dream you can't accomplish, no mountain
you can't climb.
So activate your love and faith, you can
change.

Stand up, grab ahold, give everything
you've got.
When the road is dark and cold, walk on
fearing not.
Get your life in order, clean house, and
rearrange it.
Raise your voice and make a choice
Committed now to tear the damn dam down
And change it.
Change it.

Little Dolly Parton with a show on Broadway: Talk about dreaming big dreams. I'm posing with, from left, Stephanie J. Block who played "Judy," Allison Janney, who played "Violet," and Megan Hilty, who played "Doralee." The cast album was nominated for a Grammy, and *9 to 5* is still a big road-show attraction, I'm happy to report. Now, I'm working on another musical.

Here's another one of my advice songs, and in fact, it's one of my favorites. I wrote it for *9 to 5: The Musical*. When I was writing for the three girls, I was writing for each of them. "Change It" was written for "Doralee Rhodes." They all sang on it, but she had the featured part in it.

When I wrote for the musical, I know people were expecting big things. I wanted to rise to the occasion. I had to challenge myself in so many ways. I had to write all of these songs for all of these different characters. When I wrote for "Roz," it was for her to do a sexy song. I was having to act it out.

I think I had the most fun writing songs for "Mr. Hart." Even though he was a turd, in order to write for him I had to get inside of him and know what he was thinking. Because, of course, he thought he was right.

I have a little lake house out on Old Hickory Lake [near Nashville]. I remember going out there to write for the musical. There was this little staircase there, and I would swing around on it, pretending to be "Mr. Hart." I was getting down and dirty with "Mr. Hart." I was all by myself and thinking, "Lord, if anybody could see me, they'd think I'm absolutely insane."

I guess because it was such a challenge, I overwrote. I probably had five or six songs for "Mr. Hart" when they only needed one. I just wanted to make sure I covered all the bases. I've got tons of extra stuff that I wrote. Maybe someday I'll do a whole album of the ones that didn't make it into the show. Because some of the ones I wrote I thought were better than the ones we wound up using.

A Woman's Right 2018

THIS LIGHTHEARTED LYRIC SALUTES THE passage of the Nineteenth Amendment to the Constitution, which gave women the right to vote in 1920. Dolly's song was accompanied by an animated video. "A Woman's Right" appeared on an album titled *27: The Most Perfect Album,* which featured songs inspired by the twenty-seven amendments.

First they said we couldn't dance,
Then said we couldn't drink.
And unless some man allowed it,
They said we couldn't think.
They said we shouldn't speak
'Til we were spoken to.
Well, there was just so much back then
We weren't allowed to do.

CHORUS
But the first bite of that apple
I guess revealed the truth.
That's when Eve got smart
And that's why Adam don't like fruit.
But that ol' tree of knowledge
Had some limbs that broke.
We had to fight for women's rights,
They said we couldn't vote.

We've carried signs, we've cussed at times,
Marched up and down the streets.
We had to fight for women's rights,
Wore blisters on our feet.
We got tired of seein' all our dreams go up in smoke,
Burdens more than we could tote
Having lies crammed down our throats.
But that ol' dam finally broke
When women finally got the right to vote.
Do-do, Do, Do, Do-de-de-do, Da-da-da, da-da

They said a woman's place
Was staying in her hut.
Washin', cookin', cleanin',
Wipin' baby's butts.
They said she'd never see the day
We'd equal up to them.
But here we are, we've come so far.
I guess we sure showed them.

REPEAT CHORUS

We were defiant, I'll admit;
But we all knew we couldn't quit.
'Cause the suffrage amendment must be passed.
We protested, we cried out,
Finally it came about
Ratified by Tennessee, we won at last.

REPEAT CHORUS

They thought we were a joke.
They tried to dash our hopes.
With every word they spoke
They tried to revoke
A woman's right to vote.
But we made it!

People often ask me, "Are you a feminist?" I don't like labels. Does being feminine make me a feminist? I don't think so. I really just live who I am. I'm a woman and proud of it. And I believe every woman should have the right to be anything she can be capable of.

I didn't think I had to march in the streets to prove anything. I would write it in my songs and live it as a woman in business. I never felt like I had to do it any differently than that. Everybody has the right to do things their own way.

I got approached to do this song for an album they were making about the constitutional amendments. I said, "Let me write about a woman's right to vote, but in my own way." I wrote it tongue-in-cheek and clever, but still making a point. The fact that Tennessee was the deciding state to get the vote across gave me a little extra pride, so I wrote that in there, too. It has some really fun lines, and I was proud to be part of that project.

In 2020, we celebrated the one hundredth anniversary of women getting the right to vote in America. I've been celebrating women for years, sometimes in the privacy of my own yard at home.

There'll Be Love

With Porter Wagoner (Dolly Parton / Porter Wagoner) 1971

THIS SONG WAS INTRODUCED on the *Two of a Kind* album by Porter Wagoner and Dolly Parton.

There'll be love love love oh precious love

Just as long as there's two people there'll
be love
In spite of hate that fills the land
Love will always have command
As long as there's two people there'll be love

God created man and woman at the start
And He placed inside of them a lovin' heart
But it wasn't God that made the hate and lust
But as long as there's two people there'll
be love
There'll be love love love . . .

For every person somewhere there's a mate
It's the force for survival that brings hate
For even though the going might be rough
As long as there's two people there'll be love

You can lock a man behind a prison wall
And you may think that he has no love at all
But there's someone somewhere that he's
thinking of
For as long as there's two people there'll
be love

There'll be love love love . . .

There's a lot of bad in this world, a lot of darkness. But there's a lot of good and a lot of light. I agree with the idea that we're all born good, because we're all God's children. God is good. God is love. And I think it will always come back to that, to love.

It's awful how we corrupt ourselves, our children, and our world and make meanness the new norm. That's not how it's supposed to be. We are supposed to be loving, caring people. Sometimes, you need to write songs that make people rethink and try to do better.

I wrote this song with Porter Wagoner many years ago. I was with Porter when he was dying [in 2007]. I forgave him, and I thanked him for all of the opportunities he gave me. I wanted him to know exactly how I felt. I told him everything was fine and asked him that if there was anything he needed to forgive me for, please do. I wanted him to be free of anything that he might have been worrying about.

He was in hospice and wasn't coherent at the time. But I squeezed his hand, and he made a move to say he understood. He died just a few hours after we visited.

Why

With Mavis Staples 2018

DOLLY SINGS THIS ON THE SOUNDTRACK ALBUM for *Dumplin'* with pop-gospel great Mavis Staples, famed for such hits with the Staple Singers as "I'll Take You There," "Respect Yourself," and "If You're Ready (Come Go with Me)."

I often wonder what I'm doin' here.
There must be a reason, it's not always clear.
Why was I born, what's my purpose in life?
There must be an answer and I wonder why.

CHORUS
I wonder why we can't love and be free,
Let everyone be all that they need to be.
Judge not lest we be judged, let Heaven
decide.
Still we don't do it and I wonder why.

I know I'm not perfect, but nobody is.
Things more important are topping my list,
Acceptance and kindness and doin'
what's right.
We could if we would and I wonder why.

REPEAT CHORUS

I wonder why we don't do as we should,
Why we don't go about makin' things good.
Looking beyond faults, see what's inside.
God loves us all I bet He wonders why.

We can't love one another the way that
we are.
Why we are blinded from seein' that far?
Let's light our love lamp, spread radiant light.
We're walkin' in darkness and I wonder why.

REPEAT CHORUS

We could if we would and I wonder why.
Love is the answer to the question why.

I have loved Mavis Staples ever since her days with the Staple Singers, her family, and her dad who played that great guitar. I mean, I have followed her all the way. When we were doing the *Dumplin'* soundtrack album, we were getting different people to sing on different tracks. I said, "I bet she's still around. I'm going to find her." It turns out that she works all the time, just like I do. She was on tour overseas, but I got a message to her.

I said, "Would you come and sing on one of my songs? I have been inspired by your family for years. Some of my songs, like 'The Seeker,' have a Staple Singers attitude. I've written a song that I think you would be really good on. In fact, I stole some of your flavor for it." She said, "I would love to come sing on your song."

She did, and we had the best time. I just love her to death, and she did a great job on "Why." A year later, she sang my music when they honored me at the MusicCares Person of the Year banquet. I'll always treasure that.

I am a huge Mavis Staples fan. Her heart and her spirit are as big and soulful as her voice is.

Better Day 2011

THIS IS THE TITLE SONG of an album filled with optimistic messages.

All that's blue ain't sky and sea
Some of that blue's gonna fall on me.
But the blues don't come to stay,
They'll move away on a better day.

Troubles and woes and misery
Ain't gonna get the best of me.
Lift the shades, fix my gaze
On a better day; clear away, clear away.

Better days just up ahead
When sorrow ain't sleepin' in my bed,
When people ain't messin' with my head.
There's a better way, there's a brighter day.
Oh, there's a better day with clearer skies
Hope and promise on the rise.
Oh, the future, well, it's lookin' bright; there's a better day.
Look away, look away.

There's a better day, better days just up ahead
When sorrow ain't sleepin' in my bed,
When people ain't messin' with my head.
There's a better day, there's a better day.
Oh, all that's blue, it ain't sky and sea
Some of that blue's gonna fall on me;
But it won't always be that way.
'Cause there's a better day, look away, look away.

I love to write songs like "Shine Like the Sun" and "Better Day," because they are "attitude" songs. They are like preaching, in a way. I know I sound like an evangelist sometimes. Aunt Dorothy Jo, Grandpa Jake, and my uncle Orville were preachers. My mother might as well have been one, because she was always preaching to us about one thing and another. So I come by it naturally. So those songs are like sermons, in a way, trying to reach people.

Every day, I ask God to help me lift people up and to glorify Him. That's my mission, to lift mankind up if I can and to make people happy. If there's any light shining on me, I'd rather direct it at Him. I get a little scared sometimes when people act like I'm someone they're worshipping. That's an idol God, and I don't believe in that. I don't believe in idol worship of any kind. People often do that to show business people, and that's scary to me. That's when I say, "No. Look higher. Look up there. It ain't me." Let me radiate His light, so that people see Him, not me.

Every now and then, someone will burst into tears in front of me. I go, "Oh, cut it out. I ain't 'all that.' I ain't even all 'there'!"

If We Don't

(Dolly Parton / Linda Perry) 2018

DOLLY WAS JOINED BY BLUEGRASS STARS Alison Krauss and Rhonda Vincent on this recording. It appeared on the *Dumplin'* soundtrack.

Look around and see what's goin' on,
What's goin' on, what's goin' on.
To me it seems to be so very wrong,
So very wrong, can't get along.
We can find the answers to the questions if
And when we do I do believe
We could do a whole lot better
If we walked this life together.
Who will make a difference in this world
. . . if we don't?

I'd like to think there is a better way,
A better way, a brighter day.
I'd rather think like this than to be swayed
The other way and only say
There's no point to even try, be content to
    live a lie;
But I have the faith.
When we decide to we can change it,
Take our world and rearrange it.
Who is gonna ever change it, change it
. . . if we don't?

Take a look inside ourselves,
See what I can do.
Make a step to be of help,
So much we can improve.
Try to make a difference in this world
Before we're through.
Who will do it, who will do it, who will
    do it, who
. . . if we don't?

Look around and see what's going on.
Everything just seems to be so wrong.
If we'd just open up our eyes
We could see a better life.
I still believe.
There's a place for all of us
If we'd reach out
And touch the love
Nothing's gonna ever change it much
. . . if we don't.

If I don't, if you don't,
If we don't, if I don't.
If you won't, if we don't.

This is one of the songs that Linda Perry and I wrote together for the *Dumplin'* soundtrack. She decided to give it a Johnny Cash guitar sound, which I loved. I thought, "Who can I get to be on this record? I've got to get two country girls." Rhonda Vincent and Alison Krauss are two of the best bluegrass girls ever, and I love them both. Rhonda played the fire out of the mandolin on the track. Alison played the fiddle. We all sang it and did our harmonies. It's one of my favorites on the soundtrack, and it has a great message, too.

I have always thought of Alison Krauss as my little sister, or maybe the daughter I never had. Our voices seem to blend just perfectly.

When Life Is Good Again

(Dolly Parton / Kent Wells) 2020

WHEN THE CORONAVIRUS PANDEMIC HIT in the spring of 2020, Dolly pledged $1 million to fund research for a vaccine. She launched a web series called *Goodnight with Dolly* in which she read bedtime stories for homebound children. The Nashville music community lost stars Joe Diffie and John Prine to COVID-19, and Dolly's *Wild Texas Wind* pal Ray Benson was among those diagnosed. The US death toll passed 100,000 the week she released this song. She concluded its video with the words, "Be safe, be respectful, wear your mask, lead with love. —Dolly."

When life is good again
I'll be a better friend
A bigger person when
Life is good again

More thoughtful than I've been
I'll be so different then
More in the moment when
Life is good again

I'll open up my heart
And let the whole world in
I'll try to make amends
When life is good again

We've been brought to our knees
We've been so ill at ease
There are no guarantees
But you know life goes on
This too shall pass away
Bring new and different days
We need to change our ways
And right our wrongs

Let's open up our hearts
And let the whole world in
Let's try to make amends
When life is good again

I'll open up my doors again
And hear the message in the wind
Repent of all my sins (Hallelujah)
When life is good again

I'll try to be someone
On which you can depend
A helping hand to lend
Let's open up our eyes
And see what's goin' on
If we're to move along
From where we've been

Let's open up our hearts
And let the love shine in (Shine in)
We've all got knees to bend
And we'll just pray 'til then
Ask God's forgiveness when
Life is good again

And it's gonna be good again (It's gonna be,
it's gonna be)
It's gonna be good again
It'll be alright (It'll be alright)

God's the reason for all things
You want rainbows, you get rain
We'll all be forever changed (Forever
changed)
I'll sail my boat and fly my kite
Walk in the park, go out at night
And hold my loved ones extra tight
When everything is on the mend
I'll even drink with my old friends
Sing and play my mandolin
We'll make it through this long dark night
Darkness fades when faced with light
And everything's gonna be alright
When life is good again

If I'm gonna wear a mask, it's gotta have guitars on it, right? I can't stay still: Even during the pandemic, I was working on new projects all the time. While practicing social distancing with my people, of course.

Try 2014

DOLLY INCLUDED THIS SONG ON HER *Blue Smoke* collection of 2014. "Try" is also a cornerstone song on the soundtrack of a 2020 Netflix original musical *Christmas on the Square*.

I have chased after rainbows;
I've captured one or two.
I've reached for the stars;
And I have even held a few.
I've walked that lonesome valley,
Topped the mountains, soared the sky.
I've laughed and I have cried;
But I have always tried.

'Cause I've always been a dreamer,
And dreams are special things.
But dreams are of no value
If they're not equipped with wings.
So secure yourself for climbing,
Make ready for the sky.
Don't let your chance go by,
You'll make it if you try.

So try to be the first one up the mountain,
The highest-flying dreamer in the sky.
And try your best to be an inspiration
For others that are still afraid and shy.
And try to make the most of every moment
'Cause if you never try, you never win.
So try each day to try a little harder
And if you fail, get up and try again.

You know nothin' is impossible
If you can just believe.
Don't live your life in shackles
When faith can be the key.
The winner's one that keeps
Determination in his eyes.
Who's not afraid to fly,
And not afraid to try.

So try to be the first one up the mountain.
And try to be the first to touch the sky.
And don't let somebody tell you you
can't do it.
And if they say that, show 'em it's a lie.
And if you fail at first, just keep on trying
'Cause you are not a failure in God's eyes.
So spread your wings
And let the magic happen
'Cause you'll never really know
If you don't try.

And the first step is the one that's always
hardest.
But you'll never really know if you don't try.
You have to try.

I wrote this as the theme song for the Imagination Library when we started it twenty-five years ago. Now I think of it as being my version of Frank Sinatra's "I Did It My Way" that sums up who I am. It's like my testimony in song. "I have chased after rainbows / I've captured one or two / I've reached for the stars / And I have even held a few / I've walked that lonesome valley / Topped the mountains, soared the sky / I've laughed and I have cried / But I have always tried." And like the song says, I've always been a dreamer, no matter what has happened.

I'm planning to use it in a musical that's my life story. Whenever I go to one of the Imagination Library roll-outs, I take my little guitar and I sing this song. I sang it when I did my commencement speech for the students at the University of Tennessee [in 2009]. It's good for young people to hear its message that you have to get out there and make it work. Go out and do your thing.

I think it's going to become "my song." It has kind of developed a life of its own. And I hope that it will live on and on.

I can't explain why, but I know that I am blessed that the songs just keep on flowing out of me. I hope they always will.

The Secret Song

THERE IS A LOCKED BOX in a display case at Dollywood's DreamMore Resort that contains a mystery Dolly Parton song.

I had dreamed of the resort for many years before it became real [in 2015]. They try every year to come up with something that will draw the interest of the press. They thought up the idea of a vault-like box that people could see as they walked by. They asked me to write a song to put in there. It would be a song that will never be heard until thirty years from the time we opened the resort.

They said, "You'll be long dead." I said, "Well, maybe not. I'll be ninety-nine. I've seen people live to be older than that."

They told me that it had to be a secret song and that I couldn't use it until they open that box. I said, "That's like burying one of my kids, putting it on ice or something, and I won't be around to see it brought back to life."

So I wrote this song, and I can't say what it is. It's just burning me up inside that I have to leave it in there. I put a CD player in the box, too. Because the song is on a CD, and there's no telling what music is going to be by then. Hopefully, it will play and the whole thing ain't rotted.

It's in a chestnut-wood box that my uncle Bill made. The chestnut was a mighty tree that got wiped out by blight. Bill has spent the past twenty or thirty years of his life working really hard trying to make it come back with a blight-resistant chestnut. They've come a long way with that. I'm really proud of him for that work. I even once wrote a song for him as a promotion called "The Chestnut Tree."

The chestnut was an American icon, a giant in the Smoky Mountains, and the most wonderful wood. So I thought it was appropriate to be the box.

Anyway, it's kind of weird or strange that they would ask me to write this mystery song. I don't know if I want to live to be one hundred or not. But you never know. I might, and if I do, I'm going to be at that opening.

This plank of wood is from Dolly's first stage, the front porch of the Tennessee Mountain Home where Dolly first dreamed of being a star.
This chestnut "Dream Box" is a repository of Dolly's memories and wishes for the future. It will not be opened until Dolly's 100th birthday on January 19, 2046. The Dream Box itself is a tribute to her original mentor and uncle, Bill Owens, who has worked tirelessly to preserve the American Chestnut tree. As a final tribute, Dolly has placed a song which she has written to be released as her last. Entitled, "My Place in History," only Dolly knows its melody and content until 2046.

Song Index

Credits

All songs published by Velvet Apple Music, BMI, with the exceptions of the following: "Puppy Love" (p. 40) published by Round Hill Music/BMG, "Wait 'Til I Get You Home" (p. 208), "White Limozeen" (p. 244) and "Country Is as Country Does" (p. 361) published by Velvet Apple Music / Songpainter Music, BMI. "Girl in the Movies" (p. 256), "Red Shoes" (p. 356) and "If We Don't" (p. 370) published by Velvet Apple Music / Deep Dark Robot Music, BMI. "Better Get to Livin'" (p. 359) and "When Life Is Good Again" (Ch. 14) published by Velvet Apple Music, BMI / Clear Shot Music, ASCAP. "Country Road" (p. 278) published by Velvet Apple Music / Gary Scruggs Music, BMI. "Family" (p. 282) published by Velvet Apple Music / Brick Hithouse Music, BMI. "Straight Talk" (p. 249) published by Velvet Apple Music and HolPicMusic. "Fish out of Water" (p. 331) published by Velvet Apple Music and HolPic Music. "Livin' a Lie" (p. 229) published by Velvet Apple Music and HolPic Music. All rights on behalf of Velvet Apple Music administered by Sony Music/ATV Music Publishing LLC. All rights reserved. Print rights for "Girl in the Movies (p. 256)," "If We Don't (p.366)," and "Red Shoes (p. 352)," courtesy of Peer Music. Print rights for "Wait 'Til I Get You Home (p. 208)," "Country Is As Country Does (p. 357)," "White Limozeen (p. 244)," "Better Get To Livin' (354)," "When Life Is Good Again (p. 368)," "Country Road (p. 278)," "Straight Talk (p. 248)," "Fish Out Of Water (p. 330)," & "Livin' A Lie (p. 328)" courtesy of Hal Leonard.

P. 1: Courtesy of Chasing Rainbows Museum
P. 3: Courtesy of Chasing Rainbows Museum
P. 6: Photos by Antonis Achilleos
P. 8: Photo by Antonis Achilleos
P. 9: Photo by Les Leverett; permission by Grand Ole Opry
P. 10: Photo by Antonis Achilleos
P. 12: Photo by Antonis Achilleos
P. 13: (Dolly) Courtesy of Chasing Rainbows Museum
P. 13: (background) Used under license from Shutterstock.com
P. 14: Photo by Trey Fanjoy
P. 16: Photo by Antonis Achilleos
P. 18: (lyrics) Photos by Antonis Achilleos
P. 18: (album) Original photo by Les Leverett; permission by Grand Ole Opry and Sony Music Entertainment; photo by Antonis Achilleos
P. 19: Photo by Antonis Achilleos
P. 20: Photo by Antonis Achilleos
P. 22: (crib and table) Photos by Antonis Achilleos
P. 22: (album) Original photo by Louis Owens; permission by Sony Music Entertainment; photo by Antonis Achilleos
P. 23: Photo by Antonis Achilleos
P. 24: Photo by Antonis Achilleos
P. 26: Courtesy of Chasing Rainbows Museum
P. 27: (family photo) Courtesy of Dolly Parton
P. 27: (license plate) Courtesy of Tennessee Department of Tourism; photo by Fran Strine
P. 28: Photo by Antonis Achilleos
P. 29: (bag) Photo by Antonis Achilleos
P. 29: (Dolly and Dr. Robert F. Thomas) Courtesy of Dolly Parton
P. 31: Courtesy of Chasing Rainbows Museum
P. 33: Courtesy of Dolly Parton
P. 35: Photo by Raeanne Rubenstein; permission by Country Music Hall of Fame
P. 37: Photos by Les Leverett; permission by Grand Ole Opry
P. 38: Courtesy of Dolly Parton
P. 39: Courtesy of Dolly Parton
P. 41: (photo) Courtesy of Dolly Parton
P. 41: (album) Photo by Antonis Achilleos
P. 43: (Dolly Parton in dress) Courtesy of Chasing Rainbows Museum
P. 43: (portraits 1, 2, and 3) Courtesy of Dolly Parton
P. 43: (portrait 4) Courtesy of Chasing Rainbows Museum
P. 44: Courtesy of Chasing Rainbows Museum
P. 47: Photo by Antonis Achilleos
P. 47: (background) Used under license from Shutterstock.com.
P. 49: Courtesy of Chasing Rainbows Museum; permission by Chet Atkins Estate
P. 50: Courtesy of Dolly Parton
P. 51: Courtesy of Chasing Rainbows Museum
P. 53: Photo by Michael Ochs; permission by Michael Ochs Archives and Getty Images
P. 55: Photo by Hope Powell; courtesy of The Hope Powell Collection by Singleton/Curb, Kitty Wells Estate, and Roy Acuff Estate
P. 57: Courtesy of Dolly Parton
P. 58: Courtesy of Chasing Rainbows Museum
P. 60: Photo by Les Leverett; permission by Grand Ole Opry
P. 61: (dress) Photo by Antonis Achilleos
P. 61: (album) Original photo by Fred Foster; permission by Sony Music Entertainment and Fred Foster Estate; photo by Antonis Achilleos
P. 63: Photo by Les Leverett; permission by Grand Ole Opry
P. 65: Photo by Les Leverett; permission by Grand Ole Opry
P. 67: Courtesy of Chasing Rainbows Museum
P. 69: Courtesy of Chasing Rainbows Museum
P. 70: Photos courtesy of Chasing Rainbows Museum
P. 71: Original photo by Les Leverett; permission by Grand Ole Opry and Sony Music Entertainment; photo by Antonis Achilleos
P. 73: Original photo by Les Leverett; permission by Grand Ole Opry; photo by Antonis Achilleos
P. 74: Photos by Les Leverett; permission by Grand Ole Opry and Porter Wagoner Estate
P. 77: Photos by Les Leverett permission by Grand Ole Opry and Porter Wagoner Estate
P. 79: Photo by Les Leverett; permission by Grand Ole Opry and Porter Wagoner Estate
P. 81: (photo on left) Courtesy of Dolly Parton
P. 81: (photo on right) Courtesy of Chasing Rainbows Museum
P. 83: Original photo by Les Leverett; permission by Grand Ole Opry, Porter Wagoner Estate, and Sony Music Entertainment; photo by Antonis Achilleos
P. 85: Photo by Antonis Achilleos
P. 86: Original photo by Les Leverett; permission by Grand Ole Opry, Porter Wagoner Estate, and Sony Music Entertainment; photo by Antonis Achilleos
P. 87: Photo by Antonis Achilleos
P. 89: Photo by Antonis Achilleos
P. 91: Photo by Antonis Achilleos
P. 93: (lyrics) Photos by Antonis Achilleos
P. 93: (photo) Photo by Les Leverett; permission by Grand Ole Opry and Porter Wagoner Estate
P. 94: Courtesy of Dolly Parton
P. 96: Original photo by Les Leverett; permission by Grand Ole Opry, Porter Wagoner Estate, and Sony Music Entertainment; photo by Antonis Achilleos
P. 99: (top left) Photo by Hope Powell; courtesy of The Hope Powell Collection by Singleton/Curb

P. 99: (top right) Photo by Hope Powell; courtesy of The Hope Powell Collection by Singleton/Curb
P. 99: (bottom left) Photo courtesy of Dolly Parton
P. 99: (bottom right) Courtesy of Chasing Rainbows Museum
P. 101: Photo by Caleb A. Rawstron; permission by Grand Ole Opry and Porter Wagoner Estate
P. 103: Photo by Les Leverett; permission by Grand Ole Opry and Porter Wagoner Estate
P. 104: (top left) Courtesy of Dolly Parton
P. 104: (top right) Photo by Doug Smith
P. 104: (bottom left) Courtesy of Dolly Parton
P. 104: (bottom right) Courtesy of Dolly Parton
P. 106: Photo by Hope Powell; courtesy of The Hope Powell Collection by Singleton/Curb
P. 109: Photo by Michael Ochs; permission by Michael Ochs Archives and Getty Images
P. 110: Photo by Michael Ochs; permission by Michael Ochs Archives and Getty Images
P. 113: Courtesy of Dolly Parton
P. 115: Photo by Antonis Achilleos
P. 116: Photo by Antonis Achilleos
P. 118: Original photo by Hope Powell; courtesy of Hope Powell Collection by Singleton/Curb and permission by Sony Music Entertainment; photo by Antonis Achilleos
P. 119: Photo by Hope Powell; courtesy of The Hope Powell Collection by Singleton/Curb
P. 120: Photo by Antonis Achilleos
P. 121: Photo by Antonis Achilleos
P. 127: Courtesy of Chasing Rainbows Museum
P. 129: Photo by Les Leverett; permission by Grand Ole Opry
P. 130: Original photo by Hope Powell; courtesy of The Hope Powell Collection by Singleton/Curb and permission by Sony Music Entertainment; photo by Antonis Achilleos
P. 131: Photo by Hope Powell; courtesy of The Hope Powell Collection by Singleton/Curb
P. 132: Photo by Les Leverett; permission by Grand Ole Opry
P. 135: Photos by Antonis Achilleos
P. 137: Photo by Antonis Achilleos
P. 138: Courtesy of Chasing Rainbows Museum
P. 139: Courtesy of Dolly Parton
P. 141: Photo by Antonis Achilleos
P. 143: Courtesy of Dolly Parton
P. 145: Permission by Warner Bros. Pictures and Queen Latifah
P. 147: Courtesy of Dolly Parton
P. 149: Courtesy of Sandollar and Dolly Parton; permission by Kenny Rogers Estate
P. 150: Courtesy of Chasing Rainbows Museum
P. 152: Courtesy of Chasing Rainbows Museum
P. 153: Photos courtesy of Dolly Parton
P. 155: Photo by Alan Mayor; courtesy of Alan Mayor Estate; permission by Tammy Wynette Estate and Loretta Lynn
P. 156: Photo by Alan Mayor, courtesy of Alan Mayor Estate
P. 158: Photo by Hope Powell; courtesy of Hope Powell Collection by Singleton/Curb
P. 161: courtesy of Chasing Rainbows Museum
P. 163: Photo by Raeanne Rubenstein; permission by Country Music Hall of Fame
P. 165: courtesy of Dolly Parton
P. 171: (album) Original photo by Les Leverett; permission by Grand Ole Opry and Sony Music Entertainment; photo by Antonis Achilleos
P. 171: (dress) Photo by Antonis Achilleos
P. 173: Permission by Grand Ole Opry
P. 175: Original photo by Les Leverett; permission by Grand Ole Opry and Sony Music Entertainment; photo by Antonis Achilleos
P. 177: (guitar case) Photo by Antonis Achilleos
P. 177: (Dolly Parton with Avie Lee) Courtesy of Chasing Rainbows Museum
P. 178: Courtesy of Sandollar and Dolly Parton; permission by Merle Haggard Estate
P. 181: Courtesy of Sandollar and Dolly Parton; permission by Stella Parton
P. 183: Photo by Michael Ochs; permission by Michael Ochs Archives and Getty Images
P. 185: Courtesy of Chasing Rainbows Museum
P. 187: Courtesy of Dolly Parton; permission by Emmylou Harris
P. 189: Photo by David Gahr; permission by the Estate of David Gahr and Getty Images
P. 191: Courtesy of Sandollar and Dolly Parton; permission by Brenda Lee
P. 193: Photo by R. Diamond; permission by Getty Images; permission by Waylon Jennings Estate
P. 195: Photo by Les Leverett; permission by Grand Ole Opry
P. 196: Photo by Hope Powell; courtesy of The Hope Powell Collection by Singleton/Curb
P. 199: (guitar) Photo by Antonis Achilleos
P. 199: (Dolly Parton) Photo by Hope Powell; courtesy of The Hope Powell Collection by Singleton/Curb
P. 201: Courtesy of Chasing Rainbows Museum
P. 202: Courtesy of Sandollar and Dolly Parton; permission by Willie Nelson
P. 204: Photo by Les Leverett; permission by Les Leverett and Grand Ole Opry
P. 205: Courtesy of Sandollar and Dolly Parton; permission by Willie Nelson
P. 207: Courtesy of Sandollar and Dolly Parton
P. 209: Courtesy of Sandollar and Dolly Parton; permission by Mac Davis
P. 210: Photo by Hope Powell; courtesy of The Hope Powell Collection by Singleton/Curb
P. 212: Photo by Hope Powell; courtesy of The Hope Powell Collection by Singleton/Curb
P. 213: (photo) Courtesy of Dolly Parton
P. 213: (background) Permission by Shutterstock
P. 215: Photo by Hope Powell; courtesy of Hope Powell Collection by Singleton/Curb
P. 217: Photo by Hope Powell; courtesy of Hope Powell Collection by Singleton/Curb
P. 218: Photo by Antonis Achilleos
P. 220: Photo by Antonis Achilleos
P. 221: Photo by Antonis Achilleos
P. 223: Photo by Herb Ritts; permission by Herb Ritts Estate
P. 224: Photo by Antonis Achilleos; collection of Cross-Eyed Critters Watering Hole at Graduate Nashville Hotel
P. 227: Courtesy of Dolly Parton
P. 228: Permission by FOX Films
P. 230: Permission by FOX Films, Jane Fonda, and Lily Tomlin
P. 232: Photo by Antonis Achilleos
P. 233: Permission by FOX Films
P. 235: Courtesy of Dolly Parton
P. 237: Photo by Antonis Achilleos
P. 238: Permission by FOX Films and Sylvester Stallone
P. 241: Permission by FOX Films and Sylvester Stallone
P. 243: Courtesy of Sandollar and Dolly Parton
P. 245: (dress) Photo by Antonis Achilleos
P. 245: (album) Original photo by Robert Blakeman; permission by Robert Blakeman and Sony; photo by Antonis Achilleos
P. 246: Courtesy of Dolly Parton; permission by Ricky Skaggs and Wolfman Jack Estate
P. 247: Photo by Antonis Achilleos
P. 249: Permission by Hollywood Pictures
P. 253: Photo by Antonis Achilleos

P. 257: Photo by Justine Feldt; permission by Justine Feldt and Linda Perry
P. 259: Photo by David Gahr; permission by the Estate of David Gahr and Getty Images
P. 261: Courtesy of Dolly Parton; permission by Sandy Gallin Estate
P. 263: Photo by Michael Buckner; permission by Getty Images
P. 264: Photo by Robert Blakeman; permission by Robert Blakeman, Emmylou Harris, Linda Ronstadt, and Warner Music Nashville
P. 267: Courtesy of Chasing Rainbows Museum
P. 270: Photo by Antonis Achilleos
P. 271: Original photo by Robert Blakeman; permission by Robert Blakeman, Emmylou Harris, Linda Ronstadt, and Warner Music Nashville; photo by Antonis Achilleos
P. 275: (Dolly Parton and others) Permission by Sony, Kathy Mattea, Mary Chapin Carpenter, Tanya Tucker, Billy Ray Cyrus, and Sony Music Entertainment
P. 275: (Dolly Parton and Kathy Mattea) Courtesy of Dolly Parton; permission by Kathy Mattea
P. 278: Photo by Antonis Achilleos
P. 281: Photo by Alan Mayor; permission by Alan Mayor Estate, Tammy Wynette Estate, Mark Collie, and Loretta Lynn
P. 283: Courtesy of Dolly Parton; permission by Carl Perkins Estate
P. 284: Photo by Antonis Achilleos
P. 285: Photo by Randee St. Nicholas; permission Randee St. Nicholas and Sony Music Entertainment
P. 286: Permission by Sony Music Entertainment
P. 289: Courtesy of Dolly Parton
P. 291: Courtesy of Sandollar and Dolly Parton
P. 297: Photos courtesy of Dolly Parton
P. 301: Photo by Jim Herrington; permission by Jim Herrington
P. 302: Photo by Antonis Achilleos
P. 303: Photo by Dennis Carney
P. 305: Photo by Jim Herrington; permission by Jim Herrington
P. 306: Photo by Dennis Carney
P. 309: Photo by Antonis Achilleos
P. 311: (Dolly Parton with Bill Monroe) Permission by Grand Ole Opry
P. 311: (Dolly Parton and Charlie Daniels) Photo by Scott Hunter; permission by Charlie Daniels
P. 312: Photo by Robert Blakeman; permission by Robert Blakeman, Emmylou Harris, Linda Ronstadt, and Warner Music Nashville
P. 313: Photo by Antonis Achilleos; permission by Emmylou Harris, Linda Ronstadt, and Warner Music Nashville
P. 315: Photo by Jeremy Westby
P. 317: Courtesy of Dolly Parton
P. 318: Photo by Antonis Achilleos
P. 325: Photo by Alan Mayor; permission by Alan Mayor Estate
P. 326: Photo by Cheryl Riddle; permission by Cheryl Riddle
P. 326: (background) Used under license from Shutterstock.com.
P. 329: Photo by Randee St. Nicholas; permission by Randee St. Nicholas
P. 331: Permission by Hollywood Pictures
P. 332: Photo by Kii Arens; permission by Kii Arens and Dolly Records
P. 333: (Dolly Parton in boat) Photo by Kii Arens; permission by Kii Arens
P. 333: (Dolly Parton with doll) Photo by Hope Powell; courtesy of The Hope Powell Collection by Singleton/Curb
P. 333: (doll) Photo by Antonis Achilleos
P. 336: Photo by Antonis Achilleos
P. 337: Photos by Antonis Achilleos
P. 339: Courtesy of Dolly Parton; permission by Kris Kristofferson
P. 341: Courtesy of Sandollar and Dolly Parton
P. 343: (Dolly in denim) Courtesy of Chasing Rainbows Museum
P. 343: (Dolly and Carl at army base): Courtesy of Dolly Parton
P. 345: Photo by Jim Herrington; permission by Jim Herrington
P. 346: Photo by Ron Hoffman; permission by Sony Music Entertainment
P. 349: Permission by Grand Ole Opry and Porter Wagoner Estate
P. 351: Permission by Dollywood
P. 353: Photos by Antonis Achilleos
P. 355: Photo by Kii Arens; permission by Kii Arens
P. 359: (photo) Photo by Justin Stephens; permission by Bob Greenblatt
P. 359: (playbill) Permission by Bob Greenblatt
P. 361: Photo by Raeanne Rubenstein; permission by Country Music Hall of Fame
P. 363: Photo by Justine Feldt; permission by Justine Feldt and Mavis Staples
P. 365: Photo by Fran Strine
P. 367: Permission by Sandollar & Alison Krauss
P. 369: Photo by Steve Summers
P. 371: Photo by David McClister
P. 373: Photo by Antonis Achilleos
P. 375: Photo by Jim McGuire; permission by Grand Ole Opry

Acknowledgments:

I thank God for the gift of songwriting. I also want to thank everyone who worked so hard to put this book together. I am blessed to have a great group of people around me, and all of them went beyond the call of duty. A special thanks goes to the photographers who allowed us to use their photos. I especially want to thank Bob Oermann, my partner in rhyme. He is my hero and friend. Without him, this book would not be what it is. We present it to you with love and joy.

—Dolly Parton

First Chronicle Books LLC paperback edition, published in 2023.
Originally published in hardcover in 2020 by Chronicle Books LLC.

Library of Congress Cataloging-in-Publication Data

Names: Parton, Dolly, author. | Oermann, Robert K., author.
Title: Dolly Parton, songteller : my life in lyrics / Dolly Parton ; with Robert K. Oermann.
Other titles: Songs. Texts. Selections. | Songteller : my life in lyrics
Description: San Francisco : Chronicle Books, 2020. | Includes index.
Identifiers: LCCN 2020031352 | ISBN 9781797205090 (hardcover) | ISBN 9781797211817 (hardcover)
Subjects: LCSH: Country music--Texts. | Parton, Dolly--Portraits. | Women country musicians--Portraits. | Women singers--United States--Portraits. | Country musicians--Portraits. | Singers--United States--Portraits. | LCGFT: Country lyrics.
Classification: LCC ML54.6.P38 S66 2020 | DDC 782.421642092 [B]--dc23
LC record available at https://lccn.loc.gov/2020031352

ISBN 978-1-7972-2473-2

Manufactured in China.

MIX
Paper | Supporting responsible forestry
FSC™ C008047
FSC www.fsc.org

Design by Jacob Covey.
Additional typesetting by Liam Flanagan and AJ Hansen.
Cover lettering illustration by Jessica Hische.
Original photographs for this book by Antonis Achilleos; assistance by Russell Kilgore.

10 9 8 7 6 5 4 3 2 1

Chronicle Books LLC
680 Second Street
San Francisco, California 94107
www.chroniclebooks.com